REASONS WE FIGHT

REASONS WE FIGHT

Tejanos and American Wars, 1836–1972

ALEX MENDOZA

UNIVERSITY OF OKLAHOMA PRESS : NORMAN

Publication of this book is made possible through the generosity of Edith Kinney Gaylord.

Library of Congress Cataloging-in-Publication Data
Names: Mendoza, Alexander, 1970–author
Title: Reasons we fight : Tejanos and American wars, 1836–1972 / Alex Mendoza.
Other titles: Tejanos and American wars, 1836–1972
Description: Norman : University of Oklahoma Press, [2026] | Includes
   bibliographical references and index. | Summary: "This work examines the
   experience of Tejanos in the American military and their reasons for engaging
   in these conflicts."—Provided by publisher.
Identifiers: LCCN 2025039453 | ISBN 9780806196541 (hardcover)
Subjects: LCSH: Mexican American soldiers—United States | Mexican American
   soldiers—Attitudes | Mexican Americans—Ethnic identity | Mexican
   Americans—Texas
Classification: LCC UB418.M48+ M46 2026 | DDC 355.00896872073—dc23/
   eng/20250826
LC record available at https://lccn.loc.gov/2025039453

The manufacturer's authorized representative in the EU for product safety is Mare Nostrum Group B.V., Mauritskade 21D, 1091 GC Amsterdam, The Netherlands, email: gpsr@mare-nostrum.co.uk.

For my son, Justin Alejandro Mendoza
I give this part of me for you . . .
Nunca te olvides

CONTENTS

ACKNOWLEDGMENTS

This study on Tejanos in the military has been long in coming. Anyone who deals with writing and researching history understands how important the scores of archivists and librarians are to studying the past. Thank you all. Of course, this study, like all works of history, relies heavily on the works of other scholars. I have been strongly influenced by a wide number of historians of US military history, the Texas-Mexico border, Mexican Americans, and the Civil War era, to name a few. Yet, for any errors and misinterpretations that remain, I alone am responsible. I also would like to extend a special thanks to Andrew Berzanskis, Riley Hines, and the rest of the staff at the University of Oklahoma Press for their patience, care, and attention.

A special thanks also goes to those Tejano families who shared their stories and their photos: Magda Martínez, Raúl Pérez, the Contreras family, the Valls family, Vásquez family, the Vela family, the Páez family, the Pérez family, the Soto family, the Teniente family, the Garza family, and the Cantú family, respectively. Also deserving special acknowledgment is José A. Ramírez, author of *To the Line of Fire: Mexican Texans and World War I* (2008). He proved invaluable in helping me understand the lives of Tejanos in World War I through his own award-winning study. Significantly, too, José shared some critical archival and newspaper material that helped me start my own research. Our professor, Jerry Thompson, also deserves special mention for helping me immeasurably along the way.

Closer to home, thanks to my friends and colleagues at the University of North Texas (UNT) History Department. At the top of the list is my former department chair, Rick McCaslin. A nod also goes out to Harold

Tanner for his support. Thanks, too, to UNT's Faculty Developmental Leave, which allowed me one semester free from teaching classes to visit repositories crucial for this book. Other colleagues and former colleagues were also extremely helpful. Some even feigned interest in my project and that was good enough for me. Randolph "Mike" Campbell, Don Chipman, Andrew Torget, Walt Roberts, Chad Pearson, Gus Seligman, Mike Leggiere, Guy Chet, and Geoff Wawro have all supported this project in one way or another, as did others who offered a kind word or a funny joke. Geoff was kind enough to share galleys of his book, *The Vietnam War: A Military History* (2024), which helped me refine some ideas in the last stages of writing about the cold war era.

Other friends have also provided support for my work. At the top of the list is my former colleague, Dan Murphree. While he remains dedicated to his own work at the University of Central Florida, he is only an email or text message away from cheering me on. I miss him and his family, Mary Beth and Taylor. Thanks, too, to my former thesis chair, Peggy Hardman, who was kind enough to read and critique the manuscript from her home in Kentucky. A thank you also goes to my former cross country rival at the University of Arkansas, Gilbert Contreras. Gilbert was kind enough to share some info about his family and Company E. I should also thank David Snead, my former dissertation committee member. Finally, I give special recognition to Charles Grear, my co-editor on *Texans and War: New Interpretations of the State's Military History* (2012) and former graduate-school colleague. Chuck's help and friendship proved invaluable during the years I worked on this project. Thank you, Chuck.

I owe a debt of thanks to some of my dear friends. Of special note is my former college roommate and teammate on the University of Texas at Austin cross country team, Steve Sisson. During the final year of writing, we mourned the loss of his father, Tom, a man I loved dearly. I thank him immensely, too, for always showing an interest in my life and my projects. Also, to Robert Cantú, my former college roommate, who also pursued the path of history, Longhorn football, and Black Sabbath: I thank you so much for everything you have done for me and my family, but most of all for being a true friend. A nod of appreciation goes to a couple of my San Antonio friends, Monica McGettrick Walters and Elizabeth Coronado, for providing help from the Alamo City. Tiffany Stevens (and Ester), right here in Dallas, also provided a lot of support, making me eternally grateful. Tiffany's thoughtfulness is immeasurable. Also in Dallas, thanks to my *primos*, Lauro Mendoza and Juan Martínez, for their support. From Denver, Stacey Chaston also brought a smile to my face each time I received a message or a photo from the Rocky Mountain State. Our runs together in Dallas, Boulder, or wherever there was a NCAA cross country meet, remain meaningful in many ways. I thank you for bringing a huge smile to my face each time we saw one another. Also, my little, black dog, Baby Malcolm, gets some love too. Too many weekends I disappeared into my home office to write this book. Thanks to him, I relished every chance to leave the house and enjoy the outdoors. A lot of thinking and strategizing about this book occurred during those father-dog walks. For that, I remain grateful.

My ex-teammates on the University of Texas at Austin cross country team, David Angell, Oscar Vela, Ernie Shepard, and Brad Patterson, provided me with goals and aspirations to break the monotony of writing. Our Dallas Marathon relays in December were so much fun. Thank you all for the laughs and group texts. Other former Longhorn distance runners also provided a break from history through shared runs, coffee, beers, and music. Thanks go to Dan Castro, Chris DeGroot, Randal Grizzle, and Donnie O'Neal for everything. Dan deserves a very special acknowledgment. A talented artist and graphic designer in his own right, he contributed an original piece of artwork to this book, an interpretation of the famous compañía volante. Thank you, DC! Thanks, too, goes to Hunter Hall, another Texas Ex distance runner and truly special friend who only thinks about my joy and happiness. I appreciate our friendship, Hunter.

I also appreciate my photographer friends who shared advice on how to take better photos, some of which made their way into this manuscript. Cuate Santos, Andy González, Ronnie Sunker, and Ashleigh Young, please know I appreciate talking photography with you every chance I get. Finally, a special nod to all my other friends who just wanted to watch a football game or drink a beer. You did more for my sanity than you realized A special nod goes to my friend, Ryan Schumacher, for the copyediting.

Finally, I must thank my family. Until she passed away in January 2025, my mother never really understood what I do for a living because I did not go to work five days a week, eight hours a day like she and my father did. Yet my parents always provided me with support and a love for reading that I can never repay. ¡Mil gracias por todo! My sister, Elva Mendoza Brewster, is worthy of individual acknowledgment and recognition for her help in making this project a reality. She has long remained a steadfast supporter and an enthusiastic cheerleader. I am continuously amazed at her generosity and kindness toward siblings, cousins, and nephews. I firmly believe she is the soul of the Mendoza family.

Most importantly, this study is dedicated to my son, Justin Alejandro. Now in college and pursuing his own path, he probably does not remember me writing my first or second books. History was always part of his life growing up, though sports and music have since taken over. Now as a young adult, he knows that when I disappear to write he is always welcome to interrupt with an update about football, a debate about Alice in Chains, or even share a reference to *The Sopranos* or another piece of pop culture. The laughter alone is always worth the break in writing. I also thank him for taking care of Baby Malcolm so I could finish that one last paragraph or run off to Austin to take photos at track meets. He also listened patiently as I told him about Tejanos of past generations. He was there from the start of this project to its conclusion, asking patiently when we would have our celebratory steak dinner. Few people understand our sense of humor and we wouldn't have it any other way. Even though he knows I love him dearly, I think it is important to remind him yet again: he means the world to me. This book is dedicated to him and the deep, special, unbreakable bond that we share. Que nunca se te olvide.

INTRODUCTION

Tejano military service is a rich and complex topic. Korean War veteran Raúl M. Chavarría thought nothing of flying two flags, those of the United States and Mexico, outside his Laredo home when I visited for an oral-history interview. The two national flags flapping together in the hot summer air quickly captured my attention. Looking at the Stars and Stripes and *El Tricolor*, both weather-beaten by the South Texas sun, I wondered how a veteran of the US Army could honor two nations. I had observed Chavarría's devotion to his military service on prior occasions, noting how he proudly displayed his status as a Korean War veteran on a black embroidered baseball cap. I asked him why he flew the Mexican flag. His response was simple yet definitive. "Mi corazón le pertenece a los dos países (my heart belongs to both countries)!" he exclaimed. He explained that he had watched a CONCACAF Gold Cup match between the two countries a few weeks prior, a 5–0 victory by "El Tri" (the Mexican national team), and he had cheered himself hoarse rooting against the *Yanquis*. He smiled when he said he always rooted for Mexico in these contests.[1]

Chavarría is just one example of the complexity of military service for Texans of Mexican descent. The idea Chavarría spoke about—bicultural status and loyalty to two nations—fascinated me. Chavarría was born in Mexico in the 1930s but moved to the United States as a young adult. In his later years, he remained steadfast in his conviction that he was part of two nations, Mexico and the United States, though he acquired US citizenship years prior. For most of his life, he celebrated both the Fourth of July and the Dieciséis de Septiembre (Mexico's independence day). He spoke fluent Spanish and broken English. Though he embraced many of the notions and values of the United States and the US Army during the

1

Cold War era, he remained rooted in his love for *La Patria* well into his retirement from the import-export trade. Historian Arnoldo De León points out that this was a common occurrence during the mid-twentieth century as several forces "fanned the flames of Mexican nationalism" in Texas.[2] These included movies, cultural events, religion, music, and newspapers, just to name a few. In the border region where Chavarría lived, the presence of Mexican culture remained more pronounced than other parts of Texas.

The experiences of veterans like Chavarría and others notwithstanding, Tejanos of the mid-to-late twentieth century moved toward American ideals and values more firmly than previous generations. They became champions of the federal government and stalwart supporters of capitalism. Through military service, Tejanos sought to include themselves in the nation's war stories and martial commemorations. "Mexican Americans did not want to upend the dominant historical narratives of the nation, but only to include themselves in the established plots," writes historian Aaron E. Sánchez. "In terms of Texas history, Mexicans were not present at Valley Forge, Lexington, or Concord, but they were present at the Alamo and San Jacinto. They may not have ridden with Washington, but they did fight with Houston. These efforts in the Texas Revolution were just as important as participation in the American Revolution."[3]

The themes of Tejano patriotism resonate in the twenty-first century. In 2008, Major General Freddie Valenzuela, a native of Refugio and former commander of the US Army South, published *No Greater Love: The Lives and Times of Hispanic Soldiers*, a book that explored "the legacy of Hispanic Americans in the military." In his introduction, Valenzuela stated he was "an American first, and foremost," arguing that Hispanics are special to the American armed forces because they have always been confronted with questions about their "loyalty to this country and willingness to contribute to American progress." Valenzuela maintains that Hispanic soldiers love and cherish their country. As such, they join the armed forces not just for educational and economic opportunities, but because they represent the very embodiment of what America stands for: sacrifice, selflessness, and hard work. "Hispanic soldiers by and large do not join for self-aggrandizement or personal gain. . . . [M]ost of these soldiers want to be among comrades, getting to get the job done. We learned to be workhorses, not show horses."[4]

While Major General Valenzuela's views on Hispanic soldiers are grounded in the experience of a rich military career that spanned more than thirty years, the history of Tejano military service offers notable exceptions to his assertion that they did not view military service through the prism of personal gain. To be certain, honor and patriotism proved to be common sentiments among Tejanos. Yet, the full breadth of the Tejano military experience since the Texas Revolution indicates that additional factors influenced how they viewed military service. The desire to assimilate was a strong driving force behind the disproportionate number of high enlistments of the twentieth century.[5] But that notion was not always prevalent in earlier wars. In the wars of the nineteenth century, the loyalty and allegiance of Tejanos was predicated more on local circumstances than patriotism and national identity. It was not until World War II that Mexican Texans began to truly identify themselves with the American dream and what it could mean for their community and their families.

Tejano military service before the World War I era often had less to do with patriotism than the soldiers' local allegiances, defense of home, escape from peonage, a sense of adventurism, and desires for economic improvement. The First World War proved a watershed for Tejano identification with the American cause. By World War II, Mexican Texans found additional motivations to fight, including patriotism and the desire to refute their second-class status. Many Tejanos joined the military to demonstrate that through sacrifice in battle, they were entitled to the full rights of citizenship. In essence, Tejanos who joined the military in the twentieth century shed their "Mexicanist" identity and adopted the characteristics of American nationalism. But many remained bilingual and fluid in their identities. The notion that Tejano military service is nothing more than simple American patriotism is more of a modern construct than a historical reality.

The motivations of Tejano military service in the wars of the twentieth century evolved through time. Each successive war provided Tejano servicemen and their communities a platform to address the inequities of the political and socioeconomic worlds they knew. Military service provided a way of challenging the discriminatory practices in the state and nation as Mexican American veterans demanded the medical and political benefits that martial citizenship had earned them.

Tejano military service cannot be understood simply through prisms of assimilation and patriotism. Rather, Mexican Texans altered their motivations in the various wars since the nineteenth century, shifting their views based on a complex set of values. In recent years, as parks, memorials and buildings have been named for Hispanic soldiers, their motivations have been simplified. Yet, Tejanos who fought in various wars over the last two centuries showed a wide range of motivations.

This book is organized chronologically, tracing the origins of the Tejano military experience in colonial Texas. Chapter 1 analyzes how Texans of Mexican descent fought in numerous conflicts before the Republic of Texas gained its independence in 1836. In the eighteenth century, officers from the Spanish Royal Army trained local volunteers in units known as *compañías volantes*, or "flying companies." These local militia units had supplanted the national military's cavalry squadrons in matters of local defense by the eve of the Texas Revolution.[6] Later, during the war for Texas independence, some Tejanos identified with the mostly Anglo rebels; three Tejanos signed the Texas Declaration of Independence. Others remained loyal to Mexico. Some Tejanos tried to remain neutral during the conflict's early stages, perhaps hoping to later align themselves with the winning side. Hundreds of Tejanos were active participants in the struggle for Texas independence. Yet, after the Revolution, doubts about Tejano loyalty and the desire to remove Mexican Texans from positions of power caused friction, confusion, and conflict.

Chapter 2 traces the impact of this erosion of leadership on the Tejano community during the antebellum period. Tejano enlistment in the Mexican-American War proved dismal in 1846–48. Even though more than 8,000 Texans volunteered to fight south of Río Grande, only a few Tejanos joined the fight, most serving as guides or spies. Most Tejanos simply chose to await the outcome of these latest hostilities, as less than two dozen Spanish-surnamed volunteers served in the ranks of Texas forces, all of them in the enlisted ranks. By the time Confederate forces fired on Fort Sumter in April 1861, the Tejano population stood at approximately 25,000, mostly concentrated along the border and in Central Texas. The onset of hostilities placed the Mexican American population in a precarious position, forcing them to choose between Union and Confederate loyalties. Tejanos ultimately joined the ranks of both forces as more than 2,500 enlisted in the Confederate army, while approximately 958 Tejanos fought on the side of the Union forces. Yet throughout this conflict their loyalty was always in question by both the Union and Confederate war departments.

After the Civil War, as Texas struggled to regain its place in the nation during Reconstruction, Tejanos continued to serve in military campaigns against Indigenous people in the western part of the state.[7] Chapter 3 examines how Tejanos served as a paramilitary force and even joined the Texas Rangers to protect their communities from threats to settlement and prosperity. However, when the US Army returned to take over the security of the frontier, Tejanos slowly moved away from participating in their state's military conflicts, and Anglo Texans further questioned their loyalty. After the Spanish-American War began in 1898, some Tejanos volunteered to fight in one of the four infantry regiments and one cavalry regiment authorized by the government. Out of the approximately 4,000 soldiers the Lone Star State provided to support the war, less than 1 percent were of Mexican descent. Questions of loyalty loomed once more for the Tejano community.

Chapter 4 studies the watershed events of the World War I era. The Great War once more thrust the Mexican Texan population into the maelstrom of an American conflict. While many Mexican Texans, eager to demonstrate their loyalty to the United States, chose to enlist for service, other Tejanos fled the state to avoid military service. By and large, Tejanos of all classes answered the nation's call to arms during the Great War. Individual reasons may have varied, but they generally revolved around similar motivations: patriotism and support for the American cause, a desire to escape the economic morass of poverty, ethnic pride, and the desire for adventure in a foreign war.

Exploring how Tejanos fought for civil rights and for their country during World War II is the cornerstone of chapter 5. US entry into World War II after the Japanese attack on Pearl Harbor on December 7, 1941, once again presented Tejanos with a choice to join the conflict. But unlike in past wars, the Tejano community responded with the patriotic fervor of their Anglo-American neighbors. As many as 750,000 Texans served in the armed forces during the war. Of those, it is estimated that more than 100,000 Tejanos served in the United States armed forces. The war, and the resulting GI Bill, which expanded educational and economic opportunities for Mexican American veterans, gave many Tejano servicemen the hope that racial discrimination would become a thing of the past as they viewed themselves as Americans rather than Mexicans. Military service gave these Tejano servicemen a stake in the American dream.

Chapters 6 and 7 examine the Cold War–era conflicts in Korea and Vietnam. Following the Second World War, the Tejano population returned from Europe and the Pacific anxious to reap the rewards of their civic duty and contributions to fighting the "Good War." However, some grew disenchanted that the same biases and discrimination remained in the Lone Star State and elsewhere after 1945. As the nation pivoted to fight the spread of communism, Tejanos continued to make choices. In some respects, the patriotic fervor that marked enlistment in World War II was absent from the Korean War (covered in chapter 6), even though nearly 148,000 Tejanos served in the military during the conflict. During that period, Tejanos found themselves in an improved social, political, and economic climate. But a sense of second-class status irked many veterans and civic leaders during the postwar era. Still Tejanos proved willing to demonstrate their loyalty and nationalism, despite reports that a disproportionate number of Hispanic soldiers suffered casualties in Vietnam (as covered in chapter 7).

This study concludes with the commemoration period of the twenty-first century. It does not delve into the wars in the Middle East of the late twentieth and early twentieth-first centuries. While interviews and oral histories are plentiful for the wars in Iraq and elsewhere in the Middle East, not enough time has passed to offer proper historical perspective. Yet, there is a lot to be learned from exploring the role of Tejano military service from the Texas Revolution to Vietnam. While historians have examined specific conflicts, such as Jerry D. Thompson's extensive work on Tejanos during the Civil War or José Ramirez's award-winning work on Mexican Texans in World War I, no single work provides a comprehensive overview of the Tejano military experience. This book gives readers the first systematic understanding of the role Tejanos played in the American wars of the last two centuries.

For generations, Tejanos were often adaptable in their identity, demonstrating a sense of belonging to both Mexico and the United States. It was not until the midpoint of the twentieth century that Tejanos said no to Mexico and embraced American opportunities. My hope is that modern readers will recognize and accept that flexibility as they examine the reasons why Tejanos fought.

CHAPTER 1

"SOME ENVIED MY POSITION, AS HELD BY A *MEXICAN*"

Tejano Military Service Under Spain, Mexico, and the Republic of Texas

On September 20, 1835, Mexican General Martín Perfecto de Cos landed with five hundred troops at Copano Bay, near present-day Rockport, Texas, in Refugio County. Cos had the unenviable task of investigating and subduing recent resistance to Mexico City's efforts to resume collecting taxes and strengthen Texas's defenses against American encroachment. General-President Antonio López de Santa Anna, Cos's brother-in-law, had ordered him to disarm all unruly colonists and to expel troublemakers.

The Texans who drew the ire of Santa Anna were wary of the intruding Mexican army, and it did not take long for hostilities to erupt. On October 2, the Mexican commander at San Antonio de Béxar ordered a small number of troops to retrieve a cannon from the residents of Gonzales. The Texans resisted and claimed victory after a brief skirmish. By October 11, they had elected empresario Stephen F. Austin as their commander and prepared for further hostilities. Among the citizenry who joined the nascent rebellion were Tejanos,[1] or Mexican Texans, who would serve as cavalry. As William T. Austin (no relation to Stephen) explained, "These mexicans [*sic*] being well acquainted with the country, were of important service as express riders, guides to foraging parties &c."[2]

Austin's emphasis on how Tejanos could provide a valuable service to the Texian[3] cause underscored how volatile the situation had become north of Río Grande. As historian Stephen L. Hardin suggests, these early Texas colonists were far too familiar with war and conflict. Tejanos, who had lived through the tumultuous independence movement and fought Indians on the frontier, did not shy away from this latest struggle in Texas.[4] Through the prism of the Texas Revolution, historians have recognized the complexity of shifting national loyalties of Tejanos. While scholars have generally considered the role of Mexican Texans to be a corollary to the larger narrative of Texas independence, recent work has shown a fuller range of Tejano military service in the nineteenth century. Tejanos often straddled their loyalties in the various American conflicts of the 1800s, uncertain of which side to take as they remained conscious of their native land of Mexico. Many Tejanos held a border identity, one in which true loyalty was to the region and not the nation-states with their flags or national symbols. These sentiments were forged through time by generations of individual and local negotiations.[5]

It is understandable why William T. Austin would hold Tejano horsemen in such high regard in 1835. After all, like Anglo settlers who moved eastward to Texas, Tejano colonists who arrived north of the Río Grande were accustomed to conflict. As historian Andrés Tijerina notes in his study of nineteenth-century Texas, the Tejano community remained unified by the military purpose of their settlements. In the seventeenth century, when authorities in New Spain ordered colonization of the northern frontier, they used a precedent set on the Iberian Peninsula: buffer zones, which had been used to block Moorish invaders who came across the Strait of Gibraltar from North Africa. Mexico City officials hoped that these settlements—the municipalities, the missions, and the presidios—would work in unison to provide security on the *frontera* and form a barrier to foreign settlers and other intruders.[6]

By the 1680s, rumors of French and British forces near Texas forced Spanish officials to act. By the early seventeenth century, Spanish officials determined that Texas settlements would protect the northern borders of New Spain and defend the trading hubs in the colony's far north against

foreign invasion. These officials, however, had no control over the inhabitants of the region. In fact, the Spanish presence in San Antonio had
encroached upon the southern edges of territory generally controlled by
the Lipan Apaches.[7]

The Apaches had been present in what is now the American Southwest
since the fourteenth century. When they acquired horses from the Spanish
in 1608, they adopted a nomadic lifestyle and raided settlements with
impunity. For the next several decades, the cycle of hit-and-run attacks
and counterattacks marked the Texas region. As historian Randolph B.
"Mike" Campbell, notes, the "conflict between Spanish and Apaches
developed from several causes." Primarily, the Apaches viewed Spanish
trading with the Caddo people of East Texas and attempts to convert
Natives to Catholicism as hostile acts that would only benefit their enemies
and rivals. As such, the Apaches raided the Spanish in the San Antonio
region. Second, as the Spanish counterattacked hostile Apache bands, the
arrival of the Comanches to Texas during the 1730s only exacerbated the
already tense conflict between the Spanish and Native peoples. Spanish
efforts to subdue the Indigenous people of the region failed, and warfare
continued to disrupt Texas.[8]

During the last decade of the eighteenth century, Spain encountered
new challenges from a newly founded nation, the United States of America. Spanish officials worried about what American independence would
mean for their possessions in Florida, Louisiana, and Mexico.[9] The steady
growth of the United States in the decade following the Revolution only
exacerbated those fears: the American population eclipsed that of New
Spain by 1790.[10]

The Spanish response included attempts to regulate commerce and
promote immigration. For Americans, the opportunity to receive Spanish
land grants and access to the Mississippi River drove them westward across
the Appalachian Mountains to Louisiana. Spain's immigration policies
did not apply to Texas, however. There, Spanish officials attempted to keep
Americans from trading with the Native population and keep them out
of the region due to concerns that Americans would attempt to inspire
the population to rebel. When Spanish soldiers confronted American

Philip Nolan in March 1801, he only seemed to confirm their fears. Nolan, who had already made several trips into Texas to trade for mustangs, had drawn the suspicion of Spanish officials. They believed that he aspired to take control of the region through a filibustering expedition. After several trips into Texas, he returned in 1800 with more than two dozen men to acquire horses. Yet, in 1801 a Spanish contingent met Nolan, shot him in the head, and imprisoned his supporters.[11]

Nineteenth-Century Texas

The security of Texas remained a principal concern for Spanish officials at the turn of the nineteenth century. Indian raids, foreign intrusions, *contra-bandistas* (smugglers), and the loss of Louisiana first to France and later to the United States, all alarmed Spanish authorities. Though the Texas population still languished with only 3,169 Spanish-speaking inhabitants in 1790, Spain planned to buttress its northern *frontera* with thousands of settlers and a new military command. The Spanish crown failed to send any additional reinforcements due to events in Europe, however. Thus, it fell on the commandant general of the Interior Provinces, Nemecio Salcedo, to take on the task of securing Texas.[12]

To supplement the military aspect, Salcedo ordered the Compañía Volante de San Carlos del Álamo de Parras to march to Béxar in December 1802.[13] The compañía volante, or flying squadron, originated in the early seventh century as a tool to protect New Spain's northern *frontera*. The men who composed these mounted units numbered anywhere from two dozen to as many as seventy. They were lightly armed and focused on punitive expeditions against hostile Indians. By 1773, Teodoro de Croix, the commandant general of the northern provinces, formalized the compañía volante when Spain issued the New Regulations for the Presidios. Each unit would be composed of approximately seventy local men who understood the terrain. Training from Spanish professional soldiers instilled a semblance of military standards. Yet, ultimately, each trooper had to be responsible for his own equipment, including a carbine rifle, two pistols, a saddle, spurs, and multiple horses. The spare horses proved an essential part of the squadron's ability to relentlessly pursue

La Compañía Volante by Daniel Castro, San Antonio. Compañías Volantes, or flying squadrons, were light mobile cavalry units operating in New Spain's far northern regions during the eighteenth and nineteenth centuries. They continued to operate into the early Mexican period as a means of local defense by citizen militias.

its targets on the *frontera*. Borrowing on the tactics of Native American warriors, the squadrons employed mobile tactics and the doctrine of *vatir y perseguir* (strike and pursue) as they patrolled the region. As historian Stephen L. Hardin notes, these units attacked the enemy in their own camps and thus took the war to their adversaries.[14]

The men of these units helped define their communities. The compañía volante of San Carlos, for instance, arrived for permanent military duty in San Antonio around 1803. Tlaxcalan Indians made up most of its members. The Tlaxcalans, originally from central Mexico, had allied themselves with the Spanish and fought against the Aztecs in the sixteenth century before moving and settling in northern Mexico. Upon arrival in San Antonio, the members of the company soon intermarried with the locals. As Andrés Tijerina argues, the Tlaxcalan troops who came with the company quickly contributed to the racial mixing, or *mestizaje*, on the *frontera* by marrying with the Spanish and mestizos in San Antonio.[15] Upon arrival the Compañía Álamo immediately got to work buttressing San Antonio de Béxar. By 1805 the cavalrymen had converted the mission's old convent into a military barracks and built the first military hospital, which treated soldiers and civilians alike.[16]

For obvious reasons, the cavalrymen were popular with the residents of New Spain. They aided in thwarting Native tribe raids, helped capture fugitives, and even served as an impediment to smuggling operations on the frontier. Their duties were all encompassing, as they also served as couriers and escorts for Spanish authorities. In 1809, when rumors of an American invasion reached New Spain, the Tejano horsemen of the Compañía Álamo prepared for an attack by buttressing the defenses around San Antonio, which included the walls of their bastion. While no invasion occurred, it demonstrated their ability to remain vigilant in case of attack. Although their original orders stemmed from fears of an external invasion coming from the east, the men of the compañía would ultimately have to deal with internal rebellions.

Between 1809 and 1811, insurrections and revolutionary activity marked Texas and all of Mexico as struggles for independence led to bloody conflicts. While events continued to simmer in central Mexico, Bernardo Gutiérrez de Lara, a former merchant and blacksmith from Tamaulipas, traveled to Washington, DC, in late 1811 to request aid for the rebel cause in Mexico. Though rejected, Gutiérrez went to Louisiana to recruit men for a revolt against the Spanish government. There, he met and received the aid of Augustus William Magee, a native of Boston and a graduate of the United States Military Academy, to raise a small army. Calling themselves the Republican Army of the North, the 130-man contingent advanced on Nacogdoches, Texas, on August 8, 1812, causing the royalist supporters to flee in all directions. Governor Salcedo organized an army to meet a rebellion. The Spanish fought the rebels on-and-off until February 1813, when they retreated toward San Antonio. The rebel army defeated the Spanish at the Battle of Salado, and Gutiérrez gained control of San Antonio on April 1, 1813. Gutiérrez declared Texas independent five days later. He remained in power for three months until Joaquín de Arredondo, commandant of the eastern division of the Provincias Internas, led a force of 2,000 royalist soldiers against the rebels. At the resulting Battle of Medina, on August 18, Arredondo's army decimated the rebels, killing more than one thousand and executing more than three hundred. Though the leaders of the rebellion escaped capture, the lesson of executing rebels was not lost on one of Arredondo's junior officers, Antonio López de Santa Anna.[17]

For the soldiers in the compañía volante, the revolt revealed the difficulties in choosing national identity. For the commandant of the Álamo de Parras Company, Lieutenant Vicente Tarín, it meant he had to choose between a new political power or the world he had always known. As historian Raúl Ramos points out, during the early nineteenth century, the concept of a nation-state remained unknown to the inhabitants of Texas. The fact that they would ultimately live under five flags up to the Civil War era would only complicate things. After the Battle of Medina, those troopers who remained ambivalent about the rebellion renewed their loyalties to Spain. Those who refused to acquiesce to the Spanish flag, fought, fled to Louisiana, or avoided capture by retreating to a place on the Texas-Louisiana border called the Neutral Ground to plot their next move. San Antonio's compañía volante practically ceased to exist for the next five years, left in disrepair and without funds as raids and uncertainty continued to mark the Alamo City until after 1817.[18] San Antonio's lack of security and military preparedness during the 1810s was echoed throughout the sparse Texas frontier. The independence struggles that started in 1810 hampered the ability of officials in Mexico City to respond.

Under the Mexican Flag, 1821–1835

Once Mexican independence had been won in 1821, Tejanos continued to take part in military service. In Laredo, 150 miles south of San Antonio, residents joined the ranks of the Compañía Cívica de Laredo, a volunteer militia unit organized to protect the town from hostile Native bands. According to records in the Laredo archives, more than eighty volunteers joined the company in the half decade following Mexican independence. These men engaged in a sporadic, if not frustrating, war with the Native people. Laredo Tejanos tried to find ways to coexist with Indigenous groups on the frontier, including peace treaties.[19] Nevertheless, broken treaties and military incursions marked the decade, showing that an independent Mexico fared no better than Spain in protecting its citizenry from the *indios bárbaros* ("savage" Indians).[20]

Texas had long been a buffer for New Spain's northern frontier. Yet with Mexican independence, frontier security had to account for a daunting challenge. The new Mexican empire was immense. Encompassing the viceroyalty of New Spain, it stretched north to Texas and California in the present-day United States all the way to Central America. The vast frontier added to the maelstrom of issues the nascent nation had to deal with, including unemployment, lack of agricultural production, and depleted revenues. The burden was too much, and anti-imperial soldiers marched toward Mexico City. After ten months, Agustín Iturbide's experiment with a Mexican monarchy came to an end as he abdicated his throne in February 1823.[21]

Just before Mexican independence, Spanish officials gambled on a new scheme to populate and control the frontier. In 1821, the commandant general of Monterrey granted Moses Austin of Missouri permission to settle approximately three hundred Catholic families in Texas. When Austin died before the move could be initiated, his son, Stephen, took on the responsibility and was granted permission by the Mexican government to settle families in Texas. They were supposed to be of good moral character, adopt Catholicism, and agree to abide by Mexican laws.

Officials struck similar bargains with other empresarios, although none would ever be quite as successful as Austin. To fend off Indian attacks and generally secure the frontier, Mexican authorities implemented an immigration policy that rewarded settlers with land in exchange for honorable citizenship. Adding to the enticements, colonists could receive additional land for their slaves, and they would be exempt from Mexican taxes for a period of approximately seven years. By 1827, there were more than 10,000 US citizens living in Texas, outnumbering the Mexican population more than twofold. While Mexican officials hoped that the immigrants from the United States would provide a much-needed economic and social boost to the region, the Americans remained ambivalent about adopting Mexican laws and customs.[22] For almost a decade, Anglo-Americans flooded into the region, brought their slaves, and overlooked Tejanos. The latter, their population equaled by the Anglo newcomers by the mid-1820s, soon saw their own numbers eclipsed by the burgeoning slave population within another decade.[23]

Unsurprisingly, by the late 1820s, grievances on both sides—Mexican and Anglo Texans—began to materialize. Texans lamented that their province was attached to the state of Coahuila. The capital was in Saltillo, more than one hundred miles south of the Río Grande. Mexican officials, too, began to recognize that problems in Texas were slowly getting out of hand as some Americans sought to acquire additional Texas land by revolution or theft. In 1826, a dispute between two American empre-sarios, Haden and Jonathan Edwards, and Mexican authorities near Nacogdoches resulted in the forfeiture of their grant and a rebellion designed to carve out an independent republic in East Texas. The so-called Fredonian Rebellion in December 1826 rallied disgruntled settlers under the rallying cry of "Independence, Liberty, Justice." Mexican authori-ties, along with Austin and his colonists, rallied and forced the rebels to flee by January 1827. Yet that incident and a follow-up investigation convinced Mexican officials to buttress Mexican control over their far north. The resulting Law of April 6, 1830, prohibited all further American immigration, strengthened Mexican garrisons, and encouraged Mexican colonization in Texas.[24]

The Law of April 6, 1830, served as a catalyst for a monumental shift in the political and cultural landscape of Texas. Within a few years, Anglo Texans clashed with Mexican authorities over the collection of taxes. By 1832, some Anglos clamored for separating Texas from Coahuila or at least moving the capital to San Antonio. For their part, Tejanos found themselves in a precarious position. As they saw it, the Anglo-Texan peti-tion for statehood was possibly illegal. Even Stephen F. Austin's entreaties could not convince the Mexican Texan population to acquiesce. In San Antonio, prominent Tejanos drafted a petition to the state government that fell short of demanding a separation of Texas from Coahuila. By the end of 1832, Tejanos and Anglo Texans found themselves demanding greater rights under the Mexican flag but not full independence.[25]

The political turmoil in Texas mirrored the growing instability in Mexico City as centralists and federalists debated the country's future. In 1831, President Anastasio Bustamante ordered the execution of former president, Vicente Guerrero, who was accused of treason. While the death of Guerrero seemed to quench desires for vengeance, the social structure of Mexico and Texas remained unchanged. In Texas, the influx of additional American immigrants only intensified despite the Law of April 6, 1830. The Indian threats continued, and corruption and illiteracy persisted in Mexico's far north. Tejanos and Anglo Texans tried to define their own notions of what liberty meant for them, but in many ways, they remained apart. As historian Andrew Torget argues, though Anglos and Tejanos "communicated, collaborated, cooperated, and traded," they remained physically and ideologically segregated.[26]

The Road to Revolution

The early Mexican republic was cast in further turmoil when Antonio López de Santa Anna declared himself in rebellion against President Bustamante in 1832. Santa Anna, who had helped defend Mexico from a Spanish invasion in 1829, promised to return Mexico to its federalist-leaning Constitution of 1824. Yet, Santa Anna had already shown a certain political flexibility. After being part of Arredondo's army in 1813, Santa Anna threw his support behind Iturbide's independence movement only to help overthrow the Mexican emperor two years later. At the height of Bustamante's regime, Santa Anna used his influence to overthrow the Mexican president and force new elections in 1833. Despite winning the election, Santa Anna retreated to his hacienda in Veracruz and allowed his vice president, Valentín Gómez Farías, to lead the country in his stead. Farías's liberal reforms proved unpopular, and Santa Anna returned to the presidency with the intent on spearheading a centralist republic and abandoning the Constitution of 1824.[27]

Santa Anna's ascension coincided with the upheavals in Texas. While Anglo Texans and Tejanos remained uncertain about Santa Anna's role in the future of the region, they remained optimistic. Accordingly, Austin traveled to Mexico City in July 1833 to argue for Texas statehood, separate from Coahuila. At first Austin seemed to gain support for the idea, but it stalled in the Mexican congress. Upon his trip back home, he was arrested for writing a letter recommending that the *ayuntamiento* (city council) in San Antonio organize a government independent of Coahuila. For that serious error in judgment, Austin served near a year in prison before receiving amnesty and returning to Texas in the fall of 1835.[28]

When Austin returned to Texas, things had changed since the last time the colonists had agitated for change. In April 1835, news of Santa Anna's brutal repression of a rebellion in the state of Zacatecas alarmed Texas colonists. After Zacatecans had balked at Santa Anna's moves toward centralization, they rose in protest. Santa Anna responded with 3,500 troops, who were ordered to suppress any dissent. When Austin reached Texas on September 8, he blamed the authorities in Mexico for the instability. Accordingly, he endorsed colonists' efforts to call for a Consultation of Texas representatives at Washington-on-the-Brazos on October 15. While independence was not an absolute goal for most colonists, the planned meeting represented the opinion of many Anglos and Tejanos that the Mexican government had treated the far northern province unfairly.[29]

As residents in San Antonio (more commonly known as Béxar at this time) celebrated Mexican Independence Day on September 16, a whirlwind swirled around Texas. For months, Béxar's military commander, Colonel Domingo de Ugartechea, attempted to play the role of intermediary between the Texans and Tejanos and the Mexican government, reassuring residents that peace could be achieved if they merely submit to Mexican authority. In the summer of 1835, Ugartechea suggested Mexican troop reinforcements could ensure peace. On September 17, his superior, General Martín Perfecto de Cos, arrived in Matamoros with five hundred additional soldiers before making his way to take command of Ugartechea's garrison.

With the growing tension palpable, Ugartechea ordered a small detachment of men to march to the town of Gonzales about seventy-miles east of San Antonio to retrieve a cannon that had been loaned to the town to ward off Indian attacks. Lieutenant Francisco Castañeda led a one hundred-man force to take the cannon, arriving at Gonzales on September 29. Weather and an unfordable river allowed the town's residents enough time to rally a force of about 150 men. On October 1, the Texians raised a white banner emblazoned with a black cannon and the words "Come and Take It." At dawn the next day, the Texian force charged the Mexicans, firing the cannon, and yelling wildly. Castañeda, without orders to engage, immediately withdrew, despite losing a couple of men. The Texians, for their part, were emboldened by their actions.[30]

Historians have chronicled and argued the causes of the Texas Revolution for generations. Yet despite the complexity of events that led to the fighting in the fall of 1835, one constant remains: even though the skirmish in Gonzales was not at the level of Lexington and Concord, contemporaries viewed it as the start of their own Revolutionary War. A week later, Texans under George Collingsworth moved against the presidio at La Bahia and the town of Goliad, attacking the depleted troops there on October 10 and forcing their surrender. Once word reached out to the Texas settlements about the events in Gonzales and Goliad, additional volunteers rushed to join the cause. Undoubtedly the confrontation at Gonzales proved to be the catalyst for war.[31]

Texas Revolution

After the Texians took Goliad, war fervor intensified when Stephen F. Austin arrived the following day and the colonists decided to advance on San Antonio. Their numbers soon swelled to approximately four hundred men by October 20 as they trudged toward Salado Creek, just five miles east of San Antonio, ready to lay siege to the city.

The Consultation at Washington-on-the-Brazos, originally scheduled to meet on October 15, had been organized with the idea of trying to determine what Texans and Tejanos would do next in their growing confrontation with Mexican authorities. The hostilities at Gonzales and Goliad had changed all that, however. Instead, leaders decided to postpone that meeting until the following month. In the interim, Austin urged each district to send a representative to San Felipe. This so-called Permanent

Council only lasted three weeks, disbanding by November 1. Though it had no long-term effect on military events, this small group of representatives did try to increase support for the cause against the Mexican government. Yet it was not until November 7 that the fifty-five delegates who attended the Consultation determined the course of action for the rebellion. Falling short of an outright call for independence, the delegates instead called for a restoration of the Constitution of 1824 to appeal to Mexican federalists. Significantly, too, the Consultation created a provisional government for Texas and replaced Austin as commander of its army, appointing Tennessee native Sam Houston in his stead.[32]

The Consultation was just as uncertain in military affairs as it was in politics. By replacing Austin with Houston, the delegates recognized that the empresario was more of a statesman than a commander and directed him to travel to Washington, DC to obtain help for their cause from the United States. In its attempt to create a military force, the Consultation instructed that two-year volunteers fill its ranks. The only troops currently on hand for Houston to command were those at San Antonio. The rabble of men in the environs of that city were brave and resolute. Yet, they were not ideal soldiers. The men had failed to heed Austin's orders and calls for discipline. They found the monotony of a siege too much to bear and resorted to drinking excessively and firing their weapons at nothing in particular. The lack of discipline among the Texians was not lost on Austin who delayed his departure from the army lest they disband or do something even worse. Hoping to inspire his men to action, on November 23 Austin ordered them to attack the city. To his dismay, most of the volunteers refused. This embarrassing episode led Austin to reevaluate his role in the Texian military force. Determining that his men would continue the siege if they could simply choose their own commander, Austin thanked the men for their service before departing for San Felipe and later, Washington, DC.[33]

The scene around San Antonio reflected a larger, more pressing issue for Houston's Texian army: it truly did not exist. The men who had rallied against Mexico after the battle at Gonzales were irregular soldiers. They were free to come and go as they pleased. In sum, it was a loosely

Juan Seguin. Courtesy of the State Preservation Board, Austin, Texas.

organized militia barely held together by emotions and Austin's efforts as commander in chief. For Anglo Texans, the decision to join the cause fluctuated between their own self-determination and the safety of their homes, as the Mexican threat was not the only one on the isolated Texas frontier. For Tejanos, it proved a bit more complicated, with additional pressures. Though the events at Gonzales had united Anglos Texans and Tejanos against the centralist Mexican government, Texans of Mexican descent remained wary. This was not lost on Austin in the early stages of his command. In his bid to ensure the rift with Mexico did not end up being defined in racial or ethnic terms, Austin appointed Juan Seguín of San Antonio, a leading Tejano, to the rank of captain in October 1835, and instructed him to raise a company of vaqueros (cowboys) to aid as mounted troopers. Austin insisted that the "revolt was being fought against centralism, not for independence."[34] For his part, Seguín had already reached out to his neighbors, "satisfied that the beginning of the revolution was close at hand."[35]

The fight against centralism brought other Tejanos into the fold during the early stages of the conflict. In Victoria, Plácido Benavides, the alcalde and a prominent landowner, joined the federalist cause in October 1835. Born in 1810 in Reynosa, Tamaulipas, Benavides moved to the colony of Martín De León in Texas at the age of eighteen. He served as a land agent for De León for several years, and he married the daughter of the empresario in 1831. After his father-in-law passed away two years later, Benavides and his three brothers ascended to positions of prominence in Victoria. The Mexican government relied on Benavides to serve as colonial administrator and recruit additional settlers.[36]

In his position of leadership Benavides demonstrated an uncanny knack for military tactics when defending his colonists from Native American attacks around Victoria. In 1834, Benavides led a company of Tejanos and Anglos in a running battle against Karankawas at Green Lake, about ten miles south of Victoria in what is now Calhoun Country. Routing the Native force, Benavides basked in his role of militia commander, even building a fort, called the Round House, for the defense of Victoria. During that time, animosity between Tejano and Anglo settlers in the colony began to surface as the number of Anglo settlers eclipsed the number of Tejanos in the region. While both groups were steadfast in their support of federalism, a growing rift between them emerged by 1835. Yet, once the fighting began at Gonzales, Benavides determined he would throw his hat in the ring on the side of the federalist cause. Riding toward Gonzales with another Victoriano, John J. Linn, the two men tried to rally support for a plan to capture General Cos, who was marching from Goliad to reinforce Ugartechea in San Antonio. Failing to inspire support, Benavides and Linn instead joined the Collingsworth volunteers already set on capturing Goliad. Benavides led some thirty Tejanos in the capture of La Bahia that October.[37]

Like Seguín, Benavides was appointed captain in Austin's "Army of the People" after Goliad. Benavides led a company of twenty-six Tejanos in the siege of San Antonio. These Tejanos proved invaluable to Austin's army as they served in the role of mounted scouts, providing them with the eyes and ears they needed to lay siege to the Mexican forces in the city. Soon after arriving near San Antonio, Benavides joined his company with men under Colonel James Bowie, a native of Kentucky who had moved to Texas in 1830. Bowie and Benavides patrolled the area south of San Antonio searching for Mexican threats.[38]

Benavides, a steadfast federalist supporter, saw the conflict in strict terms, even against his fellow Tejanos. According to one account, Benavides and his men detained a local herder under the suspicion that he was hiding horses for the Mexicans. When the herder denied the accusations, Benavides implored Bowie to torture the Tejano by hanging until he revealed the location of the horses.[39] Benavides's treatment of the herder how prevalent class distinctions were in 1830s Texas. Benavides belonged to the elite class: landowners, ranchers, businessmen, and members of prominent families. On the opposite side, the *peones* (commoners) were of mixed-blood and performed the drudgery of manual and unskilled labor. Benavides demonstrated the complexity of Tejano identity during the revolutionary conflict.[40]

Other Tejanos had to make difficult choices during the Anglo-led struggle against Mexican authorities. Tejanos could align themselves with the Texians or the Mexicans, selecting rebellion or loyalty. Or they could cite long-standing social relationships and dependence on trade or other economic factors and cooperate with Mexico or the upstart rebel forces. Other choices included ignoring the immediate situation and remaining neutral during the conflict's early stages; perhaps they could later align themselves with the winning side. More importantly, there were various degrees of loyalty that moved beyond simply supporting or rejecting the notion of a Texas secession movement. As a historian of the period notes, "Tejano identity . . . needs to take into account the multiple roles played by Tejanos and their underlying role as mediators in a culturally complex place."[41]

While Benavides and Seguín seem to have had little internal conflict when they made their decision to support the rebel cause, the choice was harder for other prominent Tejanos. José Antonio Navarro, for instance, found the immediate circumstances of the rebellion more complicated. Navarro was only eighteen years old when he supported the Gutiérrez-Magee expedition of 1813. But, when the filibustering expedition failed and Spanish soldiers executed hundreds in retribution, Navarro was forced to flee to the United States. He returned three years later and settled in San Antonio to practice law. His family also supported the federalist cause. Yet, in the wake of the Gonzales skirmish, Navarro packed up his family and quickly left town, certain that additional fighting would follow. Navarro and his family traveled to their ranch in Atascosa, about twenty miles south of San Antonio. When General Cos advanced to San Antonio in early October, the governor of Texas and Coahuila, Rafael Eca y Múzquiz, instructed Navarro to assist Cos and Ugartechea with their duties. Navarro complied, despite placing him at odds with his federalist leanings and the allegiance of his neighbors to the growing rebellion. Cos, too, noted that Navarro's sympathy lay with his fellow colonists, and he testified that Navarro remained on his ranch during the hostilities.[42]

During the two-month siege in San Antonio, the Texian forces struggled just as much as the besieged. With Seguín and Benavides patrolling the southern approaches to the city, Austin's force of approximately 300 men remained numerically inferior to Cos's 650 soldiers garrisoned in the crumbling Spanish mission, San Antonio de Valero, simply known as the Alamo, and its surrounding presidio complex. Though the Texians ultimately succeeded in isolating Cos from communicating with Santa Anna's army in Mexico, the monotony of the siege began to wear on the Texas forces. They received reinforcements from the United States and an additional one hundred Tejanos joined the ranks by November, placing them at near parity with Cos's forces. On October 28, Cos attempted to break the siege, attacking an isolated force of Texians upriver, near the Concepción Mission. The Texians soundly defeated the 275-man Mexican force, inflicting more than seventy-five casualties, while suffering only two. From this point, Cos remained in a defensive position, awaiting reinforcement as Austin's army continued their siege. By November, the paucity of food and increasingly cold weather forced some of Austin's men to reevaluate their dedication to the cause. As such, when they refused Austin's orders to attack, they chose their next commander, Colonel Edward Burleson from North Carolina, a veteran of the War of 1812 and an experienced commander of various militias in the American South. Even Burleson's leadership was not enough to overcome the growing frustrations around San Antonio. In late November, the two forces clashed in the so-called Grass Fight, when Mexican forces abandoned horses, mules, and hay meant for Cos's cavalry. The skirmish was another Texian victory, but it did not dissuade the growing despondency around the Texian volunteers.[43]

Burleson's hold on the Texas forces in San Antonio continued to wane by early December as morale plummeted due to short rations and colder weather. As threats of desertion increased, Burleson made plans to assault Cos. As they had done under Austin, some of the men refused. On this occasion, however, one volunteer, Ben Milam, a native of Kentucky, convinced Burleson that three hundred men could lead the assault while the remaining four hundred volunteers remained in reserve. On December 5, Texian forces launched their assault, capturing houses north of the city plaza. The fighting stalled for the next two days until Ugartechea returned to the city with an additional six hundred men as reinforcements, including Tejanos from Laredo, about 150 miles south. Most of these troops were untrained and arrived without supplies, placing an additional burden on Cos. By December 8, both sides teetered on the brink of exhaustion, the Texans having lost Milam to a sharpshooter and feeling despondent that Mexican reinforcements had arrived. The Mexicans, too, struggled without supplies. As some Texans considered retreating eastward, one last push was made and house-to-house fighting on the night of the eighth forced Cos and his men back to the Alamo. In the wake of this setback, the Mexican forces began to dissolve into the night, deserting the Mexican commander. Cos, realizing he could not hold on, sent officers to discuss surrender terms on the morning of December 9. With generous surrender terms, Cos and his men left San Antonio, bound south toward the Río Grande.[44]

The Texans' victory at San Antonio gave the rebels the sense that victory against Mexico was within their grasp. More than a hundred American volunteers stood near the Alamo, under the command of Colonel James C. Neill, anxious for what lay next. The bulk of the men who forced Cos to surrender had already gone home, to tend to their farms, businesses, or families. Over in Goliad, Philip Dimmitt urged a drive against Matamoros to inspire more Mexican federalists to the cause.

The truth of the matter is that many of the volunteers who favored additional action against Mexico were newcomers to Texas, had no loyalty to Mexico, and viewed the conflict through the prism of race. Austin had made inroads to ensure that Tejanos joined the cause to avoid this perception, but the revolutionaries had other ideas. On December 13, 1835, Provisional Governor Henry Smith issued a proclamation for Texas settlements to send delegates to the town of Washington-on-the Brazos the following spring to write a constitution for a permanent government. A week later, on December 20, the Goliad garrison issued a declaration of independence from Mexico. It directly contradicted what the Consultation had urged the previous month and further alienated Mexican and Tejano federalists who might rally to the cause.[45]

The perceptions that the battle for San Antonio was just the beginning of a larger conflict was concerning to most Texas leaders. Yet, many new volunteers remained grandiosely optimistic. The sense of self-importance was evident in the words of one volunteer at Gonzales, David B. Macomb, who suggested that the Mexicans "did not want to fight the Anglo-American of Texas" during the confrontation over the canon. Later, Macomb insisted that the "Anglo-American spirit appears in everything we do; quick, intelligent, and comprehensive; and while such men are fighting for their rights, they may possibly be overpowered by numbers, but if whipped, they won't stay whipped."[46] In late December, the General Council (the provisional government of the Texian rebels) authorized the expedition to Matamoros, much to General Houston's chagrin. Beset by chaos and confusion, the operation remained stillborn. At the same time, news reached Texas that Santa Anna was on his way to Texas and intended to respond to the hostilities in the same way he dealt with Zacatecas.[47]

While the Texian army decided what to do next, Cos's defeated soldiers trudged home toward the Río Grande. The demoralized troops reached Laredo on Christmas Day 1835. Once more the soldiers secured sustenance and mounts in the border town as they made their way across the river toward Saltillo. Tejanos in Laredo worried more about the implications of Indian attacks and privation than Santa Anna's march north or the war fervor of Texian volunteers.

The Tejanos who joined the Texian army in the fall of 1835 did so for personal and ideological reasons. The ascension of Juan Seguín convinced other Tejanos to volunteer. In the case of Seguín's unit, many of these men were close in age and had grown up together in the area surrounding San Antonio. Since Seguín had aligned himself with Stephen F. Austin even before the rebellion, it was easier for these young Tejanos to rally behind the Anglo-Texan leaders and their movement. Beyond these personal motives, Tejanos also joined because of their ideological beliefs in their regional autonomy. As historian Arnoldo De León has suggested, the Texas frontier had instilled a certain identity in Tejanos that underscored local autonomy and independence, concepts that aligned themselves with the federalist promises of the Mexican republic. For many of these Tejanos, joining the army meant they were protecting the Constitution of 1824 and fighting for freedom from the regulations of Mexico City.[48]

The fervor for attacking Matamoros notwithstanding, the Texas volunteers who laid siege to Cos's army at San Antonio practically disappeared by late December. Out of the more than seven hundred volunteers who bore arms, only about one hundred remained, now under the command of Lieutenant Colonel J. C. Neal, the Texian artillery commander during the siege. In January 1836, James Bowie, a native Kentuckian who had made his way to Texas years earlier, arrived with another thirty to forty men. Bowie had orders from Houston to destroy the Alamo to allow Texian forces to concentrate in the east. Yet, soon after arriving, Neil convinced Bowie that the Alamo could be reinforced, and the latter deferred. While the commanders prepared the Alamo for the siege to come, on February 3, Colonel William B. Travis rode into town with an additional thirty men. Neill abdicated his command on the fourteenth when urgent family business called him away, turning over leadership to Travis. Not to be deterred, Bowie's men insisted that a vote be held for the role of commander. Travis and Bowie ultimately decided to share the command, but when Bowie fell ill a few days later, Travis assumed overall command. A famous folk hero, soldier, and politician from Tennessee, Davy Crockett, rode into town with more prestige than any of the Alamo volunteers. But he deferred all accolades and insisted on serving with the rank and file as an enlisted man.[49]

While the commanders of the Alamo worked out the defense plans for the Béxar bastion, Santa Anna marched north with an army of 6,018 men. In January, Santa Anna instructed General Cos, his brother-in-law, stationed in Monclova, to disregard his previous surrender terms with the Texians and to join his Army of Operations after a brief respite. Santa Anna planned to crush the Texas rebellion with a pincer movement. As he marched toward San Antonio, General José de Urrea would cross the Río Grande at Matamoros and advance on Goliad with a smaller army of 550 men. On February 16, 1836, Santa Anna crossed the river near present-day Eagle Pass, approximately 110 miles southwest of the Alamo. Seguín's scouts noted the Mexican army's movements and reported them to Travis, who had received so many reports that the enemy had reached Texas that it proved easy to dismiss most of these accounts. Significantly, too, these latest reports—though accurate—came from Tejanos. Travis, who held anti-Mexican views, dismissed these reports from people he suspected as favorable to the centralists. His suspicion might have grown as Tejanos in Béxar began to evacuate their homes by February 20, likely fearing the battle ahead. The next day, fifteen Tejano volunteers notified Travis that they were terminating their service. On 23 February, the Texian commander noted the advance elements of Santa Anna's army on the outskirts of San Antonio.[50]

Travis's feelings about Tejanos were not rare. In fact, they were part of a shifting paradigm of how some Texas leaders had grown suspicious of the loyalty of Mexican Texans. With Austin in Washington, power tilted toward men like Travis and Henry Smith who did not trust Tejanos. In December 1835, Smith wrote to the General Council about his suspicions and whether they should include Tejanos in Texas's representation. He noted that during the siege of Béxar few Tejanos joined the Texian cause and suspected they remained enemies of Anglo Texans.[51] "I consider the fact plan and evident: I consider they who are not for us must be against us," Smith wrote.[52] At the onset of the Revolution, the Tejano population numbered approximately four thousand and was concentrated in five areas: Nacogdoches, Victoria, Goliad, Béxar, and Laredo. The complexities of the conflict, the uncertainty of alliances, fears of retribution, and the shifting dynamics of power as the number of Anglo newcomers in Texas grew all played a role in how Tejanos tried to negotiate with the world around them. Yet, at the beginning of 1836, despite the growing rhetoric and suspicions, Tejanos such as Navarro, Erasmo Seguín, Francisco Ruiz, and Gaspar Flores still held positions as delegates bound for the convention on Washington-on-the-Brazos, scheduled for March 1, 1836. In the meantime, Texas had no true government while Santa Anna positioned his forces around San Antonio.[53]

When the Mexican army arrived at the gates of San Antonio, Santa Anna had no real strategic need to take the city, just hubris. The "Napoleon of the West" could have easily bypassed San Antonio and moved eastward, toward the more tangible military and political threats. But the need to avenge Cos's December defeat and the desire to inflict fear on anyone who supported the rebellion proved too great for Santa Anna to overcome. By February 23, the advance elements of the Mexican army had begun their siege on the Alamo. Two days later, recognizing that he could not hold the fort with the 150 men at his disposal, Travis sent pleas for help to Colonel James Fannin at Goliad. On the night of February 28, Seguín left the Alamo with another request for reinforcements. Santa Anna's cavalry had been

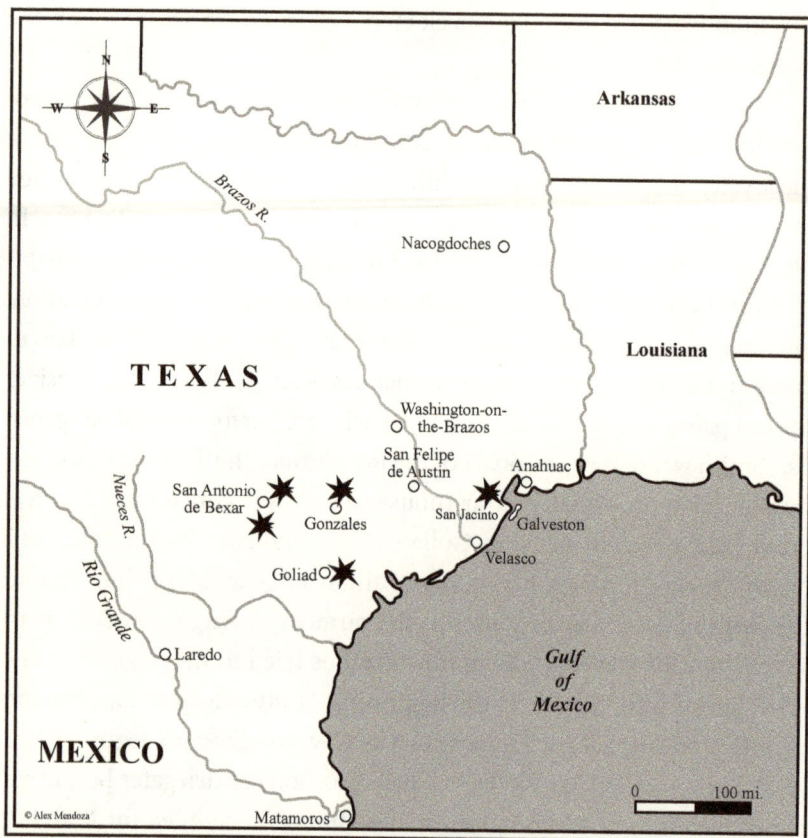

The Texas Revolution, 1835–36

able to slow the flow of couriers in and out of San Antonio, but Seguín got through. Fannin's efforts to bring relief ended in failure, and he returned to Goliad with his men. The only reinforcements that Travis received came when thirty-two volunteers from Gonzales. In the meantime, Santa Anna grew restless as he waited for his heavy artillery, which could easily break apart the Alamo's adobe walls. By March 3, the Mexicans succeeded in knocking out a few Texian guns. Inside the Alamo, hope faded quickly as the men recognized the daunting force surrounding them.[54]

On March 5, Travis gathered his men for a conference. Travis had already sent an emotional letter to the delegates at Washington-on-the-Brazos, and supplies were short as the Alamo defenders faced formidable odds. Certainly, the Texian volunteers, including the twelve Tejanos, inside the Alamo were not suicidal, but they knew that Santa Anna had established a no-quarter policy for the rebels. While Texas lore is rich with inspiring speeches that Travis delivered to his men, including one account in which the Texian commander drew a line in the sand with his saber and asked his men to join him on the righteous side for the cause of Texas independence, it is difficult to precisely chronicle what exactly happened.

Santa Anna did not want a peaceful surrender, that is for certain. He ordered his men to assault the Alamo defenses on the sixth. Just before dawn, the Mexican forces launched their assault at four different points on the Alamo's walls. Travis was one of the first to die when a bullet struck him in the forehead as he stuck his head over a rampart. Bowie died later, shot in his bed because he was too weak to stand. The battle, which lasted approximately one hour, included fierce hand-to-hand combat. The thirteen-day siege ended with 183 Alamo defenders dead, including nine Tejanos.[55] The Mexican army even executed any defenders who remained, as per Santa Anna's orders. Only a handful of non-combatant survivors inside the Alamo were allowed to leave to describe what had happened. The Mexican army suffered approximately six hundred casualties. Santa Anna had won the battle, but at a cost.[56]

The Texian sacrifice at the Alamo delayed Santa Anna enough to allow the delegates who met at Washington-on-the-Brazos enough time to formally declare independence on March 2, 1836. With independence secured, the convention focused on creating an army and named Houston its commander in chief. Houston immediately rode to Gonzales to see if the Alamo could still be saved. Meanwhile, the delegates at the convention continued trying to build a government for the next two weeks, including naming a recently arrived Mexican exile, Lorenzo De Zavala, as vice president. When Houston arrived in Gonzales, he found approximately 374 volunteers under the command of Edward Burleson. There, he learned about the fate of the Alamo defenders and the disastrous Matamoros expedition, which finally launched in late February only to be decimated by Urrea's forces on March 2. The only rebel force that remained in the field was with Fannin at Goliad and included about four hundred volunteers.[57]

Elsewhere, Houston remained in Gonzales only a few days before leaving on March 13, advancing east toward the Colorado River. Houston remained preoccupied by Santa Anna's maneuvers and tried to hold his own army together. His men grumbled as they abandoned Gonzales and set the town on fire. Texas civilians, too, began a hasty retreat eastward, lest they get caught in the path of the Mexican army. This so-called Runaway Scrape followed news of Santa Anna's decimation of the Alamo and its survivors. The Mexican commander intended to march across Texas using a three-prong advance: the main army led by Santa Anna moving from San Antonio toward Anglo settlements to the east, and two smaller columns, one under Urrea advancing along the coast and another commanded by General Antonio Gaona taking aim at Nacogdoches. Meanwhile, Houston had reached the eastern side of the Colorado River with about 750 men, including recent arrivals. He had given orders to Fannin to withdraw from Goliad and meet up with the main army on March 14. As usual, Fannin found reasons to delay.[58]

Fannin's decision to wait proved costly. News reached the garrison that some Tejanos loyal to Mexico had aided Urrea's force and had swooped in to attack reinforcements. A few days later, Urrea's force advanced on Goliad, trapping Fannin's force and forcing their surrender. Soon thereafter, on March 27, Santa Anna ordered the execution of all prisoners, despite protests from some of his officers. Almost 350 men were executed and only two dozen escaped to tell the tale.[59]

Among those who survived was Plácido Benavides, whose men accompanied the unit under Dr. James Grant on the way to Matamoros. Benavides managed to escape on horseback when the Mexican dragoons swept across South Texas. According to Urrea's report, his troops killed forty-two rebels, captured three, and allowed a handful to escape, including Benavides. Among the dead was the bulk of Benavides's Tejano company, as many as twenty-four men. Urrea's decimation of Grant's force wiped out this contingent of Tejanos at Agua Dulce Creek, about twenty-six miles south of San Patricio. Meanwhile, Benavides raced to

Presidio La Bahia (now renamed Fort Defiance by the rebels) in Goliad to alert them about the approach of Urrea. When he arrived at Goliad, Benavides learned the news about Texas's independence, throwing him into a quandary. He remembered what he had been fighting for since the fall of 1835: the Constitution of 1824 and federalism, not independence. Fannin released him Benavides from his service to the Texian army, and he returned to Victoria determined to remain neutral for the remainder of the Texas Revolution.[60]

Some Tejanos remained loyal to Mexico. They choose to support Mexico for a variety of reasons. In the case of Carlos de la Garza, who owned a ranch in present-day Victoria County, economics and rivalries played a role in whom he supported during the Revolution. De la Garza organized a mounted company that he called the Guardias Victorianas, which he formed to defend his holdings against Irish colonists at nearby San Patricio. De la Garza operated in a gray area, willing to negotiate loyalties and allegiances as they came up. He operated with Urrea's cavalry against the settlement of Refugio, but when Santa Anna ordered the execution of the three hundred soldiers of Fannin's command, De la Garza secured the release of several of his Irish rivals.[61]

The Texian loss at Goliad, aided by Tejanos who helped Urrea's centralist forces, and the departure of Benavides from the ranks of Fannin's unit due to conflicting loyalties serve as a microcosms of the complexities surrounding Tejanos and military service during the Texas Revolution. Mexican Texans had long accepted that national devotion and identity could be part of a two-way exchange in which they could negotiate loyalties to further their own interests. Despite the expectations, or even demands, of nation-states such as Spain, Mexico, and now the Republic of Texas, Tejanos, often left to their own economic and military devices, remained committed to regional loyalty through the start of the twentieth century. The actions of local leaders such as Plácido Benavides illustrated this regionalism, even if it was sometimes misunderstood by outsiders as loyalty to other causes. Thus, some Texas leaders such as Travis and Smith, remained suspicious of Tejanos. They failed to grasp that in their new republic loyalties could sometimes blur; viewing these complexities through the lenses of cultural and ethnic identity misses the mark. For Benavides, it was simple: he was fighting for federalism and a return to the Constitution of 1824. When the goal of the Revolution changed to Texas independence, he chose to remain neutral. Other Tejanos felt pressured to assist the Mexican army lest they suffer punishment or retribution. Santa Anna's presence suggested that this fear was not unfounded.

Houston took the news of Fannin's defeat hard. He continued his retreat eastward because he wanted to keep his army intact and wait to probe any weaknesses in Santa Anna's army. On March 28, Houston's army reached San Felipe on the Brazos. A day later, the general withdrew to another position twenty miles north, a plantation owned by Jared Groce. Seguín's Tejano cavalry had been screening Houston's retreat thus far. At Groce's plantation, the army set up camp and some earlier grumbling over Houston's withdrawal seemed to dissipate.

The provisional government of Texas, meanwhile, had retreated to Harrisburg (near the present-day city of Houston). President David G. Burnet pressed Houston to advance against Santa Anna. Intelligence reports soon revealed that Santa Anna had split his army and a contingent of about one thousand men had moved toward Harrisburg. Seeing a favorable opportunity, Houston decided to advance. With approximately eight hundred troops, Houston believed he finally had an opportunity to strike at a numerically equal force. The Texian army moved southward, marching fifty-two miles in about two-and-a-half days. The fight that the Texas volunteers had been clamoring for seemed evident.[62]

Santa Anna's army had already been at Harrisburg, hoping to capture the provisional government. The Mexican commander ordered the town burned and headed southeast to New Washington, on Galveston Bay. Failing to capture the Texas government officials, Santa Anna assumed that Houston would continue to retreat north toward Nacogdoches. But Houston remained determined to strike at the Mexican force. Pushing his men on the night of April 19–20, Houston implored his men to "remember the Alamo" as they headed toward battle. On April 20, Mexican scouts spotted the advance elements of the Texian army and engaged them in a skirmish. The next day, Houston held a council of war with his leading lieutenants before deciding to launch his assault against the Mexican army at their camp at the confluence of the San Jacinto River and Buffalo Bayou. Reinforcement swelled the ranks of Houston's forces to nearly nine hundred men. The Mexican army had been buttressed by the arrival of Cos's troops and had about 1,350 troops.[63]

At about 3:00 p.m., Houston ordered his men forward against the Mexican line, infantry and artillery marching across the undulating prairie. Seguín pleaded with Houston to allow his cavalry unit, nineteen Tejanos, to be a part of the assault. The commander hesitated at first, fearing that the Texians' resentment toward Mexicans might arouse hostility (or worse). Seguín, who remained committed to the cause of independence, insisted, and Houston ultimately acquiesced. The Tejanos went into battle with cardboard placards in their hats to distinguish themselves from the enemy.

The Texians marched quickly till they were within four hundred yards of the Mexican camp. The men charged forward with screams of "Remember the Alamo! Remember Goliad!" reverberating over the din of musketry and artillery fire. Within twenty minutes, the battle turned into an utter rout. At the end, approximately 630 Mexicans lay dead, and another 700 were taken prisoner. The Texian army suffered a mere eight casualties. Santa Anna was taken prisoner. The following day he met with Houston despite calls for his execution in response to his no quarter policy. Houston protected the Mexican president but forced Santa Anna to sign an armistice that required the retreat of the remaining Mexican armies to south of the Río Grande. With the resulting Treaty of Velasco, Texas independence had been won.[64] For his exploits at San Jacinto, Seguín was promoted to the rank of colonel. The men under his command, the Ninth Company, Second Regiment of Texas Volunteers, could return to Béxar now that the Mexican threat had been expelled and Texas independence secured.[65] In total, 183 Tejano men fought in the Texas Revolution.[66]

The Republic of Texas

The new Republic of Texas transformed the lives of Tejanos and shifted the region's power structure. In the post-independence era, Tejanos

witnessed the decline of their economic and political strength. The fact
that most Tejanos remained neutral during the conflict only exacerbated
the doubts Anglo Texans held of their loyalty. When Tejanos balked as
the Revolution changed from a fight to preserve federalism to a struggle
for independence, it merely confirmed the reservations of some Texas leaders. In the 1835 siege of San Antonio, for instance, General Cos demanded
that the Tejano populace provide manual labor and sustenance for the
Mexican army. In the eyes of Anglo Texans, Tejanos who complied with
Cos committed treason. Most Tejanos were not able to stake out a place
of economic independence during the war. Wealthy Tejanos could at
least negotiate their roles during the war. One example was José Antonio
Navarro, who fled to his ranch with his family lest he betray his friends
and neighbors. By 1836, with the Mexican army gone from San Antonio,
Navarro was one of the Texas delegates who signed the declaration of
independence in March.[67]

A paucity of sources from Tejano participants means we may never
have a clear picture of their thinking and motives during the rebellion.
But a few examples show they were complex. In Laredo, for instance,
the difficulties of maintaining neutrality became readily apparent. In
December 1835, during Cos's defense of San Antonio, Mexican officials
enlisted men and confiscated material from Laredo to provide aid. When
Cos was defeated and the Mexican army moved south of the Río Grande
the following month, mayor Don Basilio Benavides implored Mexican
officials to provide his city defense from Indian attacks as the fighting for
Texas continued to spin out of control. But not every resident of Laredo
insisted on neutrality. In the Battle of the Alamo, a Laredoan, José María
Guerrero, a forty-three-year-old private, fought to defend the iconic bastion.[68] Guerrero, who had joined the company of prominent *Bexareño*
Juan Seguín, did not leave a written record outlining his thoughts and
motives for participating in the Anglo-Texan movement. Yet, the fact that
a Laredoan cast his lot with what eventually became a secession movement
indicates the complex decision-making process that faced the Mexican
Texan population during the Revolution.[69] Though most Tejanos tried to
remain neutral, loyalty to family and friends superseded nationalism. In

San Antonio, Juan Francisco Ximenes's three sons volunteered to fight for the Texian cause alongside Seguín in 1835 and 1836.[70]

During the Texas Republic period, power devolved from Mexico to Anglo newcomers. This change was evident even before the rebellion ended as Anglo Texans began to commandeer Tejanos just like Cos's army had done in San Antonio. In Goliad, the Anglo-Texan army confiscated Tejanos' property and livestock to maintain their hold on the city. Following the war, the sense of distrust only increased as Tejano families were increasingly displaced. Mexican Texans had cast their lot with their Anglo counterparts only to witness the eclipse of old power structures.[71] In fact, some of the Tejanos in Seguín's company made claims against the Republic of Texas for their services in the war only to have those demands rebuffed.[72] The problems facing Tejano veterans were not unique. During the next few years, the Tejano population experienced a transformation of their native land. As historian David Montejano notes, "the spirit of revenge" remained present as Anglo Texans began to claim the lands of the Mexican Texans, "ally and foe alike" in the years following the Revolution.[73]

Some Tejanos attempted to resist encroachment on their lands through armed resistance. One, Vicente Córdova of Nacogdoches, tried to lead a rebellion against the Republic in 1838. Ultimately, Córdova's efforts were defeated, and the leader had to flee to Mexico. But the furor led to other Tejanos (and Córdova's Cherokee allies) losing their land in Texas. While some of the Tejano elite staved off complete displacement through economic partnerships and intermarriage, others were not so fortunate.[74]

Texas Revolution veterans Juan Seguín and José Antonio Navarro continued to serve in positions of leadership as they straddled their dual identities as Tejanos and Mexicans. While Seguín remained integral to Texas politics, serving as the only Tejano in the Texas senate, Navarro advocated the recognition of Tejano rights. His support of the Mirabeau B. Lamar administration ultimately led to his participation in the ill-fated expedition in the summer of 1841 to annex Santa Fe, New Mexico and the upper Río Grande. Even though the Texas party ultimately surrendered to Mexican authorities without firing a shot, the incident suggests that some Tejanos still believed that they could have the best of both worlds. They faced an uphill battle as animosity and mistrust based on race and greed forced many Mexican families to flee south into Mexico despite their citizenship in the nascent Republic of Texas.[75] Even Seguín, who had earned an officer's commission for his service and had parlayed that experience into becoming the mayor of San Antonio, was forced to flee Texas as suspicions arose in the 1840s that he continued to remain loyal to Mexico. In later years, Seguín explained what happened: "The rumor, that I was a traitor, was seized with avidity; by my enemies in San Antonio. Some envied my position, as held by a *Mexican*; others found in me an obstacle to the accomplishment of their villainous plans."[76]

Despite their declining political fortunes, Mexican Texans served as Texas Rangers during the era of the Republic. First formally organized by the Consultation government in November 1835, the Rangers adopted many of the principles of the compañía volantes of the previous decades. The Rangers were not a formal military organization, but like the flying squadrons, they adopted the concept of loose, independent cavalry units to provide security. Though they struggled during the Revolution, by the late 1830s and early 1840s they served the Republic by providing reconnaissance and defense against Mexico and Indigenous nations.

Tejanos played a prominent role in the evolution of the Ranger organization. One of the first commanders of these cavalrymen was Jesús Cuellar, a Tamaulipas native who moved to Texas and served in the Revolution. Even Seguín, who was offered a post as commander but turned it down, maintained an influence from his position as chair of the Military Affairs Commission in the Texas senate during 1839. In this capacity, Tejano influence on the Rangers continued during the Republic era.[77] By the mid-1840s, however, the Rangers transformed into a different type of organization as they served against Mexico during the Mexican-American War (1846–48).

During its tumultuous lifespan (1836–45), the Texas Republic continued to be marked by conflict and violence. Claiming that Santa Anna had signed the Treaty of Velasco under duress, the Mexican legislature failed to recognize Texas independence and asserted that the state remained in rebellion. Though they proved incapable of reclaiming the region due to their own domestic instabilities, Mexican leaders never wavered in their belief that Texas remained rightfully a part of their country. Tensions continued as both sides envisioned attacking the other.

The 1841 Texan expedition to Santa Fe, located east of the northern Río Grande, which aimed to give the Texas Republic control over the lucrative Santa Fe Trail, resulted in disaster for the invaders. Suffering many hardships during their march to New Mexico, the Texans surrendered to the Mexican army without firing a shot. Their lives were spared but they suffered the indignity of being marched more than 2,000 miles south to be held prisoner in Mexico City.

Mexico, too, failed in their attempts to reclaim San Antonio the following year. Panic swept the Texas Republic as militias were raised and businesses closed in anticipation of further hostilities. Though Mexican troops retreated quickly, it reminded many Texans of the precariousness of their position. The following September, another Mexican expedition to San Antonio under General Adrián Woll once again laid claim to the city. Texas volunteers would not allow the Mexican army of one thousand men to hold the Alamo City for long, and a punitive expedition of eight hundred men drove out the Mexican belligerents in November. Emboldened and refusing to follow orders to retreat from the Río Grande, some of the volunteers continued to advance into Mexico, only to be taken prisoner at Ciudad Mier in December. This ongoing conflict allowed the Indigenous tribes of northern Texas an opportunity to exploit the chaos and raid the central parts of the Republic. During this period, wars depleted both the Native population and the Texas Republic coffers, as its debts mounted while it tried to maintain a hold on its tenuous borders.[78]

While the raids on San Antonio were not successful in reincorporating Texas back into the Mexican nation, they hastened the already deteriorating status of Tejanos. During General Rafael Vásquez's raid in the spring, the Mexican commander claimed that Juan Seguín, one of the heroes of the Texas Revolution and current mayor of San Antonio, had been collaborating with the Mexican army and was serving as a spy for Mexico. Vásquez provided no proof, and because he was only in San Antonio for a few days, the revelation that Seguín was a spy held no strategic value to the Mexican army. But if he could sow discord between Tejano elites and Anglo Texans, it could only benefit the Mexican government and further weaken the Texas Republic.

During Vásquez's invasion, Seguín had gauged the size of the invading army and urged San Antonio residents to evacuate the city. That action only made some Anglo Texans question Seguín's loyalty. Newly arrived settlers from the southern United States saw no distinction between Tejanos and Mexicans and held Mexican Texans in contempt. For Seguín, the situation turned dire as calls for his arrest for treason quickly brought angry mobs that forced him to flee. His only option was escape to Mexico. After eluding capture by bands of vigilantes, Seguín made his way across the Río Grande in May 1842. Soon after crossing into Mexico, he was imprisoned as a traitor by Mexican authorities for his role in the Texas Revolution. Seguín's struggles highlighted the new reality that Tejanos faced in the land they had settled and tried to call their own. For them, questions about loyalty, security, and identity all presented dilemmas for Mexican Texans by the middle of the nineteenth century.[79]

CHAPTER 2

"NOW, IS HE A MEXICAN OR A TEXAN?"

The Mexican-American War and the Civil War

By 1844, the Tejano population had another challenge to deal with: American expansionism. The election of James K. Polk to the presidency on an expansionist platform added a sense of urgency to the project of westward expansion and the incorporation of Texas into the United States. Accordingly, the annexation of Texas in 1845 only exacerbated the brewing conflict between the United States and Mexico. President Polk ordered Brigadier General Zachary Taylor to the region in December. Taylor's force moved to the north bank of the Río Grande. After news of a cavalry skirmish reached Washington, Polk declared that "American blood had been shed upon American soil," and asked Congress for a declaration of war against Mexico, which he received on May 13.[1]

The ensuing conflict placed the Tejano population in an unenviable position. Among the more than eight thousand Texans who volunteered to fight in the war were those that still had scores to settle from the Revolution. Many of the volunteers made little distinction between Mexican Texans and the enemy as they made their way to the Texas-Mexico border looking for a fight. Despite General Taylor's orders for volunteers to conduct themselves properly, instances of looting and violence were common throughout southern Texas and northern Mexico. Tejanos remained wary about joining another conflict so soon after the Texas Revolution. Most of the Tejano population chose to await the latest outcome of hostilities.

Yet some Mexican Texans still volunteered to fight against Mexico while others served in the capacity of guides and spies, such as Chapita Sandoval who moved freely from Corpus Christi to Matamoros with information. Some Mexican-born Texans joined the fray in the numerous state volunteer units and made their way to the Río Grande. Some of those men included two members of Company E, Second Texas Volunteers, Privates Francisco Acosta and Anastacio Barrilla. More than a dozen other Spanish-surnamed volunteers served in the ranks of Texas forces, all of them in the enlisted ranks.[2]

While most Tejanos tried to stay out of the conflict, it came to them. US Army Captain Richard A. Gillespie led a group of Texas volunteers through Laredo in July 1846 en route to join General Taylor's force in Camargo, Mexico. Gillespie raised the US flag over Laredo for the first time. Other Anglo-Americans followed. In October, Bryant P. Tilden navigated a steamboat up the Río Grande all the way to Laredo. The following month, former Texas Republic President Mirabeau B. Lamar appeared in Laredo leading seventy-three Texas volunteers, the Laredo Guards, anxious to join Taylor's army in northern Mexico. Lamar remained in Laredo, enumerating the citizenry and organizing a civic government. As the American military commander in Laredo, Lamar ordered elections for the city and delineated American authority on the north and east banks of the Río Grande. By the time the Treaty of Guadalupe Hidalgo was ratified in May 1848, Laredo was part of Texas and the United States, and the county seat in a new county of Webb.[3]

Laredo Tejanos tried to make sense of the chaos around them. There are no records of Laredoans volunteering to join the Texas volunteer forces that moved south toward Mexico City. It is likely that Laredoans, like their Tejano brethren in East and Central Texas, grew anxious about the Anglo presence in the new civilian government. After Lamar's force was mustered out of service in 1848, Anglo-American newcomers filled the ranks of public office in Webb County.

In April 1848, before the Treaty of Guadalupe Hidalgo was ratified, Laredoans sent petitions to US and Mexican authorities requesting that the town remain part of Mexico. But it was too late, the treaty was ratified, and

Laredo was part of Texas and the United States. Discord over land titles, security, and the rapid ascension of Anglo-American newcomers to their political world forced some Laredo Tejanos to leave for Mexico. Lamar was dumbfounded. He could not understand why anyone would be willing to reject living under the American system. Laredoans had "enjoyed the greatest liberty, prosperity, and peace under the laws and institutions of the United States," Lamar scolded the leading men who had framed the petition. "Whatever you believe to the contrary, Mexico has lost Laredo forever." When Lamar learned that the Laredo Tejanos had attempted to contact Mexican authorities, he intercepted their communiqué, warning them "such a purpose is directly at war with the constitutional rights of Texas."[4]

Although most Mexican Texans chose to remain neutral during the war with Mexico, that did not mean that they would remain idle in the face of threats—real or perceived—from the advancing Anglo-Americans making their way south to join the war against Mexico. In one case, Tejano ranchers attacked an American supply train making its way from Corpus Christi to the Río Grande valley at the war's onset in 1846.[5] Retaliatory raids, murders, and other atrocities from US volunteers, Texas Rangers, and Mexican bandits all kept Texans embroiled in violence throughout the war. The Texas Rangers' role in the bloodshed and the intimidation of the Tejano population is exemplified by the nickname given to them, "*Los Diablos Tejanos*" (Texas Devils) during this era. In the years prior to and after the war, the Rangers served their own version of justice with impunity. Mexican Texans also retaliated, making southern Texas and northern Mexico a veritable hotbed of guerrilla activity during the war.[6]

Resistance and neutrality weren't the only Tejano responses to the war; some may have welcomed the American presence. According to historian Douglas Richmond, by the early 1840s, Mexico's far north and, by extension, the disputed land of Texas, had witnessed increasing Indian attacks on their homes and ranches. Consequently, the presence of US soldiers suggested the possibility of joint operations against hostile Comanches and other hostile tribes.[7] The presence of US troops did not mean, however, Mexican-born Texans could join the ranks of volunteers. The Old Army could hold strong prejudices against any soldiers with dark skin.

The end of the Mexican-American War, in 1848, brought an additional challenge for the Tejano population as the Treaty of Guadalupe Hidalgo as thousands of Mexican-born Texans left for Mexico.[8] Violent racial animosity endured along the Texas-Mexico border. As historian Manuel Callahan notes, even though the violence on the border "was perpetrated by lawless elements, there was a great deal of military and paramilitary activity, much of it responding to subaltern resistance throughout the region."[9] The 1850s witnessed major conflicts such as the Cart War in South Texas and the Cortina War led by Juan Cortina and his supporters in the Río Grande valley.[10] Though peace along the border was temporarily restored by 1859, the general view of Tejanos, even those born in Texas, remained largely negative. In essence, Anglos saw Mexican Americans as lazy, corrupt, and irresponsible. Those feelings did not dissipate as Texas and the United States inched closer to another conflict as the 1850s came to an end.[11]

Secession and Civil War

Texas in 1860 was a far different place than it had been thirty years before. Since the Texas Revolution, Anglo migrants from the southern United States had flooded the region, transforming the economy of the state to one that resembled the cotton culture of the Deep South. Since annexation, the total population of Texas mushroomed to about 604,215, including approximately 25,000 Tejanos. Notably, slaves made up about a third of the population, at about 182,566. Four out of five Texans arrived in the region after annexation in 1845, and the German language was now as common as Spanish in the central part of the state. The composition of the government in Austin reflected a new political reality for Tejanos: they no longer had a significant role in the state's apparatus. Throughout the state, Anglo Texans dominated the social, economic, and political systems. Only in border counties, where the Tejano population remained an overwhelming majority, were Mexican Texans able to hold onto a vestige of political and economic control.[12] In about the span of a generation, the men and women who contributed to Texas's rise during the 1820s and 1830s were relegated to minority status and witnessed the wholesale loss of their property rights and political power.[13]

The economic and social transformation of Texas came amid growing sectional discord between the North and South over the expansion of slavery to the territories. The acquisition of the American Southwest after the Mexican-American War had only exacerbated the animosities between the two sections as the debates over the future of slavery in the territories reached a fever pitch by the mid-1850s. The opposition to slavery grew so strong that it fractured the old party system and inspired the rise of the newly formed Republican Party, which campaigned on the slogan "Free Soil, Free Labor, and Free Men."

The election of Republican Abraham Lincoln to the presidency in 1860 exacerbated Southern fears about the future of slavery, and South Carolina seceded from the United States in December 1860. By the following month, five additional Southern states joined the secession movement. In March, Texas voted in favor of secession after a convention of delegates voted overwhelmingly to leave the Union, 166 to 8. By March 5, Texas had joined the six other states in forming a new nation, the Confederate States of America. After Confederate troops fired on Fort Sumter in South Carolina on April 12, four additional states seceded and joined the Confederacy. The Civil War had begun.[14]

Secession was a dramatic crisis, even for Mexican Texans. They supported the call for leaving the Union in overwhelming numbers. In Webb, Zapata, Cameron, Starr, and Hidalgo Counties, where the Mexican Texan population remained strongest, the secession ordinance won by a tally of 1,124 to 41.[15] The complex relationship that Tejanos had with the institution of slavery remained multifaceted. Most Tejanos did not own or aspire to own slaves.[16] Some of the wealthier Mexican Texans did own slaves, including prominent San Antonian José Antonio Navarro, who owned approximately six to nine slaves according to census records. Navarro's son, Ángel, served in the Texas legislature and signed off on the ordinance of secession, casting his lot with pro-slavery majority.[17] Overall, Tejanos owned sixty slaves, all in the San Antonio area.[18]

Yet on the eve of the Civil War, Anglo Texans generally suspected that Tejanos assisted runaway slaves escape into Mexico in the form of an Underground Railroad headed south to Mexico instead of north to Canada. In the mid-1850s, white citizens in Guadalupe County passed a resolution barring Mexican "peons" from entering the county due to their alleged sympathies with slaves. In San Antonio, the local newspaper suggested that it would be best to pass a local ordinance requiring anyone of Mexican descent to register their business and intentions with local authorities to avert potential slave escapes. If a business was found suspicious, these Tejanos would be required to leave town. Rumors of Tejanos aiding slaves continued for the next several years. In 1858, residents of Gonzales thwarted a plot by Mexicans to assist slaves escape into their country. By the following year, the presence of runaway slaves coupled with the violence of the Cortina War created a tense environment on the border that only exacerbated Anglo suspicions of Tejano disloyalty even further.[19]

But an incident in South Texas, near Rio Grande City, belied the idea that Tejanos as a whole opposed slavery. Two slaves recently brought in from South Carolina had run away, claimed *The Ranchero*, a Corpus Christi newspaper, in March 1860. The paper speculated that it was "strange that they should attempt to make their way to Mexico" without any real knowledge of the land or the geography. Positing that other slaves provided critical information to the two runaways, the writer urged slaveholders to take caution. Nevertheless, the fact that they had been captured by a Tejano, Rodrigo Hinojosa, earned accolades from *The Ranchero*. "The prompt action of the Mexicans in restoring the fugitives to their owners is deserving of merited praise," the article noted. "All must admit that some of our Mexican population are of service to the community at large, as well as being law abiding citizens."[20]

Further north along the Río Grande, the capture of runaway slaves earned Laredoan Santos Benavides praise from his fellow Texans. Benavides was the great-great-grandson of Laredo's founder, Tomás Sánchez de la Barreda y Garza, and the nephew of longtime Laredo alcalde, Basilio Benavides. Santos Benavides had achieved his own degree of prominence, winning election as mayor of Laredo and chief justice of Webb County. More importantly, Benavides symbolized the very essence of Tejano existence on the frontier. Benavides proved this through his leadership in business and frontier combat, where he demonstrated courage fighting against Indigenous bands. During the 1850s, Santos led other members of his family, including brothers Refugio and Cristóbal, fighting against Native tribes and catching runaway slaves fleeing into Mexico.

In one account, in November 1860, *The Ranchero* heaped heavy praise on Benavides when the Laredoan crossed the Río Grande, with ten of his friends, in pursuit of a purported runaway slave passing himself off as a free Black citizen of Mexico. Once in Nuevo Laredo, Benavides "in the face of the entire population of the place" seized the fugitive and returned by boat to Laredo. At the river's edge, the Mexicans fired on the Benavides's party, and the ensuing gun battle left one Laredoan wounded. But Benavides and his men made it back to Laredo. The newspaper commended Benavides for his bravery, noting that this was not the first time the Laredo Tejano "distinguished himself in restoring runaway slaves to their owners." Peers described Santos Benavides as "daring and fearless." To John S. "Rip" Ford, a soldier and statesman of Texas, the Benavides family was "of great influence" and they appeared to understand "the questions upon which the South differed from the non-slaveholding states of the Union."[21]

Despite the commitment shown by Tejanos like Hinojosa and Benavides, the doubts that most Anglo Texans held about Tejano loyalty regarding slaves evolved into uncertainty about their role in military service and support for the newfound Confederate nation. In March 1861, the Texas Committee on Public Safety authorized volunteers to wrest control of the federal forts in the Lone Star State. Colonel Henry E. McCulloch took control of all federal installations from Central Texas to the Red River. Meanwhile, Colonel Ford led a contingent of men to Brownsville, where they gained control of Fort Brown before moving up the Río Grande and took every federal bastion all the way to El Paso. The ineptitude of US Army commander in the Department of Texas, General David Twiggs, contributed to the ease of the Confederate acquisition of all federal properties in the state, which amounted to nineteen forts and an arsenal with about 10,000 muskets. In exchange for coordinating the abandonment of all federal properties, Twiggs requested that he and his men be allowed to keep their small arms and be allowed to evacuate to the Gulf coast. A few months after surrendering Texas, Twiggs joined the Confederate army, but he resigned soon thereafter and retired to his native Georgia.[22]

In April, after the firing on Fort Sumter, Lincoln's request for 75,000 volunteers to put down the rebellion led Confederate President Jefferson Davis to issue his own call for a force of 100,000 volunteers to serve up to one year. A few Texans had already begun to take up arms the previous month when they volunteered to be part of the state militia. State militias would soon be incorporated into the Provisional Army of the Confederate States of America before it morphed into the more permanent Army of the Confederate States of America on April 29.[23]

The first volunteers to rally to the Texas cause joined the First Texas Mounted Rifles in San Antonio. Within a month they were incorporated into the Confederate army. These early volunteers demonstrated zeal and enthusiasm. Texans, like their Southern brethren, believed that they had a stronger martial spirit than Northerners due to their rural upbringing and frontier experience. In San Antonio, the *Semi-Weekly News* urged volunteers to flock to Confederate service because it is "almost certain that Texas will be immediately invaded."[24]

These young soldiers had no uniforms and had to furnish their own weapons as they began their rudimentary exercise and drill. As most had no real military experience, the men often resented receiving orders. Making things more difficult, the common soldier of the Civil War grudgingly respected authority, and many officers had difficulty gaining the respect of their men. The individualist spirit of Texas volunteers was reflected in their choice of weapons, which ranged from shotguns and squirrel guns to whatever weapon could be found. Such lack of resources similarly showed in the ways soldiers dressed, as many preferred their own headgear. Anglo Texans chose to wear wide-brimmed hats, while Tejanos opted for their traditional sombrero. It was not until the following year that Texas volunteers adopted a more standardized uniform.[25]

Confederate Tejanos

When Texas decided to cast its lot with the Confederacy, the call for troops placed Tejanos in a quandary. On the one hand, Tejanos could aid Confederate Texas and the state that had regarded them just slightly better than the slaves and the institution that Anglo Texans were fighting to preserve. On the other hand, they could join the United States Army and support the nation responsible for westward expansion, Manifest Destiny, and the transformation of the Mexican far north into the American Southwest. With the latter option, they could, in essence, fight against Texas and the decline of Tejano political and economic influence it represented. Either way, the decision would not be easy. After all, they had fought on the winning side and lost before.

Historian Charles Grear examines the motivations of Tejanos and maintains that the Mexican Texan population was split into two distinct groups at the onset of the war: those who had established favorable economic and political ties with Anglo Texans and those who remained outside this relatively elite group. Accordingly, several factors influenced Tejano volunteers as war came to their native land for the third time in a generation. The need to defend their homes and families defined one motivating factor as Tejanos joined the various volunteer forces throughout the state. Others joined the ranks of the Union or Confederate armies for the simple notion of viewing military service as an economic opportunity, which was also a motivating factor for Billy Yank or Johnny Reb. Others followed the path of their local political or economic leaders in hopes that their service would be rewarded following the war. Most of the Tejano community tried to avoid the conflict because they had no ideological or political motivation to fight on either side. This proved a challenge for Texas, as Confederate authorities attempted to rally support for their cause.[26]

Historians have chronicled the motivations of Civil War soldiers for generations. Broad themes such as fighting to defend property rights and the emphasis of self-government marked some of the motives behind why Johnny Reb enlisted in the army. Billy Yank might have cited the ideas of defending the Constitution or preserving the liberty of the republic and the spirit of 1776. In Texas, men volunteered for both the Union and Confederate armies—especially the latter. The few Unionist sympathizers in Texas generally came from the German population belt in Central Texas, which included towns such as Fredericksburg, New Braunfels, and Martindale. Non-German Unionists were found in other parts of the state as well. These men leaned toward the Union cause because of their principles and frowned upon slavery. In their accounts, Texas soldiers wrote about the need to defend home and hearth while highlighting the themes of liberty and self-government. Tejanos, on the other hand, did not indulge in romanticizing the war and fighting in their limited accounts of why they joined the Rebel cause.[27]

It is difficult to broadly attribute Tejano motives since so few sources exist from the Civil War era. The concepts of loyalty and identity were much more complex during a time and place where borders, nation-states, and allegiances had shifted dramatically in just a few decades. To view nationalism and loyalty as a stark, black-or-white phenomenon in which Tejanos could have been free to pick one identity or another—Mexican or American, Confederate or Union—is not quite accurate. Instead, recent scholarship takes a more wide-ranging view and places the Tejano perspective at center stage. It offers a more multifaceted approach, in which individual motives could be negotiated by time, place, and personal experience. Certainly some Mexican Texans moved toward viewing themselves as Texan or American despite enduring second-class status during the antebellum period. Because Texas remained rather isolated from the rest of the South and the nation, many still viewed their identity and loyalty through the concept of regional identity.[28]

The Tejano elite tended to support the Confederate cause for a variety of reasons. After the Texas Revolution period, one way Tejanos tried to maintain their hold on economic and political power was through intermarriage with Anglo newcomers.[29] The political inclinations of Mexican Texans during the 1850s also made elite Tejanos strong allies of Southern Democrats and secessionists. Elite Tejanos were race conscious, just like wealthy Southern landowners and likely to support slavery. Finally, the long-standing regionalism of Mexico's far north—and later, the Texas frontier—struck a chord similar to Southern states' rights philosophies.[30] These sentiments clearly aligned certain segments of the Tejano population with the Confederate cause and placed them at odds with disenfranchised and dispossessed Tejanos in Central and South Texas.

Yet, Tejanos' Confederate sympathies were not absolute, as the case of San Antonio shows.[31] By February 1861, on the eve of Texas joining the Confederacy, the Union-supporting San Antonio newspaper, the *Tri-Weekly Alamo Express* proclaimed, "It is beyond doubt that our county and city are Union in sentiment, and that they can easily be carried against secession."[32] Elite Tejanos in the city did tend to support the Union cause, especially those tied to anti-secession Governor Sam Houston. Houston, in fact, directed Ángel Navarro, slave owner and scion of the prominent *Bexareño* José Antonio Navarro, to serve as a liaison during the 1859 Cortina uprising. Navarro was happy to report to the authorities in Austin that Cortina and his minions were acting as individuals and not part of a larger Tejano movement against the government.[33] When the San Antonio vote came in approving secession, it was by a close margin of 827 to 709.[34]

The Unionism seen at the onset of 1861 quickly faded. San Antonians, like most of the state's residents, soon came to embrace the Confederate cause, sometimes to the point of violence. On May 13, a pro-Confederate mob broke into the *Alamo Express* offices and burned the building to the ground. The following day, the editor, James Newcomb, left San Antonio for Mexico carrying three guns for self-defense. The rival paper, *The Daily Ledger and Texan*, remained unapologetic, claiming the *Alamo Express* should have been destroyed long ago. "We will not brook the presence of traitors nor tolerate the existence of nuisances," their editorial warned.[35]

In the Alamo City, Tejano elites Joseph Rafael de la Garza and Manuel Yturri answered the call and were among the first to volunteer for the Confederate war effort in March 1861. Both men were bilingual, educated, and hailed from prominent Tejano families. The twenty-three-year-old de la Garza went to school at St. Joseph's College in Bardstown, Kentucky, before coming back to San Antonio and helping his father, José Antonio, run one of the largest landholdings in Bexar County. Yturri was also

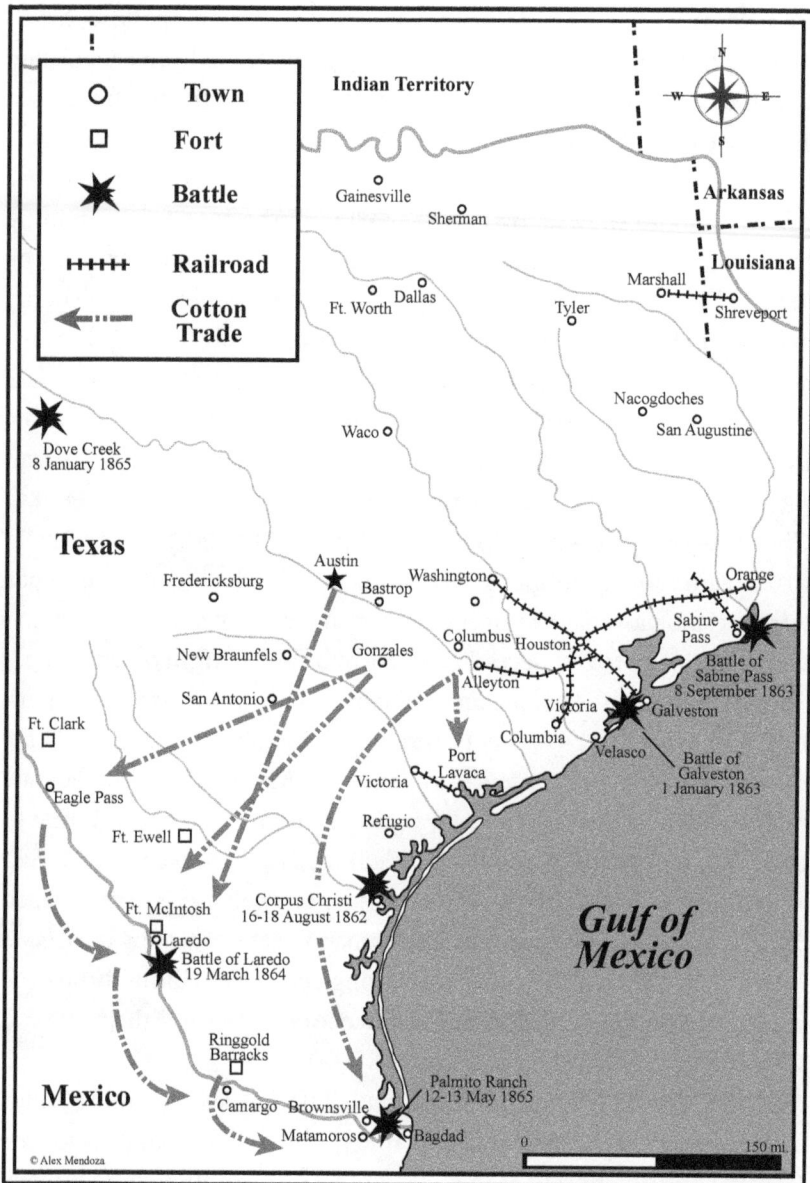

○	Town
□	Fort
✳	Battle
┣━━┫	Railroad
◀╌╌╌	Cotton Trade

Indian Territory

Arkansas

Louisiana

Gainesville

Sherman

Marshall

Shreveport

Ft. Worth   Dallas

Tyler

Nacogdoches

San Augustine

Dove Creek
8 January 1865

Waco

Texas

Austin

Fredericksburg

Bastrop

Washington

Orange

New Braunfels

Gonzales

Columbus Houston

Sabine
Pass

Alleyton

Battle of
Sabine Pass
8 September 1863

San Antonio

Victoria

Galveston

Ft. Clark

Columbia

Velasco

Battle of
Galveston
1 January 1863

Eagle Pass

Port
Lavaca

Ft. Ewell

Victoria

Refugio

Gulf of
Mexico

Ft. McIntosh

Corpus Christi
16–18 August 1862

Laredo

Battle of Laredo
19 March 1864

Ringgold
Barracks

Mexico

Camargo Brownsville

Palmito Ranch
12–13 May 1865

Matamoros   Bagdad

0   150 mi.

© Alex Mendoza

Civil War Texas, 1861–65

twenty-three years old and went to school at St. Joseph's before transferring to the University of Pennsylvania. The two young Tejanos established a familial tie when Yturri married one of De la Garza's sisters, Elena. Both men enlisted in Captain Samuel W. McAllister's Alamo Rifles for three years or the duration of the war. The Alamo Rifles would ultimately be transferred into the Confederate army's Company K, Sixth Texas Infantry. De la Garza enlisted as a captain while Yturri joined as a private. Though both the De la Garza and Yturri families were well off in comparison to most other Mexican Texans, neither family owned slaves, like the Navarros. Yet, the De la Garza family had established kinship ties through intermarriage to men from the slaveholding South and thus were sympathetic to the Confederate cause. At the same time, the De la Garza and Yturri families certainly recognized how being perceived as disloyal to the Anglo majority could lead to ostracism and loss of political and economic prestige like their compatriot, Juan Seguín.[36]

De la Garza's unit remained stationed in Texas at Victoria before marching to Arkansas, near Pine Bluff, in 1862. In his observations during the first year of the war, the young Tejano officer made no mention of a larger cause he was fighting for. He did lament, however, that the men in Arkansas "were not very patriotic" for the Confederacy.[37] De la Garza missed his friends and family, noting that he would prefer to serve his duty in Texas. He wrote about the Yankee armies, the movement of the Rebels in Virginia, and the general boredom of serving as a junior officer.[38] By 1863, De la Garza recognized the growing disaffection for the Confederacy among his compatriots, but he remained resolute in his letters home. "When I went into the service," he wrote, "I determined that I would go through and I am of the same mind yet with the help of God."[39]

In his letters, Yturri also expressed the normal enthusiasm for soldiering early in the war. When he transferred to Captain James Duff's Thirty-Third Texas Cavalry ("Duff's Partisan Rangers") in 1862, he told his wife that he appreciated Duff and Lieutenant James R. Sweet, stating, "I will never get out of it until the war is over, or die in it by their side."[40] Though his feelings would change later, Yturri, like De la Garza, expressed concern about his hometown and expressed his strong desire to remain in Texas and not fight elsewhere. He resented the idea of potentially being transferred east of the Mississippi River.[41] As he dealt with the challenges of soldiering in the Confederate army, Yturri remained cognizant of his fellow Tejanos and wrote about how they fared in the unit. "I am in the same mess where Y. Cassiano, José García, and Severo Losoya are, and all seem to be very well satisfied and pleased with the company."[42] His attachment to Texas suggests that Yturri, like many Texas soldiers in the Confederate army, viewed his service more as a means to defend the Lone Star State from Yankee invaders than defending any particular political principle or constitutional theory. Nevertheless, Yturri, like other wealthy Tejanos of his era, remained hostile toward African Americans during his service.[43]

For Texas to succeed in the Civil War, the authorities in Austin would need the cooperation and support of the Tejano population, particularly the elite class who held influence over poorer Tejanos. Certainly, the conflict between Confederate Tejanos and other Tejanos or *Mexicanos* did not take long to materialize. On April 14, 1861, twenty-two Laredo Tejanos joined the sheriff of Nueces County, Captain Matthew Nolan, at Fort McIntosh as he rode to the town of Carrizo (later, Zapata), approximately fifty-miles downriver, in Zapata County, to put down an uprising led by thirty-nine-year-old rancher, Antonio Ochoa. Frustrated by several factors, including political disfranchisement, Ochoa led his men—which included *Mexicanos* from the town of Guerrero, across the Río Grande from Carrizo in Mexico—against the Confederacy and the Anglo-dominated government that had been the source of discord for his band of supporters. Leaving nothing to chance, at dawn on the fifteenth, Nolan ordered his men, who now included residents of Zapata County, to attack Ochoa's men who had taken up a position around the Rancho Clareño. The battle at Rancho Clareño proved a decisive defeat for the band of Cortinistas, some of whom were shot while trying to surrender. Investigators from the 1873 Mexican border commission later described the events at Rancho Clareño as a massacre. Even though Ochoa himself escaped unharmed having been across the river when Nolan ordered his assault, the battle indicated how blurred the lines of Tejano/Mexican loyalty could be in the early days of the Civil War.[44]

Refugio Benavides, Atanacio Vidaurri, Cristobal Benavides, and John Z. Leyendecker, Confederate officers from Laredo, Texas. Courtesy of Special Collections, the University of Texas at San Antonio (ITC 072-3258).

The following month, reports reached Texas officials that Juan Cortina had advanced to the Texas border from the interior of Mexico to take advantage of the turmoil in Texas and launch what was ultimately regarded as the second Cortina War. The authorities in Carrizo, worried about Cortina after hearing rumors that Unionists had provided him arms upon recognizing his popularity in northern Mexico. Zapata County officials asked Confederate authorities for assistance. The responsibility fell on Colonel Ford, the commander of the Military Department of the Río Grande. Ford, in turn, turned to Santos Benavides to assist the state, granting him a commission as a captain of the Partisan Rangers for Texas. Ford hoped that Santos could raise a company of one hundred men to help secure the border.[45] Santos's brother, Cristóbal, joined his company, as did his brother-in-law, John Z. Leyendecker.[46]

Cortina was rumored to have crossed the Río Grande and advanced toward Carrizo on May 20. Rumors swirled that the Mexican bandit sought vengeance for Rancho Clareño, specifically against Henry Redmond, the Anglo landowner who dominated Zapata politics and its economy. Refugio Benavides rode quickly to Redmond's ranch, joining his brother Santos, in less than a day, with thirty-six men. Cortina had already surrounded Redmond's ranch when Benavides's force reached the Zapatans. In the ensuing forty-minute fight, the Laredoans and their fellow Confederates routed Cortina's force, killing several men in the initial charge with no casualties. Following a black flag policy (no quarter), Benavides killed other members of Cortina's band as they tried to sack the Zapata County Courthouse. Another six or seven men reportedly drowned while trying to cross the Río Grande. Benavides ordered the execution of another eleven prisoners. Cortina and about a dozen men escaped the Confederate assault and returned safely to Mexico.[47]

The defeat of the Cortinistas at the hands of the Santos Benavides-led force from Laredo demonstrated the ambiguity and constantly shifting identities and loyalties that characterized the Texas-Mexico borderlands. Ever since he took the law into his own hands in response to Anglo discrimination in the Río Grande valley years earlier, Cortina had been regarded as a Robin Hood–type figure by ethnic Mexicans on both sides of the Río Grande. Anglos, on the other hand, considered Cortina as a common bandit. Therein lay the conundrum for Benavides and his band of Confederate soldiers from Laredo.

Like Benavides, Cortina was born in Mexico's far north, but a year later, in 1824. Like Benavides, Cortina was also a landowner along the Río Grande, having gained title to grants near the Brownsville area. Both men witnessed the Mexican government's efforts in the 1820s and 1830s to forge a shared sense of nationalism within its boundaries as the citizenry was inundated with the symbols and values of Mexican nationalism.[48] Both men were Mexican. Yet, they fought one another in 1861, building upon a contrasting set of values and loyalties. The outcome threatened the "peace structure" that Anglos and Tejanos had forged over the previous few decades. Benavides and his fellow Laredoans can be considered what historian Elliott Young calls *libres fronterizos* (free border people), an identity that transcended national loyalties and emphasized the inviolability of individual autonomy and liberty.[49]

Accordingly, when Benavides rode to meet Cortina, notions of nationalism or patriotic feelings were likely far from his mind. Instead, the Laredo Tejano focused on the threat that Cortina could bring to the region's economic alliances, his friendships, and, above all, the personal honor that defending one's home underscored. The importance of Cortina's defeat moved beyond simply securing the loyalty of the Tejano/Mexican populations along the Río Grande. It also ensured that Anglo Texans would no longer doubt the allegiance of Benavides and the Mexican Texans. In fact, some Anglo Confederates had doubted Benavides's loyalty until he defeated Cortina. After Colonel Ford informed Governor Edward Clark of Benavides's exploits against Cortina, the latter wrote to praise the Laredoan and gave him an engraved pistol as a token of his appreciation. Clark informed Benavides that he hoped the pistol "will always be used in defense of your country and prove an instrument of terror and destruction to her enemies."[50]

Benavides's success against Cortina and the praise heaped upon him by the Texas authorities notwithstanding, a few months later, consternation grew as the Laredo Tejanos refused to enlist in the Confederate army as other state units had done. By the fall of 1861, Benavides and his men came to the end of their six-month enlistments, and Governor Clark grew apprehensive. Ford reached out to Benavides to inform him that General Earl Van Dorn, commanding the Department of Texas, desired his company of Tejanos to be mustered into the Confederacy. Benavides openly refused; they would not enlist for three years. Benavides recognized the racism and contempt that Anglo Texans held for Tejanos and feared he and his men would be sent far away from Laredo if they enlisted in the Confederate army. Clark sent an envoy to Laredo, Charles Thorkeli de Løvenskiold, to negotiate a solution. By December 1861, new Texas Governor Francis Lubbock shared his predecessor's concerns, lest the Confederacy lose control of the vital Texas-Mexico border region. For about a month, uncertainty about Tejano service continued until finally an agreement was reached. State leaders acquiesced to Benavides's desire and allowed them to enlist for one year rather than the standard duration of the war. On January 1, 1862, Løvenskiold mustered Benavides's men into Confederate service while praising them for their heroic deeds along the border. Even though thirty-two Tejanos refused to enlist, Benavides was able to enlist more men a few months later. Even his brother, Refugio, raised a company of his own at Ringgold Barracks.[51]

After being mustered into the Confederate army, Benavides and his fellow Tejanos patrolled a two hundred-mile swath of land along the Río Grande to secure the frontier for the Rebel cause. In addition to maintaining peace and eliminating banditry, Benavides's force also had to deal with threats from Native bands, who continued to raid and steal horses from Laredo and the vicinity, and *enganchaderos*, Union agents who offered rewards to Tejanos and Mexicans who conducted raids against Confederate trade to Mexico. The rewards to the Unionists ranged between 100 pesos in gold to fifty to 160 acres of land in Texas. In response to these Unionists, Benavides's troops crossed the Río Grande in pursuit. In July 1862, the Houston *Tri-Weekly Telegraph* boasted that Benavides and his men captured more than three dozen Unionist "traitors" attempting to flee into Mexico. Benavides and his men spent the following two years securing the town's economic prosperity, protecting the now lucrative cotton trade with Mexico that had flourished in the wake of the Union blockade in the Gulf of Mexico. For his service to the Rebel cause, in November 1863, Benavides received a promotion as colonel in the Confederate army. General John B. Magruder, the commander of the Department of Texas, New Mexico, and Arizona, was impressed with Benavides, authorizing the Laredoan to impress 250 bales of cotton from which to pay his men, most of whom had not been paid in months.[52]

The Confederate military service of elite Tejanos like Benavides, Yturri, and De la Garza was an anomaly. Others, like brothers Sixto Eusebio and George Antonio Navarro, became officers in the Confederate army, while their brother Ángel served in the Ninth Texas Legislature. But most Mexican Texans who served the Confederacy were poor, illiterate, and in the lower echelons of society. Most of these approximately 2,500 men came from three counties: Webb, Bexar, and Refugio.[53] They fought for reasons that focused more on economic opportunity than political power, local defense, and loyalty to Texas. In West Texas, the fear of Indian attacks concerned most residents of El Paso County, particularly after the US Army abandoned Fort Bliss in 1861.[54]

More than fifty Tejanos served in Colonel John R. Baylor's Second Texas Mounted Rifles, who joined General Henry Hopkins Sibley's Confederate Army of New Mexico as it marched on New Mexico with designs to advance northward to Colorado and seize its mines. Sibley launched his audacious plan in January 1862 as his army marched on the west bank of the Río Grande. At the Battle of Valverde, on February 21, Sibley's men drove the Federals from the field and captured some artillery. There, Tejanos fought Nuevomexicanos in a battle that resulted in 222 Union and 183 Confederate casualties. They continued northward for another month until they were forced to retreat to Texas by Colorado volunteers who destroyed their supply trains.[55]

Tejanos also served in the Civil War's eastern theater. Tejanos enlisted in what would ultimately be known as Hood's Texas Brigade, which saw service at Gaines Mill, Second Bull Run, Antietam, Fredericksburg, Gettysburg, the Wilderness, and the Siege of Petersburg. Other Mexican Texans served in General Hiram B. Granbury's Brigade in the Army of Tennessee. These units served in major battles at Chattanooga, Atlanta, Franklin, and Nashville. Eugenio Navarro, from San Antonio, was elected lieutenant and earned the favor of the men in his Company K, Sixth Texas Infantry. Lieutenant Martiriano Rodríguez of San Antonio served alongside Yturri in the Third Texas Infantry that saw service in Arkansas and Louisiana.

Most of the Tejanos who served, however, remained in the Lone Star State. Captain Joseph Peñaloza raised a company almost entirely composed of Tejanos from the San Antonio area and received orders to defend the Texas coast near Saluria, on the north end of Matagorda Island, and Galveston. He continued serving on the coast until 1864, when he received a transfer to Santos Benavides's unit. Captain Sixto Eusebio Navarro, Company E, Eighth Texas Infantry, also served protecting the mouth of the Río Grande, at Fort Brown, until the Union gained control of the area in 1864. Navarro's brother, José Ángel, the Harvard educated lawyer who served as Houston's envoy during the 1859 Cortina uprising, had earned an officer's commission by organizing a company of men. In 1862, he was stationed in the San Antonio area before serving briefly in West Texas at Fort Davis, but within a year he moved closer to home to be near his brother.[56]

When Santos Benavides received promotion to colonel, he achieved the highest rank of any Mexican Texan in the Confederacy. Benavides's military responsibilities on the Texas-Mexico border proved almost overwhelming. In the summer of 1863, Vicksburg, Mississippi, fell into the hands of the United States. Suddenly, the Trans-Mississippi states of Texas, Louisiana, and Arkansas were cut off from the rest of the Confederacy. The Union naval blockade on the Texas coast thus placed a greater strain on the Rebel efforts to smuggle cotton and import war matériel into the Lone Star State. Keeping open the Texas-Mexico cotton trade over the Río Grande became imperative. Texas Confederates used ferries to ship cotton across to Mexico to evade the Union blockade. Ships from all over the world arrived at the mouth of the Río Grande to take on Texas cotton at Bagdad.[57]

Another challenge for Benavides were the Confederate deserters, Unionist sympathizers, and *Mexicano* bandits operating along the border. His brief became even more difficult when US troops took over Brownsville in November 1863.[58] By the end of that year, Benavides had three hundred men under his command and he constantly worried that Laredo would be attacked, giving the Union access to the cotton trade flowing into Tamaulipas, Mexico.[59] In February 1864, Benavides rode hundreds of miles between, Laredo, Eagle Pass, and San Antonio to coordinate efforts to meet the disparate challenges on the border. By the end of the month, Benavides returned to Laredo physically drained. His foremost biographer notes, "Santos returned to Laredo so exhausted from so much time in the saddle that for days he was unable to get out of bed."[60]

As Benavides recuperated and cotton continued to be stockpiled in San Agustín Plaza, rumors of a Union invasion of Laredo surfaced. On the afternoon of March 19, 1864, a vaquero rode into town and warned that the US cavalry was approaching the city along the Río Grande. Forced to end his convalescence, Benavides sounded the alarm for Laredoans to prepare for a Yankee advance. Benavides ordered his depleted force to move east of the town plaza toward Zacate Creek, a tributary of the Río Grande. He was at his defiant best. "As it is I have to fight to the last; though hardly able to stand, I shall die fighting," he maintained. "I won't retreat, no matter what force the Yankees have—I know I can depend on my boys."[61] The colonel knew his men were outnumbered by as many as ten to one. He ordered the citizenry to arm themselves and to line up cotton bales to serve as barriers in case the Federal soldiers pushed past the Rebels. Benavides left instructions that his house be set on fire should it fall into the hands of the enemy. More than 5,000 bales of cotton were also to be destroyed. Meanwhile, the Tejano colonel ordered a rider to patrol Zacate Creek, blowing his horn at every chance to give the impression that the Confederates had more men than they really had.[62]

US Army Major Alfred E. Holt led a two hundred-man expedition, half of whom were from the Tejano Second Texas Cavalry Regiment, up the Río Grande from its base near Brownsville. The troops marched on the Mexican side of the river to avoid detection before crossing to the Texas side as they approached Laredo. As they neared Zacate Creek, the Confederates met them with the bulk of their force near a large rock. A small Rebel detachment was left in town in case Benavides would have to retreat. The Union cavalrymen dismounted as they approached the Confederate positions and fired. Benavides's men responded in kind, pausing only to reload. The Federals attacked and were repulsed three times. For about three hours, the battle raged on along the banks of the Zacate. After the three assaults, the Federals took their wounded and retreated east, crossing Chacon Creek about a mile away. Sporadic firing continued into the night as Benavides wrote dispatches to Ford urging him to come to the border. Confederate reinforcements arrived that night, and with rumors swirling that a larger Federal force was preparing to attack the town the next day, Benavides planned to go on the offensive. At daybreak, the Rebel Tejanos advanced past the previous day's battle site

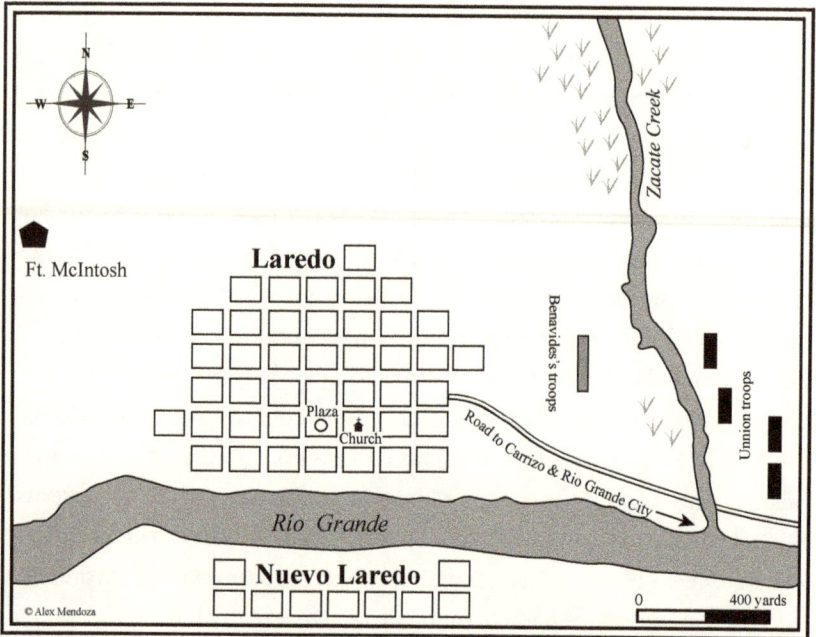

The Battle of Laredo, March 19, 1864

but found the Union camp deserted. The Federals left no record of their disastrous Laredo campaign, but Benavides's men rejoiced in their success against the invading force. For the remainder of the war, no other Union offensive would reach as far as Laredo. In his official report, Benavides proclaimed that the Yankees "all had left in a stampede" after they realized reinforcements had arrived.[63]

In the months following the battle for Laredo, Benavides believed he had earned a promotion to brigadier general in the Confederate army. In his estimation, he had campaigned tirelessly for the Confederate cause. Benavides had used his contacts along the river to apprehend Unionists, had rejected entreaties attempting to lure him to the Union army, drove off various Federal forces along the border, and continued to serve as the political and economic broker of power in Webb County.[64] In a January 1864 report to his superiors, General Magruder described Benavides as "perfectly faithful" to the Confederate cause. Magruder had to reassure authorities who still may have doubted Benavides's loyalty. The promotion never arrived, however, as Benavides and Ford began to feud. At issue were the Tejano colonel's propensity to ignore Ford's directives and Ford's suspicion that Benavides was recruiting men from his regiment. Certainly, Benavides did possess an independent streak that chafed at Ford. At one point, Ford grew so frustrated with Benavides that he ordered his arrest in October 1864. Finally, an emissary settled the dispute. Yet, the promotion to brigadier general that Magruder had promised never came for Benavides and he always blamed Ford for sabotaging his command.[65]

Through the previous months, Benavides's ability to cross the river with ease had befuddled allies and foes alike. In late November 1863, Benavides and twenty of his men faced a US Army detachment near Ringgold Barracks. Fearing he could be flanked, Benavides crossed the border into Mexico, much to the frustration of US Army General N. J. T. Dana, who sought clarification as to diplomatic relations with Mexico and extradition. "Now, is he a Mexican or a Texan?" Dana asked, genuinely perplexed by a Tejano who identified as both.[66] What Dana and others did not understand was that many Mexican Texans along the border negotiated their identity daily, crossing physical and ideological borders. When Benavides refused to follow Ford's commands and the Confederacy's desires to enlist for the duration of the war, the Tejano's resistance went beyond his character and sense of personal independence. In a broader sense, he followed the philosophy covered by the phrase *"obedezco pero no cumplo"* (I obey but do not comply), which dates to the Spanish Texas era. The identity of borderlands Tejanos transcended national loyalties and emphasized individual autonomy and liberty. They were free, in other words, to build upon the various allegiances and loyalties available to them along the Río Grande. They were American but Mexican at the same time. They negotiated their loyalty, one in which their true allegiance was to the region and not the nation-states and their competing national symbols.[67]

Unionist Tejanos

Benavides exhibited dual national loyalties when it suited him, but he remained faithful to the Confederacy. Other Tejanos, such as Adrián

Vidal from Brownsville, switched loyalties and ultimately abandoned Texas altogether. Born in 1845 in Nuevo León, Mexico, Vidal moved to Texas as a young boy when his mother married a businessman from Brownsville. After the outbreak of the Civil War, Vidal, who had already gained a reputation as a gambler and drinker, enlisted as a private in the Confederate army in October 1862. For the next year he served in the lower Río Grande valley and earned recognition for helping capture a Federal gunboat near Brownsville. He received a promotion to captain. Yet, Vidal remained unhappy with the Confederacy. He was unable to communicate effectively in English (a common problem for many Tejanos), and he lamented the paucity of pay and supplies. Finally in October 1863, he snapped and led a mutiny of Tejanos against his fellow Confederates. Vidal and his mutineers killed one Rebel soldier and evaded capture as they robbed and plundered their way to Mexico. He resurfaced the following month when the US Army gained control of Brownsville. Vidal and his men joined the Union army, with Vidal earning commission as captain of Vidal's Independent Partisan Rangers. For the next several months, Vidal's Tejanos reconnoitered for the Yankees. The same issues Vidal faced in the Confederacy surfaced once more with the Federals as he chafed at the discrimination he faced from Anglo soldiers and his inability to learn English. By the spring of 1864, Vidal attempted to leave the Union army and requested a discharge. By the time the US Army was ready to rid itself of the discontented Tejano, Vidal and his men had already fled to Mexico. Remarkably, he was not done fighting yet, as he joined Juan Cortina, now leading a Mexican army in Tamaulipas at war with French imperialist forces. In 1865, French forces caught Vidal and executed him, despite attempts by his family to pay a ransom and secure his release.[68]

The rich and complex story of Adrián Vidal fighting for three different armies during the Civil War is unique in Texas history. But the fact that more than 958 Mexican Texans fought for the Union in a state remained a part of the Confederacy reveals the divided loyalties found in Texas.[69] While the Texas secession vote was overwhelmingly popular, strong pockets of Unionist sentiment remained. Unionism grew out of shared experiences and relationships that bound many Texans, including Tejanos.

Others valued the roles of the US Army in protecting the frontier and the federal government in helping in the state's economic development. However, slavery remained the most salient issue dividing residents of the Lone Star State. Because many Texans remained indifferent to the Confederacy, Unionist ideas continued to circulate.[70]

Tejano Unionists had few alternatives but to leave their homes and head for Mexico with other Texas exiles who feared retribution from state authorities or local Confederate sympathizers. By the summer of 1862, groups of these Unionists had begun to arrive on the Texas-Mexico border and included a few Tejanos. Andrew J. Hamilton of Austin had led a group of fifteen men to Matamoros in July. Edmund J. Davis, a former state judge in Laredo and Corpus Christi, also found exile at Matamoros. Other bands of Texas Unionists attempting to flee into Mexico were caught by Confederate authorities that fall. On August 10, 1862, near the west fork of the Nueces River, about twenty miles from Fort Clark and ten from Eagle Pass, a group of nineteen Unionists, mostly German, but also a few Mexican Texans, were ambushed by Confederates. Only seven Unionists managed to escape into Mexico as the Confederates executed any wounded German or Tejano they could find.[71] Texas Unionists arriving in Mexico were helped by Leonard Pierce, the US consul in Matamoros, who fed them, gave them clothes, and coordinated with Mexican authorities. Much to the chagrin of the Confederate General Hamilton P. Bee, who complained that Pierce was recruiting troops for the US Army, the Confederates were helpless to do anything about the creation of Federal regiments across the Río Grande.[72]

In some respects, the motives of Tejano Unionists are easier to analyze than those of their Confederate counterparts. These Tejanos were not fighting directly against the institution of slavery nor were they thinking of postwar politics. Instead, they mostly fought for the $300 bounties paid by the US Army. For Mexican Texans, this was a huge sum of money and far eclipsed what most Tejano laborers could earn each year working the agricultural fields of the Lone Star State. Since approximately a third of all Tejanos were unskilled laborers, it was a strong incentive.[73] Others joined the ranks of the Union blue to exact a semblance of revenge against the authorities in Texas and the people they believed had perpetuated their political and economic ostracism. They aimed their dissent against landowners or lawyers who they saw as being responsible for the loss of land or their way of life over the previous years. Though their motivations remain difficult to pin down definitively, these Tejanos were recruited to fight by Anglo Texans and US officials who supported the Constitution and held anti-slavery views. Foremost among these recruiters were John L. Haynes of Rio Grande City, Edmund J. Davis, of Laredo, and Andrew J. Hamilton, of Austin.[74]

In the fall of 1862, Haynes and Davis wrote to US Secretary of War Edwin Stanton requesting his assistance for raising a regiment of Unionists along the Texas-Mexico border.[75] Once given the green light to raise a regiment of Tejanos, Haynes vouched for the "loyalty of Mexican Texans" with US Army General Nathaniel P. Banks, the commander of the Department of the Gulf.[76] Colonel Davis, later to become governor of Texas during the Reconstruction era, assumed command of Company A, First Regiment of Texas Cavalry, in October 1862. By early 1863, two additional companies were added to the unit, which was stationed in Louisiana. The men fought in various engagements in Louisiana through the end of the year, even serving on occupation duty when Union forces took control of the city of New Orleans. Like their Confederate counterparts, they, too, preferred to fight close to home. In October 1863, the first elements of the First Texas Cavalry (Union) arrived in South Texas to take the fight to their fellow Texans. By the following month, Colonel Haynes was leading a small force of two hundred men up the river to recruit more Mexican Texans to serve in the US Army. The Union offered Tejanos a $125 bounty upon enlistment, an additional bounty of $75 at the end of the war, a clothes allotment, and a monthly salary of $13. The rewards proved so enticing to the men on the lower Río Grande that the Second Texas Cavalry was quickly formed. Haynes took command of the unit in November 1863, as it began operations to wrestle the lucrative cotton trade away from the Confederates. Haynes soon encountered tensions between his men and the new recruits as the *Mexicanos* lacked discipline and did not speak English. Their lack of loyalty soon became apparent, as these soldiers faced overwhelming discrimination and began to chafe at military service when the promises made during the recruitment process failed to materialize.[77]

In February 1864, Davis wrote to General Edward O. C. Ord, commander of the Eighth Corps, Department of the Gulf, to lament how the Tejanos and *Mexicanos* in his unit had failed to work out on the lower Río Grande. Davis maintained that the supplies and clothing that was promised to the recruits had failed to arrive at the border. He claimed that the men found it too tempting to desert with whatever equipment they had: "They soon become dissatisfied with our manner of making payments, and being of Indian blood and nature, the discipline and restraint of this camp, and the value of their horses, arms, and equipments [*sic*] proving too much of a temptation, they take an opportunity to desert and carry them into Mexico, in some cases deserting from off picket." [78] The solution was to transfer the men to Louisiana, far away from the Texas-Mexico border, to make desertion more difficult. With the transfer approved, in June 1864, the regiment, except for two companies, sailed to New Orleans and up the Mississippi River until they were across from Baton Rouge. There, the Tejanos suffered in an unfamiliar land and climate, worried about their families back home, many of whom were forced to flee into Mexico to avoid Confederate reprisals.[79] By August 1864, officials consolidated the First and Second Regiments and ordered them to serve the remainder of the war in Louisiana. It was not until July 1865, after the surrender of the Confederate Trans-Mississippi Department, that these Tejano soldiers returned to Texas.[80]

Campaigning

Confederate and Union Tejano soldiers shared some of the same difficulties of racism and discrimination during the Civil War. Negative sentiments ingrained in the Anglo-Texan population since the antebellum era were shared with other Anglo-Americans who insisted that Mexican Texans and other *Mexicanos* remained a primitive people who hindered progress with their lazy, unenterprising culture. Anglos viewed Tejanos as possessing poor intellect and primitive cultures, rooted in their mixed heritage and flawed ethnic traits.[81] The discrimination against Tejanos in the decade leading up to the Civil War materialized in law enforcement and the dehumanization of people of Mexican descent. The Texas Rangers and other white Texans showed no apprehension about using lynching as a form of retaliatory violence against Tejanos.[82] Before the Civil War, Tejanos in Central Texas had suffered lynchings. In the 1850s, during a trip through Texas, journalist (and later renowned landscape architect) Frederick Law Olmsted noted that Mexican Texans had been driven from their Austin-area homes because they were alleged horse thieves. In San Antonio, Olmsted observed that "a Mexican, caught in an attempt to steal a horse, had been hung by a Lynching party, on the spot."[83]

The practice of executing Tejanos continued into the Civil War era as soldiers, Union or Confederate, noted that it occurred often. Simple disagreements, Tejanos observed, could quickly escalate into needless violence. Racist sentiments were ingrained in both Johnny Reb and Billy Yank. Lieutenant Benjamin McIntyre observed that the Second Texas Cavalry of Tejanos were not to be trusted because of their "Mexican origin." The Iowa soldier wrote in his diary that "I consider them dishonest, cowardly and treacherous and only bide their time to make good their escape."[84] General Francis Herron, commander of the Union forces at Brownsville, insisted that the Mexicans "could not be trusted."[85]

Santiago Tafolla, a New Mexican who moved to Texas as an adult, joined the Confederate army in 1862, when he saw the economic opportunity of military service as something he could not pass up, and enlisted in Duff's Thirty-Third Regiment. In the summer of 1864, Tafolla recalled that when his unit was ordered to Louisiana, a dispute arose between a *"Mexicano* and an *Americano."* He believed the conflict grew so heated that all the Anglo soldiers threatened they "would put an end to all the 'greasers' in their midst."[86] Tafolla believed that if not for him and another soldier, Fred Metzger, who served as peacemakers between the two groups that evening, a calamity would have happened. Tafolla's compatriots decided to "desert that very night." They believed the racial discrimination was too great to endure. The Tejano Confederates insisted that Tafolla join them. Tafolla was apprehensive and agreed to go with them if his fellow

Mexican Texans left the army with their own horses and did not plunder any additional livestock. Planning their escape, Tafolla and three other Tejanos, José Casillas, José Garza, and Francisco Martínez, deserted and headed for the safety of Mexico. "Not one of us had ever been on Mexican soil," Tafolla lamented. Eluding squads of other Confederate soldiers and avoiding detection by civilians, the Tejano Confederates finally crossed into Piedras Negras and Tafolla shouted "¡Que viva Mexico!" in joy.[87]

Desertion was common in the Union and Confederate armies, but for different reasons. In the Rebel units, many Tejano soldiers grew weary and tired by the war effort and the monotony of soldier life. Being ordered east of the Mississippi caused angst and consternation as it pulled the men farther away from their homes. Captain Manuel Yturri attributed "more than two hundred desertions" in his unit due to orders to cross the Mississippi River.[88] In the Union army's Second Regiment, mass desertions in 1864 prompted Davis to post a regular guard around the Texas camp to prevent soldiers escaping to Mexico. In one case, a simple rumor, which later turned out to be true, that the unit would be transferred to Louisiana prompted a mass exodus of men. The problem grew so great the Second Texas had to be re-created by 1865, this time with only ten Tejanos.[89]

For soldiers caught deserting their units, the repercussions were severe. Private Pedro García, a soldier in Company E, First Texas Regiment (Union), deserted his post in Cameron County but was caught, court-martialed, and sentenced to be executed.[90] An Iowa soldier, Benjamin F. McIntyre, recorded the harrowing account of García's execution, his eyes covered with a bandage as he was shot by a dozen muskets. The incident proved so unsettling that it was even known by the civilian population and the Confederate Tejanos in nearby Rio Grande City.[91]

In the final year of the war, desertion of Confederate soldiers proved a widespread problem that authorities in Richmond had to address. As the ranks continued to be depleted by absentees, Confederate officials adopted a more lenient policy of granting furloughs to raise morale and discourage the men from deserting. Some commanders attempted to augment their strength by granting furloughs to men who promised to bring in additional recruits.[92] Allowing soldiers brief passes to visit family and friends on the home front provided the men a brief respite from the hardships of war. Despite the lenient attitude, the Confederate high command tried to exclude Texas troops from the liberal furlough policy because they feared that temporary leave might become permanent.[93]

While desertion due to racism and discrimination was a common rationale for Tejanos to leave their units, another factor was lack of pay and equipment. The Laredo Tejanos under Benavides were practically destitute, not having been paid in more than seven months. As rumors swirled that they might leave their posts and take their sidearms with them, Confederate officials worried about border security if they lost the Tejanos. Charles Thorkeli Løvenskiold, the governor's emissary, worried about what the Mexican Texans would take with them if they were allowed to disband without his supervision. To avert a crisis, Løvenskiold managed to negotiate an agreement in which Webb County would pay the men $30 and the state would later reimburse the county. Yet, the problem of paucity of pay did not disappear for the Laredoans. In 1864, Santos's men were in such dire needs of weapons and money that General Magruder attempted to portion out a few wagons full of cotton to pay the Tejanos, only to renege a short while later.[94] Union Tejanos struggled, too, to receive timely pay and weapons. The fact that they served on the border and were deemed a lower class of men perhaps explains why the Union army so often failed to fulfill the promises made to the *Mexicanos* and Tejanos during the recruitment.[95]

In addition to pay and equipment, the language barrier often proved a source of contention. Further frustrating Tejanos was the general indifference they met from superiors who often disregarded the will of the men when they appointed unsympathetic Anglo junior officers to lead the companies. In 1864, rumors swirled in the Second Texas Regiment (Union) that George W. Paschal, from Austin, was about to be appointed lieutenant colonel of the regiment. The Mexican Texan junior officers protested that Paschal did not speak Spanish and had no field experience with the unit. A handful of junior officers promised that they were committed to defeating the Confederates but did not believe Paschal would be the right man to lead them. Despite their entreaties, the US Army proceeded to appoint Paschal as the commander of the regiment, further alienating the Tejanos.[96] Confederate Tejanos also struggled with language deficiencies and clamored to serve with Spanish-speaking officers. Private Tafolla of the Thirty-Third Regiment knew how to speak English, having served in the US Army during the 1850s. But his fellow Tejanos "begged me to word a petition to Col. Duff asking that we be transferred to the regiment of Col. Santos Benavides, who was in charge of a regiment of *mexicanos*," Tafolla later wrote.[97]

Besides some shared experiences with German and Irish soldiers, the issues of ethnic discrimination and challenges of language certainly remain unique to Tejano Civil War soldiers. But the Mexican Texans who fought for the Union and the Confederacy did share some of the complaints of their Johnny Reb and Billy Yank counterparts. One was the monotony of camp life: the lack of proper food, weather, drill, forced marches, and routine duties that wore on the men. "I've been lying down most of the day because I have a pain in my leg or bones. I believe it's due to the soakings and being in the water so much and sleeping with wet clothes," Manuel Yturri lamented to his wife in 1865. "I believe that if I were single and I knew that this war was going to last four years more, I would kill myself."[98] His brother-in-law, Joseph de la Garza, seemed more content with camp life, yet he complained about the bitter cold while serving in Arkansas. "I never suffered cold feet in my life until now. I tell you, you may roast them by the fire for three hours, turn around, step on the ground for a minute and they are cold again," he observed.[99] Their Union counterparts in the Texas cavalry had less mundane work as horsemen charged with patrolling the border. Yet, they, too, became restless as health conditions along the Río Grande were poor, and soldiers seemed to die from illness frequently. In December 1863, the soldiers of the Second Regiment cut down trees for firewood so they could keep warm only to be told not to by their officers.[100]

Like most of the common soldiers of the Civil War, the Union and Confederate Tejano rank and file focused more on the day-to-day challenges of acquiring food, keeping warm, and staying healthy than contemplating what new campaign might follow."[101] Private Tafolla recalled that to break the monotony he and his comrades "would dance with each other" to pass the time.[102] Obtaining clothing proved paramount. Since most of the men came from the lower socioeconomic classes, they struggled with a shortage of supplies and clothing. Sometimes, this prompted some creative scavenging. "And we'll see if we can take enough [clothes] from the Yankees to dress ourselves," Captain De la Garza wrote his mother in October 1862.[103] In other cases, the men took matters into their own hands and tried to seize civilian property on the lower Río Grande so they could sell it and buy their own clothes. In May 1865, some of Benavides's men tried to seize clothing from a warehouse at Ringgold Barracks.[104] The rabble had to be dispersed by Captain Cristóbal Benavides, who implored the men to wait for their clothing to be distributed. Lack of clothing and equipment bothered the men, to be sure, but they also grumbled at their sparse diets. Manuel Yturri noted that he suffered from colic during the war and attributed that affliction to the poor diet he received. "I think it's from how well we live, on lean meat and corn bread," he speculated. "What a sad life I experience as a soldier . . . Almost all the soldiers in the division suffer from diahrrea [*sic*], Meat and corn bread are the rations."[105] Every soldier felt the fear associated with combat and the deaths they witnessed. Yturri insisted that the violence and gore he had witnessed in combat was enough to last a lifetime. "I would rather be a shepherd than a soldier in the front lines," he maintained.[106] When Joseph de la Garza died in the Battle of Mansfield in 1864, a fellow soldier noted that an artillery shell hit him above the knee and he "died soon after."[107]

The Civil War ended on April 9, 1865 when General Robert E. Lee surrendered the Confederacy's foremost army to General Ulysses S. Grant at Appomattox. It took until May 1 for Texans to learn about Lee's defeat, President Abraham Lincoln's assassination, and the surrender of other Confederate armies east of the Mississippi. As the Texas soldiers in other armies trudged home to the Lone Star State, Confederates on the Río Grande were not ready to give up. General John S. Ford led one final confrontation against the Federals on May 13, 1865 at the Battle of Palmito Ranch, about ten miles east of Brownsville. Though there was racism in defying the advance of the Union army, which included units of African American soldiers, the main reason why the Rebels fought was to cross thousands of pounds of cotton into Mexico before it could be confiscated by the Yankees. The result was a victory for the Confederates, as they inflicted 111 casualties on the Union army while suffering less than a dozen of their own. Tejanos fought on both sides as remnants of Benavides's regiment and the Second Texas faced each other on the battlefield one last time. A few weeks later, General Edmund Kirby Smith surrendered the Trans-Mississippi Department to US authorities on June 2. Ultimately, the inevitable moment arrived when the Confederate army in Texas melted away as soldiers fled to Mexico or simply went home. One of the last Confederates to surrender was Santos Benavides, who did not submit his muster rolls for parole until August 1865, months after Ford had instructed him to do so.[108]

Conclusions

Even though more Tejanos fought on behalf of the Confederacy than the Union, state officials recognized the perilous dynamics of recruiting from the Tejano community. The Mexican government noted as such in an 1873 Border Commission report, stating that the "majority" of Tejanos resisted the Confederate war effort "on account of their dislike for the Confederate cause, or on account of their living among its defenders, those very persons from whom they had received so many vexations."[109] Most of the Tejanos who fought for the Confederacy or the Union did not demonstrate a notable level of nationalism or patriotism. Unlike some of their Yankee counterparts, they did not enlist to protect the Union or preserve the Constitution. Historians of the Civil War have provided scholarly analysis demonstrating the various rationales and motivations of why soldiers enlisted. Johnny Reb and Billy Yank fought for a variety of reasons, but ultimately adventure, slavery, honor, defense of home, states' rights, and different interpretations of liberty served as some of the reasons, to name a few. Nationalism and national identity also explains why people lined up on opposite sides during the war.[110]

The reasons why most of the common soldiers of the Civil War fought in the war failed to apply to Tejanos, however. Except for the elites, who

Santos Benavides, post–Civil War period. Santos Benavides was a prominent Laredo Tejano during the nineteenth century. Rising to the rank of colonel in the Confederate army, Benavides was the highest-ranking Mexican Texan during the Civil War. Courtesy of the Webb County Heritage Foundation, Laredo, Texas.

sought to further their political and economic interests with the dominant Anglo ruling class, most Mexican Texans sought to advance themselves economically through their military service. They saw their enlistment in either the Union and Confederate armies as a labor agreement that could be renegotiated or canceled later. Thus, when they were not paid or they were shipped to defend the Confederacy in a location far from their homes, they deserted. In some cases, this choice resulted in death as they were shot for abandoning their posts. For Tejanos, the border also added an additional path to escape, as life along the Río Grande had created a space where nationalism and patriotism were weak and individuals could negotiate what culture and loyalty meant to them. Mexican Texans who fought for the Union or the Confederacy were often deemed to be lacking strong ideological convictions for their respective nation-states. Yet, these Tejanos did have strong ideals. The Confederates who fought for Benavides and other regiments viewed the war as a fight for local defense and individual loyalties and not an ideological struggle for or against slavery. The Tejanos who joined the Union saw the war as an opportunity to influence their political and economic future.

CHAPTER 3

"I AM AN AMERICAN FIRST, LAST, AND ALL THE TIME"

Tejanos from Reconstruction to the Spanish-American War

Following the Civil War, Tejano soldiers returned to their homes and families, where they reflected on their years of sacrifice and prepared for the future. Since the Texas Revolution, Tejanos had seen how their participation in the past conflicts of Texas had boded ill for them, as political retaliation, violence, and property loss marked the postwar periods. The Civil War was no exception. Tejano Confederates wondered what the Federal victory would mean to them, their property, and their families.

In this case, they joined the majority of Anglo Texans who fought for and supported the Confederacy. In June 1865, as Texas prepared to turn over Confederate property to the United States, some Confederate leaders absconded in fear. Former governors Edward Clark and Pendleton Murrah, for instance, fled to Mexico rather than await US troops. Other Deep South Confederates followed suit, moving to Mexico or even farther south to Brazil to avoid the federal government's Reconstruction policies. By mid-June, US soldiers arrived at Galveston and Marshall. Among General Gordon Granger's duties upon his arrival in Galveston were the nullification of all Confederate laws, the paroling of Rebel troops, and the pronouncement on June 19 that the Emancipation Proclamation granted freedom to the enslaved people of Texas. Henceforth known as "Juneteenth," the decree transformed the political and social landscape of Texas in one swoop.[1]

As the US government and Texas leaders navigated the murky waters of what Reconstruction would entail, rumors swirled about how the federal government might deal with former Rebel soldiers. US soldiers slowly advanced up the Río Grande toward Laredo and Eagle Pass. After learning that he could be executed for sedition, Colonel Santos Benavides, the highest-ranking Tejano officer, fled to Mexico with his brothers. The Benavideses, though long-standing members of the South Texas Tejano elite, still could choose among the different identities available to them in the mid-nineteenth century. They could identify as American, Confederate, Texan, or, in this case, as they traveled to Monterrey to avoid capture by federal authorities, Mexican. Even though the Civil War and military service had allowed the soldiers of the Benavides regiment to embrace the Confederate identity of their fellow Rebels, the end of the war allowed them to pivot toward their Mexican cultural roots to avoid punishment. Consequently, only John Z. Leyendecker, brother-in-law to the Benavides brothers and the former captain and quartermaster of Santos's regiment, was left to surrender in Laredo to federal authorities in the summer of 1865. It took an additional few weeks before Cristóbal Benavides learned that federal troops would not be seeking vengeance and retribution against the former Confederates. Soon thereafter, Santos and his brothers returned to the border to resume their life in the postbellum period.[2]

The Tejano soldiers of the Civil War had a markedly different experience than their Anglo counterparts.[3] Tejano veterans stood apart from their Anglo colleagues. Many had already deserted, having joined mostly for economic opportunity. Others, disenchanted with scant food and supplies and the persistent racism in the Rebel ranks, chose to desert to Mexico rather than continue to suffer these indignities. Santiago Tafolla later recalled that he was living in northern Mexico with his family after deserting from his unit during the last year of the war. He did not learn until August 1865 that the war was over, but he was in no hurry to return. He waited until he finished harvesting his crops in October before crossing the Río Grande once more.[4] In May, near Hempstead, Texas, Manuel Yturri promised he would soon be with his family in San Antonio but feared that the enemy would take "possession of this state." He worried because the Confederate "troops are too disconsolate because of what happened on the other side of the Mississippi."[5]

The Civil War's conclusion in Texas did not end the turmoil of the previous four years. Race relations, political power, labor relations, and the state's economy were all unsettled. By the end of 1865, the Texas elite began to chafe at the palpable changes: the continued presence of the US Army in the state; the creation of the Bureau of Refugees, Freedmen, and Abandoned Lands (or Freedmen's Bureau) to help the newly freed African Americans; and the challenge that the freed slaves presented to the social order.[6] When the Texas Constitutional Convention met on February 7, 1866 to comply with the requirements of presidential Reconstruction, former secessionists and conservative Unionists outlined a path designed to restore the conditions of 1860. As such, the new legislature refused to ratify the Thirteenth and Fourteenth Amendments to the US Constitution and forged a plan to deny the African American community their basic civil rights.

The reluctance of state leaders throughout the former Confederate states to accept the generous policies of presidential Reconstruction forced the US Congress to assume control of the process. By 1867, Congress passed the Military Reconstruction Acts, which divided the former Confederate states into five military districts and placed them each under the command of a general in the US Army. Military commanders were to remove former Confederates from office, protect the rights of African Americans, supervise elections, and begin the process of having each state write a new constitution to be approved by Congress. The process of Congressional Reconstruction in Texas lasted until March 30, 1870, when the state was readmitted into the Union.[7]

As state officials battled for the future of Texas, Tejanos, too, were affected by Congressional Reconstruction. In Laredo, the alcalde and three other aldermen were removed from office. These officials included Santos Benavides, who could only find a position as a notary.[8] In San Antonio, Tejanos joined their Anglo neighbors in opposing the civil rights and suffrage protections for African Americans. In August 1868, former

Confederates and Democrats organized Los Bexareños Demócratas to uphold the notion of white supremacy. Los Bexareños included many of the city's prominent Tejanos, Manuel Yturri, Rafael Quintanilla, Juan Cárdenas, and José Ángel Navarro, to name a few. They also included several Anglo Texans. Using pamphlets and editorials in the *San Antonio Herald*, the Tejanos championed conservative causes and railed against Republican principles until Texas was redeemed from Republican rule.[9] Other conservative factions emerged soon thereafter. One such group, the Conservative Union Reconstructionists, included the elder Tejano states-man José Antonio Navarro and diverged from Los Bexareños' hardline policies. The Conservative Union Reconstructionists did not oppose the right of freedmen to vote. Yet, they feared that "negro-rule predominates" would spell the end for Texas and the nation. The cause was important to the elder Navarro, who emerged from his neutral stance during the Civil War to take on a more politically active role.[10]

But conservatives did not represent the ideals of all Tejanos. The complexity and heterogeneous nature of Tejano thinking during Recon-struction is demonstrated by the creation of the Mexican-Texas Club in San Antonio a month before Los Bexareños came to existence. By stark contrast, the Mexican-Texas Club defended the rights of African Americans and supported the US Congress as it moved to disenfranchise former Confederates and supporters of the Rebel cause. By the following year, the Mexican Texas Club had approximately four hundred members and had expanded to nearby Wilson County, southeast of the city. Tejanos like Epistacio Mondragón, Juan M. Chávez, Fermín Cassiano, and Anto-nio P. Rivas used their own newspaper, *El Mejicano de Texas*, to push their pro-Union opinions and their support for Republican policies. Though the passions of Reconstruction would fade by the 1870s, where Tejanos stood on the political ideals of the era stood in contrast and demonstrated the individual agency that Mexican Texans held in how they viewed the world around them.[11] When Reconstruction ended and Democrats regained control of the state in 1874, the "redeemed" Texas government adopted a new constitution in 1876 and the return of the antebellum elite to control the state's political and economic operations.[12]

The Texas Frontier

As Texas returned to the status quo, the problems of security on the frontier once more loomed large. One of the complaints Texans had against the federal government prior to 1861 had been the ineffectiveness of the US Army in combating banditry and Native American raids. Federal troops returned to the Texas-Mexico border after the war, and most of them were African American soldiers from the United States Colored Troops.

While the US Infantry proved woefully inadequate in handling the surge of violence along the Río Grande, the fact that some counties had no law enforcement officials to maintain order only compounded the problems. As the Kickapoos, Lipan Apaches, and Comanches wreaked havoc on Texas, many herders, travelers, and ranchers were killed during the raids. Outlaws, too, presented a challenge and often murdered people for no rhyme or reason. In 1866, the commander of Fort McIntosh, US Army Major Andrew J. Hogan, worked with Santos Benavides and more than two dozen Laredo Tejanos in a joint operation to eliminate a group of outlaws operating near Dogtown (present day Tilden).[13] Three years later, in April 1869, when Indigenous bands killed more than half a dozen citizens, the new commander at Fort McIntosh issued a call for four companies of Webb County civilians to assist the military in their response. Though this service was voluntary in nature, Tejanos feared that they might be conscripted into military service akin to what they experienced under the Confederacy. Benavides and other Tejanos ultimately rose to the challenge and helped the US Army in its attempts to restore order on the border into the 1870s.[14] The role of Tejanos in assisting the US Army echoed the Texas Revolutionary era, when the compañías volantes remained an integral part of Texas society.

The lawlessness and raids continued into the 1870s and included the return of Juan Cortina, who rustled cattle in the lower Río Grande valley. Texas officials had to act. In 1874, Governor Richard Coke, feeling the pressure to curb the disorder after a wave of violence killed more than two dozen South Texans, appealed to Refugio Benavides, then acting as mayor of Laredo, to serve as a lieutenant in the Texas Rangers. In an unprecedented move, the governor authorized Benavides to cross the border into Mexico in pursuit of bandits and Natives, if needed. This development caused consternation in the US State Department, which maintained that the governor would be in violation of federal law if Benavides and his compatriots crossed the Río Grande.[15]

In a desperate bid to restore public confidence in the state government, the legislature had approved the permanent Ranger force on April 10, 1874. The Texas Ranger badge meant little in the wave of violence that erupted in South Texas during the period. Once more failing to distinguish between Tejanos and Mexican bandits working with or alongside Cortina, law enforcement officials and soldiers dealt violence indiscriminately. Benavides, wearing the tin star of the Rangers, meted out drastic measures of his own, hanging a man in 1874 for allegedly skinning cattle.[16]

By the mid-to-late 1870s, Texas's postwar cattle boom had only intensified the violence. Indigenous bands and cattle rustlers, whether Mexican *bandidos* or Anglo-American outlaws, brought more fighting to the frontier. As pressure mounted on the US Army to eradicate the Native threat, federal soldiers would have to do more with less. Even though the US Army had mushroomed to nearly one million men in uniform by the end of the Civil War, the war's end saw rapid demobilization, which reduced the force's strength dramatically. By 1866, Congress had decided that less than 40,000 regular troops were all that the country needed. The number increased slightly in 1867 following Congressional Reconstruction, but the size of the army continued to dwindle to less than 30,000 men between 1870 and 1876. The cavalry, which made up about one-fourth of the army, averaged between 7,000 and 10,000 horsemen during that same period. But what the army lacked in manpower, it tried to make for up in facilities. By 1870, a line of forts in West Texas offered protection to settlers and officials. Officials organized these forts into four subdistricts—the Presidio, Brazos, Pecos, and Río Grande—as the US Army unsuccessfully attempted to subdue their Native foes.[17]

The US Army struggled with various administrative challenges while it dealt with the problem of Native Americans in the West. In the years after Appomattox, inconsistent policies hampered US troops on the frontier.[18]

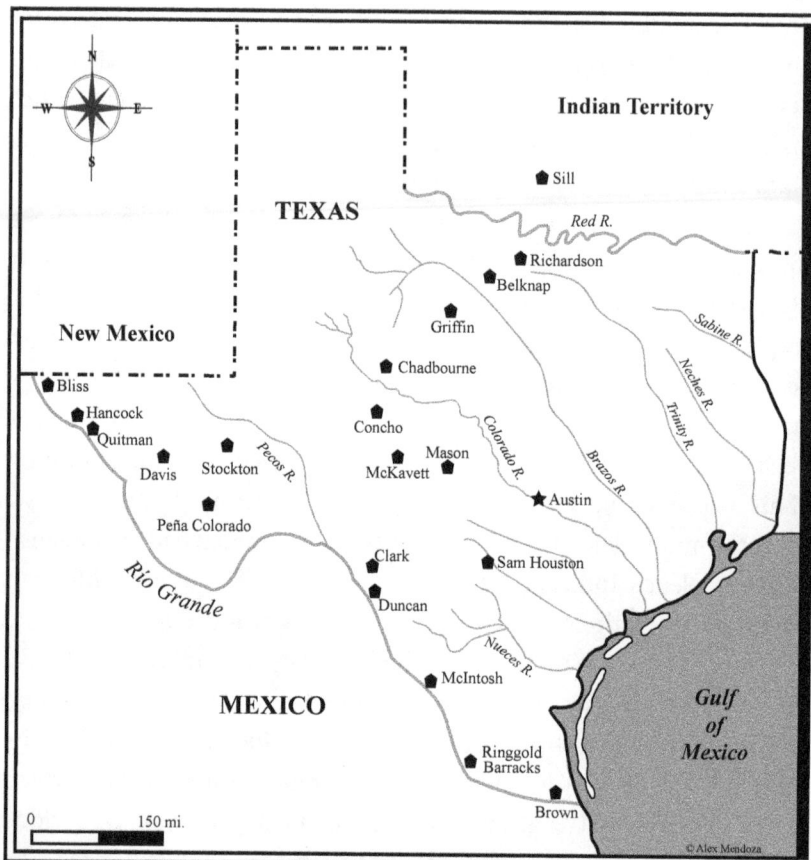

US Army Forts in Texas, 1866–90

By 1871, federal policy toward Indians took a dramatic turn. Prior to that year, Indian Bureau agents saw Indian Territory as a sanctuary for Native bands, regardless of whether they committed violence against settlers or soldiers. After 1871, however, General William T. Sherman lobbied for a change in policy. In Texas, Sherman found a capable commander in General Ranald S. Mackenzie, a West Point graduate and Civil War veteran, to lead campaigns against the Natives. Mackenzie moved his headquarters to Fort Richardson, northwest of Fort Worth, and launched a series of operations against the Comanches, Apaches, Kiowas, and Kickapoos in western Texas.[19] Using scouts from the Tonkawa tribe, a traditional enemy of the Comanches, Mackenzie's Fourth Cavalry proved relentless in its pursuit of the Indigenous bands, even chasing them into Mexico. By 1875, at the conclusion of the Red River War, the US Army succeeded in pushing the Texas Indians to reservations in the Indian Territory.[20]

The shift of the US Army from Reconstruction duty to frontier constabulary service did not provide new opportunities for Tejanos. Downsizing and racism formed barriers to Mexican-Texan military service during this era. This marked a change from previous years. In the antebellum army, Santiago Tafolla had found a place, serving in New Mexico and Texas before he left in 1861 and joined the Confederacy. Enlisting at the age of seventeen, Tafolla fought against Indians and met Jefferson Davis when he toured Texas during his stint as secretary of war. Soon thereafter, Tafolla was almost charged with desertion after an altercation with a non-commissioned officer.[21] Congress authorized six segregated regiments of African Americans in 1866 but made no such concessions to actively recruit Mexican Americans.[22]

With opportunities for service in the US Army limited by the economic and social realities of the period, Texans found alternate avenues for military service. In 1867, the US Congress banned the militia forces of Texas and eight other former Confederate states. Three years later, however, Congress allowed Texas back into the Union. State officials soon passed a bill authorizing a new state militia in June 1870, which featured two separate categories: the State Guard, which included volunteer companies, and the Reserve Military, which consisted of men between the ages of eighteen and forty-five.[23] In addition, the legislature created the Texas State Police.[24] The new laws quickly bore fruit: more than 90,000 men enrolled in the Reserve Militia and over 3,500 joined the State Guard.[25] But interest in militia service declined rapidly. By the end of 1871, the Texas adjutant general reported that the state militia had less than 75,000 men.[26]

The state militia's post–Civil War decline was symptomatic of larger trends. Outside of a few northern states, the nation generally saw a downtick of militia enlistment. Texans still chafed at Republican Reconstruction efforts and the possibility of African Americans serving in the state militia or State Police. By 1873, when Democrats regained control of the state government, a flurry of legislation eliminated the State Police and refurbished the state militia. State leaders had left the militia off the list of state agencies that received appropriations.[27] The militia had no weapons until the federal government provided the state with a thousand guns. Nevertheless, militia volunteers furnished their own uniforms and paid rent on their own armories without government aid during the 1870s.[28]

While Tejano life was marked by many continuities during Reconstruction, it was changing in important ways. By 1880, the state's approximately 70,000 Mexican Texans made up 39 percent of the state's population. They remained clustered in the same geographic areas they occupied during the Texas Revolutionary era, in the south, central, and western parts of the state. Almost half of the Tejano population (46 percent) lived below the Nueces River, while 36 percent resided in Central Texas, and the remaining 18 percent dwelled in the Trans-Pecos. Though they had not reached northern and eastern Texas in numbers, Tejanos continued to assert themselves politically and economically in areas where their numbers were significant. In South Texas, Tejanos made inroads in local and county politics and served as mayors, treasurers, and county attorneys. Historians suggest that though Tejanos showed greater interest in Texas politics and civic duty in the 1870s and 1880s, they still retained a sense of their Mexican identity.[29]

Tejanos joined the Texas militia wherever they could, but they left few records explaining why they joined. Their rationale was probably the same as other militia volunteers throughout the United States during the period: to contend for a viable place in the new political and economic order of their community. "The fact that by this time the majority of Mexican Texans were of native birth meant that the Tejano community had an increased familiarity with American institutions: schools, churches, and other mainstream agencies that helped Tejanos take advantage of new opportunities opening up in a modernizing society," historian Arnoldo De León maintains.[30] Moreover, militia service provided a way for volunteers to assert their masculinity.[31]

Two options available to Tejanos during the post–Civil War era were the Frontier Forces and Volunteers Guards. The companies paid their own expenses, rented their armories and paid for their own uniforms, which were mostly gray or blue. They joined the ranks of companies formed in Abilene, El Paso, and San Antonio, among other places. Private Ramón Treviño of San Antonio was representative of the typical militia volunteer. Treviño was born in Monterrey, Mexico, and joined Company A in October 1870 at age forty-five. He was five feet, nine inches tall, of "dark complexion," and a laborer who indebted himself to the state for one Winchester carbine, valued at thirty dollars.[32] Thirty-year-old Patricio Benavides also enrolled in San Antonio and indebted himself for a Winchester. He remained in service for one year.[33]

Tejano volunteers faced the language and literacy barriers that still hampered many Mexican Texans in the late nineteenth century. From 1860 to 1900, the Tejano literacy rate ranged between 12.4 and 25.1 percent.[34] Patricio Benavides and Cisto Castillo (from San Elizario), for instance, had to sign their name with an "X" in lieu of a formal signature in their official paperwork with the adjutant general's office.[35] But some Tejanos, such as Claude Flores (Abilene), Encarnación Martinez (Alice), and Jesús Sandoval (Brownsville), signed their full names when they joined the Texas militia.[36]

1890s Texas

By the 1890s, the militia force in Texas was on the decline. In 1891, the new adjutant general, Woodford H. Mabry, attempted to reform the organization by recommending that the legislature create a permanent training facility in northwest Austin. State officials accepted his proposal, and the installation later to be known as Camp Mabry was born. Still, the numbers of men in the state forces continued to slowly dwindle. By 1896, the numbers fell to approximately 2,500 men.[37]

For Tejanos, the decline in state militia coincided with a reluctance to join the United States Army. In 1894, Congress passed a law that required soldiers to be able to read, write, and speak English. For many Tejanos, most of whom continued to speak and communicate in Spanish, this formed a roadblock to recruitment.

With the state militia dwindling, the responsibility for frontier defense reverted to the Texas Rangers. The *Rinches*, as they were known to residents of Mexican descent along the Río Grande, discriminated against *Mexicanos* and Tejanos with equal aplomb, even though a few Tejanos had served in the Rangers' organization. In 1885, a gun battle between Rangers and respected Tejanos in Webb County and an interethnic election riot in Laredo the following year only heightened the tension and mistrust between locals and the law enforcement agency. Effectively shut out of military service, Tejanos went about their business, focusing on local matters and leaving the broader issues of security and defense to state and federal authorities.[38]

Life on the border was changing. With the introduction of the railroads, South Texas began to shift from being an agricultural region to a commercial area and trade center. Anglo and Mexican migrants arrived, hoping to prosper economically and politically. With the arrival of new citizens, too, came additional problems and alterations of the "peace structure" between Tejanos and Anglos. In the early 1890s, Francisco Ruiz Sandoval and Catarino Garza, both Mexican nationals who lived in Laredo and the Río Grande valley during the previous decade, attempted to organize Texas-based rebellions against Mexican President Porfirio Díaz. The resulting conflicts put the US Army and the Texas Rangers on high alert, made no geographical distinctions and further blurred the lines of nationalism and loyalty.

Contemporaries—both Anglo and Mexican—recognized the possibility of future violence. In 1892, Matías Romero, the Mexican minister of finance, published an article in the *North American Review* urging Anglo-Americans to take control of the border, arguing, in part, that Texans of Mexican descent were susceptible to the manipulations of men like Sandoval and Garza. Mexican Texans, Romero maintained, "have never amalgamated with their [Anglo] neighbors." The crux of the matter, according to the Mexican diplomat, was that these "people are generally ignorant, few being able to read and write, and they are easily influenced

Third Cavalry Troopers Searching a Suspected Revolutionist by Frederic Remington, 1892. The Miriam and Ira D. Wallach Division of Art, Prints and Photographs: Picture Collection, The New York Public Library Digital Collections.

by unscrupulous members of their own race, who can appeal to them in their native tongue." While Romero had a personal stake in maintaining the status quo vis-à-vis the Díaz regime, it was not difficult to sway an already nervous Anglo Texan population who already feared the conflict that Mexican revolutionaries could trigger on the border.[39]

Romero's article struck a chord with Texas's Anglo population. When US troops and state authorities could not capture Garza due to a sympathetic civilian population along the border, it seemed clear that the loyalties of Tejanos could be in question. As such, in 1891, US Army troops moved to the border with orders to destroy any Tejano community who supported the anti-Díaz revolutionaries operating in South Texas. For the US Army commander, Captain John Gregory Bourke, it was not enough to simply defeat the rebels. He aimed for a complete devastation of the border Tejano communities who may have offered support. Bourke, who had fought against the Apache bands in Arizona, brought the same brutality he used there to Tejanos along the Río Grande. US soldiers burned ranches, stole livestock, and searched houses without warrants. As historian Monica Muñoz Martinez notes, the military "strategies for defeating Catarino Garza's rebellion set a precedent for later practices by the US Army and state police alike."[40] The US Army's and Texas Rangers' wave of violence and intimidation went unchecked by state and federal authorities. By 1893, the US Army claimed victory over Garza's revolutionaries and forced their leader into exile.[41]

The swift retribution of the army and state authorities offered a clear view of the trepidation many Anglos felt toward Tejanos. Texas businessmen depended on trade with Mexico, and they feared Mexican revolutionaries could sway Tejanos with notions of racial nationalism, and overturn the gains of the last two decades. Moreover, the growing discord between the United States and Spain over Cuba marked another area of concern regarding Tejano loyalties, particularly since the virtues of the Spanish founders of Texas had long been part of the state's lore. The questions of Tejano loyalty and patriotism, and the desire to manage and control the growing Tejano population, came to a head by the late 1890s. With the 1891 death of Tejano stalwart Santos Benavides, who had

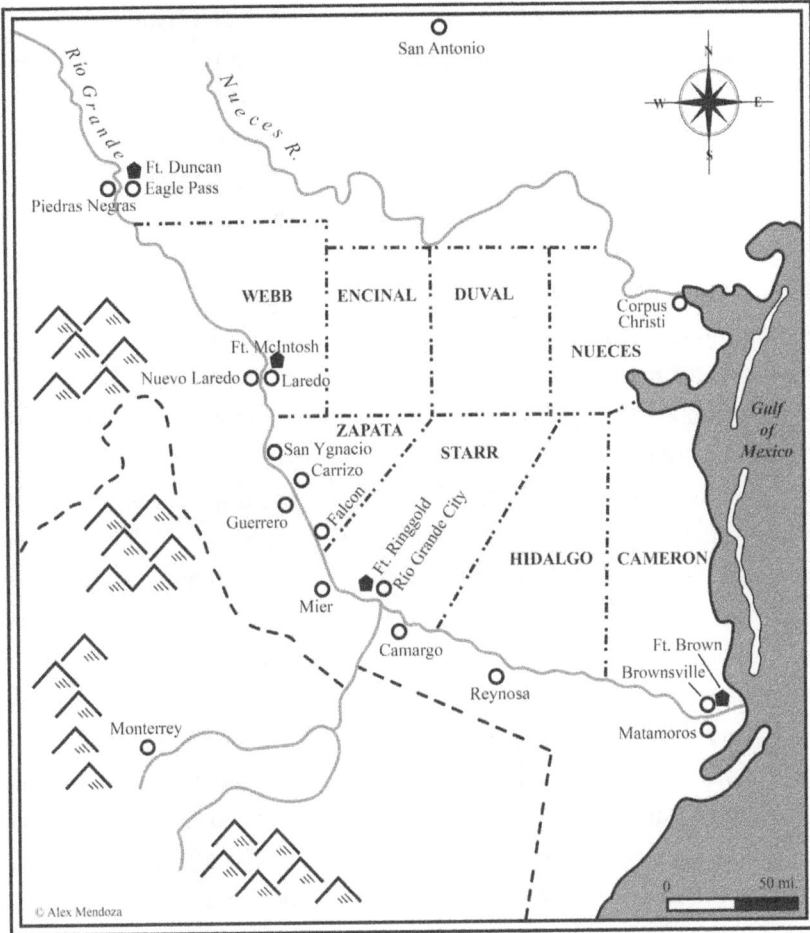

South Texas Border Region, 1860–90

served in the Texas state legislature from 1879 to 1885, it appeared as if the structure of accommodation and alliance that had marked the old Tejano and Anglo elite since the Texas Revolution would crumble.[42]

Spanish-American War

While Texans and Tejanos struggled with revolutionaries and racial tensions along the border, more than one thousand miles to the southeast, on the island of Cuba, dissidents launched an uprising against Spanish authorities aimed to topple the colonial rulers and establish independence. The rebellion was quickly suppressed by the Spanish. Nevertheless, the movement continued as exiles returned to the island and launched a coordinated military insurgency that wreaked havoc on Spanish Cuba. As the revitalized insurgency gained traction in 1896, Spanish General Valeriano Weyler y Nicolau arrived to lead Spanish troops against the rebels. Weyler arrived on the island and launched a brutal campaign. Weyler instituted a policy of reconcentration for civilians, placing them in detention camps and restricting all travel without permission. The Spanish general's rationale for his reconcentration policies were rooted in constraining civilian support for the Cuban guerrillas and eliminating casualties for his troops. Though reconcentration had been instituted along the Kansas-Missouri border during the Civil War, Weyler's policies soon attracted attention and criticism from the American press and the White House. President Grover Cleveland refused to recognize the Cuban revolutionaries in the fall of 1896, but he did mention that American investments on the island remained important and suggested that a compromise could be reached if the Spanish allowed the Cubans home rule.[43]

After he won the presidential election of 1896, Republican President William McKinley echoed Cleveland's support for the Cubans self-rule. McKinley assumed office in March 1897 preoccupied more by internal tensions caused by the Panic of 1893 than events in Cuba. Yet, the president underestimated Spain's desire to hold onto Cuba.

The Spanish viewed the very legitimacy of their once prosperous empire in question as they struggled to hold onto their last American possessions, Cuba and Puerto Rico. For the rest of the year, McKinley supported Spain in its attempts to pacify Cuba. In January 1898, the Spanish launched a few economic reforms on the island, but the insurgents, sensing weakness, refused to budge. Later that month, the US Navy ordered the USS *Maine* to Havana to protect American interests during the ongoing hostilities. But the following month, on February 8, American neutrality would be strained by the *New York Journal*'s publication of a private letter written by Spanish minister Enrique Dupuy de Lôme, which contained derogatory remarks about President McKinley. In the midst of that scandal, on February 15, the *Maine* exploded under mysterious circumstances in Havana harbor, killing over 260 sailors. Authorities in Washington ordered a court of inquiry to determine the cause of the explosion. Americans would nor wait for an official investigation as the press and politicians blamed the Spanish for the loss of American lives.

In March, Spanish and American inquiries reached different conclusions. The American court argued that a submarine mine had caused the *Maine's* forward magazines to explode and the ship to sink. The Spanish countered that it was an internal explosion. Nevertheless, the possibility for an American intervention increased dramatically in the following weeks as the McKinley administration weighed its options. After diplomatic efforts failed, Congress authorized the president to declare war on April 25, 1898, retroactive to April 21 to counter Spain's formal declaration of war on the United States on April 23. The United States and Spain were at war.[44]

In Texas, war fervor had been building up for months.[45] Brownsville's *Daily Herald* noted the arrival of the battleship USS *Texas* and the gunboat USS *Nashville* in Galveston in mid-February. Reduced railroad rates and admission fees drew patriotic visitors.[46] So many Texans arrived in Galveston for the viewing that many were unable to board the battleship.[47] In Laredo, a local fraternal group, the Improved Order of the Red Men, organized a celebration for George Washington's birthday on February 22, 1898, to "awaken patriotism on the border" and to emphasize American values and ideals. Whites and Tejanos in Laredo dressed up as Native Americans and "attacked" the "settlers," winning victory and securing a key to the city from the mayor. The celebration, which included parades and burlesque shows, lasted two days.[48] Farther north, in Austin, members of the United Confederate Veterans vowed to volunteer against the Spanish.[49] Many Texans were ready for war even before April 1898, as these accounts indicate.[50]

In late April, McKinley's put out a call for volunteers. Each state had to furnish the needed troops based on its population.[51] A month later, Texas Governor Charles J. Culberson issued General Orders No. 180, which called for three regiments of volunteers and one regiment of cavalry, a total of approximately four thousand troops.[52] The enlistment period was to be two years or the duration of the war, whichever was shorter.[53] Problems emerged almost immediately. The financial rewards for volunteering were minimal, far below what many prospective soldiers could earn at home.[54] Texas was one of the worst states for pay, coming in at a paltry $1.72 per man.[55]

Racism also hampered the war effort. Governor Culberson, like many southern politicians, feared the use of Black troops and refused to accept any Black militia units. As volunteer units reached the rendezvous point at Camp Mabry in Austin by the first week of May 1898, Tejanos across the state were once more forced to come to terms with another choice: volunteer to fight in this latest war or refuse service, like some of their Anglo contemporaries. Culberson's racism coincided with Alabama Congressman Joseph Wheeler's call for the Gulf Coast states to provide the bulk of the troops to fight in Cuba. Wheeler, a former Confederate lieutenant general, volunteered for service at the age of sixty-one. He also insisted that the white men from the Gulf Coast states do the bulk of the fighting; they were acclimated to the climate of Cuba, where yellow fever and tropical illnesses might prove overwhelming to northern soldiers.[56] Not all Gulf Coast residents agreed with Wheeler, but racism and an overreliance on Texas volunteers diminished Tejano enthusiasm.[57]

But hesitance to enlist was not unique to Tejanos. Contrary to Wheeler's expectations, in Alabama and other states of the former Confederacy, regiments had a tough time attracting volunteers. When men did enlist, they often deserted after they realized they could not keep their own units intact and that they would be subject to federal orders.[58] While volunteers from the Deep South might have had reason to resent federal authorities, Tejanos might have had similar reasons to balk at service in the US Army. Historian John L. Leffler argues that some Texans resisted fighting against Spain in Cuba because they did not want to leave their jobs and families, but they would more readily fight the Spanish if Texas were invaded.[59]

The ambivalence of Tejanos in response to the war effort showed that the state's *Mexicano* community still straddled two cultures: that of their ancestral homeland and their modern state, with its growing

Anglo-American institutions. During the border tensions of the 1890s, the loyalty of Mexican Texans came under scrutiny by state officials. Though the Spanish-language press protested the heavy-handed policies of the US Army and the Texas Rangers, these calls were unheeded due to the need to bring this region under control for economic development.[60] The fact remained that by 1898, many Anglo Texans still viewed Tejanos with suspicion. Some believed that Mexico and Mexican Texans might have underlying sympathies with Spain.[61]

Consider events in El Paso. On February 25, after the sinking of the *Maine*, the *El Paso International Daily Times* reported that American soldiers at Fort Bliss remained vigilant and ready for war against Spain.[62] Two days later, the *Times* warned that Mexicans sympathetic to Spain could provide that country with gold to fund their war against the Cubans and Americans.[63] The following month, the *Times* reported on an alleged desecration of the American flag at a local saloon. "Hundreds of persons called the *Times*' office last night . . . when it was realized that 'old glory' was about to be dishonored," the paper proclaimed. The incident turned out to be a mere rumor, but the *Times* report was symptomatic of the hyper-patriotism of the period.[64] On April 20, when The Eighteenth Infantry finally left the city for training in Florida, the *Times* asserted that "El Paso's Patriotism Stirred."[65]

With federal troops and Texas Rangers gone, attention pivoted to concerns about border security and Mexican banditry.[66] In late May 1898, local school principal W. H. T. López was harshly criticized by his fellow citizens for having sympathies for Spain and Mexico. The accusations stemmed from the fact that López had the flags of Spain, Mexico, and Texas displayed in his classroom. The incident prompted the El Paso educator to call the office of the *Times* to profess his loyalty to the United States. According to the paper, López denied the allegation that he was guilty of "disloyalty to this country and of being an outspoken sympathizer with Spain in the present war." "I am an American citizen," López claimed. "My sympathies are with my mother country the United States in its fight with Spain." He further noted that "the people of El Paso have treated me very kindly, and I do not want them to think for one moment that they have been giving their confidence to a traitor to the country of his birth."[67] The heightened suspicions likely kept some Tejanos in El Paso from volunteering for the war. While twelve El Pasoans volunteered to join Teddy Roosevelt's "Rough Riders" that month, only two Tejanos joined the El Paso Home Guards.[68]

The López incident in El Paso echoed larger concerns about Pan-Hispanicism. In the years leading up to the outbreak of the Spanish-American War, Anglo Texans feared that a "Spanish-led movement aiming at solidarity among Hispanic nations" in Latin America threatened to upset the delicate balance of accommodation between them and Mexican Texans.[69] Anglo-Americans worried that Mexico would provide a haven for Spanish exiles agitating against the American war effort in Cuba. Residents of Piedras Negras, Coahuila, across the Río Grande from Eagle Pass and Fort Duncan, raised $4,500 to send to Spain during its conflict with the United States, seeming to confirm borderlands support for the Spanish cause. In San Antonio, several Spanish-language newspapers in the city expressed sympathy for Spain.[70] Even though Mexico proclaimed a firm neutrality, White Texans feared that the hostilities with Spain might give revolutionaries an opportunity to raid into unprotected Texas. When Texas newspapers reported that Mexican authorities had broken up a plot of hundreds of Spanish sympathizers to invade the lower Río Grande valley, it alarmed Texans and even Tejanos.[71]

In Laredo, the Tejano population remained ambivalent about volunteering in this latest American war. When *The Laredo Daily Times* reported on aborted raid organized in Mexico against the Río Grande valley, it called the plot a "Spanish Conspiracy."[72] Wartime tensions threatened the accommodation that Anglo and Tejano Laredo had reached in the wake of Santos Benavides's death earlier in the decade. Border businessmen depended on trade with Mexico but feared that Mexican revolutionaries supported by Spanish would sway Tejano Laredoans and turn back Texas's political and economic progress. Questions of Tejano loyalty and patriotism underlay the desire to manage and control the Laredo Tejano majority. As historian Elliott Young argues, the goal for the Laredo elite—both Anglo and Tejano—was social control of the masses and the emphasis of American patriotism.[73] In late April 1898, *The Laredo Daily Times* newspaper launched a series of editorials designed to inspire volunteers to enlist. On April 26, the *Times* suggested that Texans were ideally suited for the climate in Cuba.[74] Two days later, the newspaper argued that Americans and Mexicans from the Texas-Mexico border had an advantage and could "get assignments in the Regular Army as interpreters and scouts" in the Spanish-speaking island of Cuba.[75] At the same time, the *Times* criticized Spanish-language newspapers for being a malign influence. They pointed to the Garza rebellion as an example of how Mexican Texans could be swayed by falsehoods and fiery rhetoric.[76] When the Laredo volunteers departed the city for Camp Mabry in mid-May, Anglo mistrust remained present. Even though a Tejano, Tomás Arispe, served as a first lieutenant in Laredo's Company K, broad support from the city's Mexican-Texan population had failed to materialize. When *The Laredo Daily Times* published a list on May 4, 1898, of businesses and citizens who had donated money to support the local volunteers in Company K, only two out of seventy-five, L. R. Ortiz and J. Correo, had Spanish-surnames. While poverty might have been partly to blame for the lack of financial support, this latest effort of Laredo Tejanos to remain neutral did not go unnoticed.

As Company K readied for service, Anglos accused prominent Laredo Tejano Amador Sánchez of being sympathetic to Spain because he failed to enlist or support the war. Born in 1866 into a wealthy ranching family, Sánchez graduated from St. Mary's University in San Antonio before being elected as the Webb County District Clerk in 1890. In June 1898, he had to deflect accusations that he was in "sympathy with Spain." In a public letter published in the *Times*, Sánchez claimed those falsehoods originated from a "political enemy" who was "capable of inventing anything." He maintained that he was loyal to the United States. He claimed that he was "anxious to go to the front," but did not do so for two reasons: his obligation to his wife and five children, and the character of the war, which he did not believe was of an urgent nature. Yet, he was proudly patriotic. "I am an American first, last, and all the time, even if my name sounds Spanish," Sánchez wrote.[77]

Just as it had during the Civil War, San Antonio served as the epicenter of military activity for the Spanish-American War. Fort Sam Houston served as the supply base for the First United States Volunteer Cavalry, better known as Teddy Roosevelt's "Rough Riders." San Antonio had mushroomed in size to become the largest city in Texas with about 50,000 people by the end of the nineteenth century. Tejanos in the city numbered more than 7,000, about 10 percent of the state's total Mexican Texas population.[78] The rich military history of San Antonio coupled with the strong Tejano presence suggested that a higher proportion of Mexican Texans would volunteer to fight the Spanish. Accordingly, the city organized three regiments (two infantry and one cavalry): Company F, First Infantry Regiment, Belknap Rifles; Company G, First Infantry Regiment, San Antonio Guard Zouaves, and Troop I, First Regiment Cavalry, San Antonio Cavalry.[79] Tejanos turned out to volunteer for the war. Alamo City natives Eleno Castillo and Henry Pérez volunteered to join Company F, while Eugene Hernández and George Chávez enlisted in Company G, First Infantry.[80] These men did not leave records as to why they joined the fight. Yet it is likely they joined for the same reason many others volunteered: patriotic duty, economic motivations, or even a sense of adventure that appealed to working-class Texans.[81]

The Spanish-language press in San Antonio recognized the service of local Tejanos On 7 May, *La Fé Católica* pointed out that a Tejano, Eugene Hernández, was a captain in the San Antonio Zouave Company of the National Guard. Hernández was at the head of the unit as it marched from the Alamo Plaza on April 30, the newspaper reported. A large public turnout saw the men of Companies F and G off to Austin for camp as music from the "best local bands" played on.[82] The praise heaped on Captain Hernández was not isolated. On May 26, San Antonio's *El Regidor* praised Alamo City native Ramón Guerra, who was attempting to organize a rifle company of Mexican Texans to go fight in the war. "Twenty young men, enthusiastically seeking war laurels have agreed to join this company," the paper raved.[83] Though Guerra's unit never saw action in Cuba or the Philippines, the notions of winning war honors and performing heroic acts of bravery resonated with nineteenth century men.

One notable Tejano recruit from San Antonio was Augustine Peter De Zavala, the grandson of the vice president of the Republic of Texas, Lorenzo De Zavala. Lorenzo died in 1836 but his oldest son, Augustine, had six children of his own, including Augustine Peter and Adina, who would later become an advocate of historical preservation (especially on behalf of the Alamo), eventually becoming a member of the Daughters of the Republic of Texas and a founding member of the Texas Historical and Landmarks Association in the 1900s. Born in 1882 in San Antonio, Augustine was typical of most of the Spanish-American War volunteers: he was in his twenties and unmarried, without a significant career to hold him back. Like his sister, young Augustine was well-educated and ambitious. After all, his grandfather had a South Texas county named after him. When young Augustine volunteered as a private to join Company F, First Infantry, Belknap Rifles, it is likely he thought of martial glory and the social and political recognition that military service would bestow.[84]

On May 18, Augustine wrote to his sister explaining his rationale for enlisting, pointing out that he had been struggling to find viable work and when war erupted; knew the head of the Belknap Rifles, Captain Solon L. McAdoo; and thought volunteering would prove a worthwhile investment for later career opportunities.[85] "I have enlisted for 2 years at the rate of $15.60 a month and maybe we will get $24 instead," he explained. "I have done wrong for joining without yours and mamma's consent," De Zavala conceded, "but I did not want to bum[,] as I said before." He further rationalized: "If after a year I want to get out, I can easily buy myself out. I also don't think that a years [*sic*] more experience would hurt me, I will just be nearly 28 years old and I can get anything to do then just as easy as I can now and much easier."[86] Even though his family worried that the twenty-six-year-old St. Mary's College graduate would find danger in Cuba, De Zavala reassured them. "I will tell you the same as I told Momma yesterday," he wrote to Adina, "there is no use to worry about me, I am all right and this will do me a great deal of good and I will get to see something [in the war]."[87]

However, the following month, when De Zavala grew frustrated that he remained a private, he suggested that his sister meet with Captain

McAdoo, who had returned to San Antonio temporarily, to see if she could help him obtain a promotion. "I also do not know who else it would be good to write to," he mused. "You might go and see Capn. McAdoo, he is in SA [San Antonio] now sick, and go see him and talk to him and what he says goes in this company." Augustine knew what he was asking for and did not want to be caught broaching military protocol by having his sister serve as his liaison, but he had been unable to visit McAdoo personally while stationed in Alabama and likely figured he had nothing to lose. "Don't make it out if I ever said a word," Augustine cautioned, "but ask him if there isn't any non-commissioned office he could give me. If you can get him to write the Lieut. here and tell them to promote me, they will do it quick."[88]

De Zavala stood out as a wealthier Tejano volunteer, but the Spanish-American War did not inspire Mexican Texans to join the US Army in large numbers. Most Texas volunteers came from populous areas of the Lone Star State such as San Antonio, Austin, Dallas, Fort Worth, Houston, and East Texas, and others organized in San Angelo, Corsicana, and Sherman. No unit from the Río Grande valley, a traditional Tejano population stronghold, was organized for the war. Even Corpus Christi, a key port on the Gulf of Mexico and a burgeoning city with a population of more than 4,000, had no Spanish-surnamed volunteer when its Kenedy Rifles, led by Captain Gerard O.C. MacManus, went off to war. The muster roll of the company, which included soldiers from nearby Beeville, did not include a single Tejano.[89] It is likely that racism prevailed there, as the *Corpus Christi Caller* reprinted Rudyard Kipling's poem "White Man's Burden" and worried about a Spanish invasion of Texas in the weeks leading up to the outbreak of war.[90] In essence, the volunteers from Corpus Christi did not represent the "overall population as would be the conscripts" of the Spanish-American War, as historian David Trask suggests.[91] For Texas that meant that out of the approximately four thousand soldiers the Lone Star State provided to support the war, less than 1 percent were of Mexican descent, a figure that did not reflect the overall population.[92]

Texans did not see much action in the war. Volunteers arrived in Austin in mid-May for organization and left by the twentieth, bound for camp near Mobile, Alabama. From there, most remained in camp, waiting for transfer to Florida before departing to Cuba. Yet, despite the war rhetoric and patriotic spirit of early 1898, only one of the five Texas regiments ever left the country. By the time the First Texas arrived in Cuba, the war was over, and they remained on the island on occupation duty from December 1898 to March 1899. At that point, they returned to Galveston, where they were mustered out and returned home. The four stateside regiments were mustered out between November 1898 and March 1899.[93]

Laredo's Company K returned to the border to be acknowledged by a "Grand Cavalry Ball" with hundreds of attendees.[94] They had been willing to do what others had not, even though they did not see combat.[95] The Mexican Texans who joined the fray demonstrated their commitment to their communities. It was an opportunity to restore a sense of masculinity that had disappeared in the post-Reconstruction era, when fighting Indigenous bands no longer proved necessary and the martial spirit declined as modernization took hold in Texas.

Though Texas's participation in the Spanish-American War was relatively minor, it illustrates how Tejanos remained wary of martial service. Though Augustine De Zavala expressed a favorable attitude early in his enlistment, he soured once he realized that it would not provide him with the economic and political advancement he desired. Like other soldiers, he groused about poor conditions. Reporting on his camp in Alabama, De Zavala went through the usual litany of complaints about food, drilling, and the monotony of camp life. He even grumbled about the lack of desks to write letters.[96]

The Spanish-American War lasted a mere four months, ending officially on August 12, 1898, with a cessation of hostilities. A few months later, on December 10, the Peace of Paris made Cuba a protectorate of the United States along with the Philippines, Guam, and Puerto Rico. Theodore Roosevelt called it a "Splendid Little War." But the fighting was not over for the US armed forces. The Spanish-American War arguably thrust the United States into world affairs for the first time, establishing it as a regional power in the Western Hemisphere and across the Pacific. US forces had welcomed the assistance of Filipino nationalist forces against Spain, and guerrillas under Emilio Aguinaldo embraced the Americans and fought with them against their colonial rulers. However, when the Americans took over the Philippine Islands after the Peace of Paris, Aguinaldo's forces were enraged that they had simply traded one colonial power for another. In February 1899, Filipino forces struck at the Americans, launching a series of attacks against the occupying forces in Manila. The resulting insurgency would last for more than three years, from February 1899 to July 1902 and cost more than 25,000 military casualties on both sides and more than 250,000 civilian casualties. The fighting would force the US Army to increase its Regular Army to more than 70,000 men as the war evolved from conventional combat to an all-out guerrilla war. Meanwhile, anti-imperialists protested the McKinley and Theodore Roosevelt administrations, howling against the idea of United States possessing overseas colonies.[97]

The logistical and manpower demands of fighting an insurgency thousands of miles away on the Philippine archipelago strained the resources of the US Army. President McKinley could increase the size of the Regular Army to meet the new demands of the war against the Filipino insurgency and the security of American interests in the new world order, or he could rely once more on volunteer citizen-soldiers. Since increasing the size of the Regular Army had historically been impossible during the nineteenth century, McKinley decided to rely on the volunteer model, but with a modification. This time, the army replaced traditional state units, with local community attachments, with federal volunteer regiments, which would be organized regionally. The 1899 Army Act authorized the Regular Army to increase its size to 65,000 men, supplemented by 35,000 volunteers. These new volunteers would combine the loyalty of state volunteers with the discipline and professionalism of regular troops. To ensure that some state volunteers were enticed to prolonging their military service, the War Department offered a $500 bonus to reenlist.[98]

Lone Star recruits would find a place in the Thirty-Third Infantry Regiment, US Volunteers, which was composed mostly of men from Texas and the American South. Led by Colonel Luther R. Hare, a Regular

Army veteran and Belton native, the unit would be headquartered in San Antonio and include a coterie of Texans in its officer corps. The Thirty-Third consisted of Anglos, Native Americans, and Mexican Americans. According to the historian of the regiment, a handful of Tejanos enlisted in the unit, most of them from San Antonio. José Castillo of San Antonio was a laborer who preferred life in the army over his daily work. Antonio Cárdenas enlisted at Fort McIntosh, in Laredo. He, too, was a laborer who saw army pay as an improvement on what he earned in menial work. The army had improved its pay: privates could earn $15.60 per month, corporals could earn $18, and sergeants $21.60. Yet not every Tejano volunteer was an unskilled worker. Two Tejanos, Nathan Bueno and Edward Torres from San Antonio, were blacksmiths. Another, Amos Chávez, also from San Antonio, was a butcher. While two Tejanos were discharged before seeing combat in the Philippines, their compatriots fulfilled their duties.[99]

Conclusions

Tejanos had a mixed military record in the four decades between the Civil War and the turn of the twentieth century. Just as they had for centuries, Tejanos after 1865 continued to perform military duties for their communities. Men like Santos and Refugio Benavides served as paramilitaries and even joined the Texas Rangers to protect their communities from Indigenous threats. However, when the US Army returned to take over the security of the frontier, Tejanos gradually withdrew from their state's martial conflicts (and were kept out of the army by racist policies). During the 1890s, as the Garza rebellion unfolded, Tejanos remained wary of federal authority and Texas law enforcement.[100]

In the wake of the Garza rebellion, Tejanos endured suspicions of disloyalty from their Anglo neighbors. Accordingly, not many Tejanos enlisted in the Spanish-American War, citing neutrality or a hesitation to fight far away from their homes for little financial incentive. The latter was not a unique complaint; many Anglo Texans shared these same sentiments. But some Tejanos, including Augustine De Zavala, signed up for service. Certainly, the desire to demonstrate honor and bravery were factors behind the motivation to volunteer for war. Additionally, military service could lead to other tangible benefits, such as economic or political opportunities.[101]

The first decade of the twentieth century brought massive changes to the Texas Mexican community. In 1900, Texas reported 164,974 residents of Mexican descent, but this figure increased to 277,331 by 1910. At the turn of the twentieth century, 43 percent of those Tejanos reported to have been born in Mexico. That figure increased slightly to 45 percent in 1910.[102]

Modernization continued apace in the new century. After the 1892 Garza Rebellion, the military campaigns of the US Army and the extralegal efforts of local law enforcement convinced observers that the South Texas border region was stable and safe for Anglo settlement. By 1904, when two railroad lines, the Texas-Mexico Railroad, which ran from Corpus Christi to Laredo, and the International-Great Northern Railroad, which linked Corpus Christi to San Antonio, were built, it brought a flood of Anglo newcomers to the region. These newcomers brought commercial agriculture, which literally and figuratively transformed the South Texas landscape.

To help gain land and maintain a low-wage workforce, Anglo land developers and Texas officials worked together to transform the political world of Texas. In what historian Monica Muñoz Martinez calls the "Juan Crow laws of segregation," Texas authorities replaced the previous generation's policies of accommodation with laws prohibiting interracial marriage and establishing new codes of social conduct.[103] Tejanos, whom opinion makers had long stigmatized as disloyal and unpatriotic, now confronted a new layer of discrimination that threatened to strip away their rights and privileges. Political machines mobilized the vote of Mexican Texans for Anglo candidates, and new disfranchisement laws in the Lone Star State aimed to keep Mexican Texans, as well as poor whites and African Americans, away from the voting booth after 1902.[104] At the turn of the century, the Tejano community would have to reconcile how to deal with both de jure and de facto segregation. Such discrimination would prove influential as the world teetered on the brink of war by 1914.[105]

CHAPTER 4

"FOR HONOR, FOR PATRIOTISM . . . FOR OUR OWN BEST INTERESTS"

Tejano Military Service During World War I

Texas greeted the twentieth century boldly, riding the crest of a wave of changes that began in the late nineteenth century. The Lone Star State was a far different place than the heavily rural one it had been fifty years before.

The catalyst for this rapid transformation was the building of railroads in the 1870s and 1880s as towns were connected by the iron rail, which altered the state with their rapid transportation of goods. By 1901, the Spindletop Oil Field, near Beaumont, sparked an oil boom, which led to the development of adjacent industries. Thousands flocked to East Texas to partake in the boom. This influx only accelerated the urbanization already taking place at the end of the nineteenth century. Towns suddenly became major cities. In 1890, no Texas city had more than 40,000 residents. Yet by 1910, Dallas, Fort Worth, Houston, and San Antonio all reached populations of more than 100,000 people. Texas remained mostly agricultural and rural during the first decade of the twentieth century, but change and modernization were evident.[1]

For Tejanos, the dawn of the new century was not as auspicious as many white, middle-class Americans of the Progressive Era would have imagined. Modernization and philanthropy by themselves were unable to fix society's flaws. Mexican Texans saw the modern era much the same way they had seen the previous century end, which featured efforts to further marginalize their community as opportunities in government, economics, and education continued to be elusive. Employers continued to pay Tejanos less than Anglos, and land displacement further eroded their economic standing.[2] Politically, Mexican Texans fared worse than previous decades. The Texas state legislature passed the poll-tax law in 1902 and the white primary the following year. These disfranchisement laws proved insurmountable for Tejanos, as many could not afford the added fees and thus failed to vote. Those who could vote fell under the umbrella of boss rule as political machines controlled the Tejano vote along the Texas-Mexico border.[3] In areas where Tejanos remained the majority, they were able to negotiate with political rings to get several Mexican Texans be elected to local offices at the city or county level. In some cases, a few Tejanos even served in the Texas House of Representatives. In other parts of the state, however, Tejanos were a voiceless minority.[4]

Tejanos remained in the political and economic shadows of the transformative changes taking place in the state in the early 1900s. In the first decade of the twentieth century, the Mexican Texan population continued to surge, exploding to more than 125,016 by 1910.[5] This marked increase was due to the push and pull factors of migration from Mexico. Though Mexican laborers had long been attracted to work in the Texas agricultural sector, the commercial farms that developed at the turn of the twentieth century proved especially alluring to many *Mexicanos*. On the other side of the border, the slowly deteriorating conditions in Mexico during the reign of President Porfirio Díaz pushed others to leave their native country to come to the American Southwest lest they remain in rural Mexico surrounded by dying villages and working as *campesinos*, or, peasant farmer, earning far less than the average American farm laborer. The lower classes were not the only ones leaving Mexico for the United States.[6] Intellectuals, journalists, and many middle-class citizens who challenged Díaz's authoritarian regime risked retribution in their native country if they stayed. Other members of the upper class simply sought temporary refuge from the instability of the Díaz dictatorship.[7] At the outbreak of the Mexican Revolution and Díaz's resignation in 1910, tens of thousands of Mexicans headed for border to escape the violence of civil war.[8]

Along with the surge in the Tejano population, Anglo newcomers continued to settle in South Texas, establishing predominantly Anglo towns and carving new counties out of old ones. The newly arrived Anglos showed little interest in their Tejano neighbors and employed tools of political and economic discrimination to further isolate the *Mexicano* classes with social segregation in schools, neighborhoods, and other public places.[9] A further insult to Tejanos was that the new segregationist policies made no distinction between poor Mexican Texans and elites.[10] To many Tejanos, being denied service at restaurants, transportation, or other public facilities was a stunning change. Even more disturbing than segregation, the Texas Rangers, local and county law enforcement officials, and other vigilante groups initiated a wave of violence against Tejanos through lynchings and murders that upset race relations in the state.[11]

La Matanza

The increased number of lynchings in the early twentieth century, many of them lost to history, proved far more devastating to the Mexican American community than the legal efforts to disfranchise and limit economic opportunity.[12] To many Anglo Texans, the growth of the Tejano population and the instability of the Mexican Revolution proved alarming and caused them to react violently to maintain control over a group they considered inferior.[13] The number of lynchings would increase through the next five years before finally declining after 1917.[14]

As anti-Mexican sentiment increased during the early 1910s, race relations deteriorated even further in January 1915, when a group of unknown authors penned a revolutionary manifesto known as the Plan de San Diego. Unidentified Mexican and Tejano conspirators signed the document in San Diego, Texas, located in Duval County approximately eighty-miles northeast of Laredo, but its true origins likely came from northern Mexico, where the Revolution still raged. The document planned for a racial war against the United States starting on February 20 and mandated the execution of every non-Hispanic male over the age of sixteen. A "Liberating Army for the Peoples" comprising Mexicans, African Americans, Japanese, and Native Americans would lead this rebellion to take the

American Southwest back from the United States.[15] Although law enforcement officials arrested one of the organizers and seized a copy of the plan before the February launch date, fear remained.[16] By that summer, Tejanos and *Mexicanos* organized paramilitary groups of up to one hundred men, launching a reign of terror against their Anglo neighbors.[17] These raids targeted farms and railroads and caused hundreds of thousands of dollars of damage and inflicted approximately sixty Anglo casualties.[18] Soon after, South Texas was paralyzed with fear as these rebels, also known as *sediciosos* (seditionists), wreaked havoc on unsuspecting victims before fleeing across the Río Grande to safety.[19]

The news of the plan and the bloody intention to launch a race war shook Texas. Though authorities initially remained incredulous that Mexican Texans could organize against their Anglo neighbors, eventually unfolding events convinced state law enforcement officials and Anglo vigilante groups to strike back. In August 1915, soon after a notable raid on Las Norias, part of the King Ranch, that left behind half a dozen casualties, the Texas Rangers launched a reprisal assault that killed approximately three hundred Mexican Texans.[20] Anglo vigilantes organized in the wake of the border raids, reinforcing the work of the Rangers. That August, the *San Antonio Express* described it as a "border war" that seemed to be "spreading" across the state.[21]

Throughout the fall, Anglo Texans launched a storm of violence and intimidation against Tejanos that reverberated across the state and reached all the way to Washington, DC.[22] Though the numbers of lynchings and murders are imprecise, it is estimated that hundreds—if not several thousand—of ethnic Mexicans were killed from August 1915 to June 1916. This period, known as *La Matanza* (the Massacre), did not discriminate between real Mexican outlaws operating in South Texas or law-abiding Tejanos trying to work and provide for their families.[23] The bodies of dead *Mexicanos* were left to decompose, and law enforcement officials brushed off any investigation, chalking up the violence to banditry and criminal activity that warranted no further explanation.[24] The impact of these murders, whether committed by law enforcement officials or vigilantes, intimidated the Tejano community, as many feared for their lives.[25] Some Tejanos, however, relished seeing the angst of white Texans.

The wave of Anglo violence and retaliation against ethnic Mexicans reverberated throughout South Texas. Texas Governor James E. Ferguson urged the authorities in Washington to send the US Army to the border. In September 1915, the US Secretary of War responded with more than 2,500 federal troops, who were stationed from Brownsville to Eagle Pass.[26] In addition, local law enforcement officials received the authority to fire across the river into Mexico to quell disturbances.[27] The border's militarization caused further stress in the Tejano community as it sought to acquiesce to authorities.[28] Those who could not accommodate left. Ultimately, thousands of *Mexicanos* read the writing on the wall, fled Texas, and headed south, into the storm of the Mexican Revolution.[29] For them, the Lone Star State remained too volatile.

While the violence in the wake of the failed Plan de San Diego uprising dimmed by the summer of 1916, problems along the border shifted toward the El Paso area that same year. From the state of Chihuahua in northern Mexico, Francisco "Pancho" Villa, served as the leader of the Division of the North, the largest revolutionary force in the Americas. By the summer of 1915, Villa's forces had suffered so many defeats that US President Woodrow Wilson officially recognized the government of Mexican President Venustiano Carranza. Villa saw this as a betrayal and lashed out at the Americans on January 9, 1916, when his forces stopped a train carrying US mining engineers and executed fifteen Americans. Two months later, on March 9, Villa raided Columbus, New Mexico, and killed eighteen Americans and burned the town. Wilson responded by ordering General John J. "Blackjack" Pershing and six thousand troops to the border on a punitive expedition to capture the rebels.[30] While Pershing floundered in catching the elusive Villa, the impact of these border raids proved immense. Authorities in Washington, DC, militarized the Río Grande and its environs as tens of thousands of national guardsmen poured in.[31] The *El Paso Daily Times* warned of "a foreign army marching through the streets of an American city."[32]

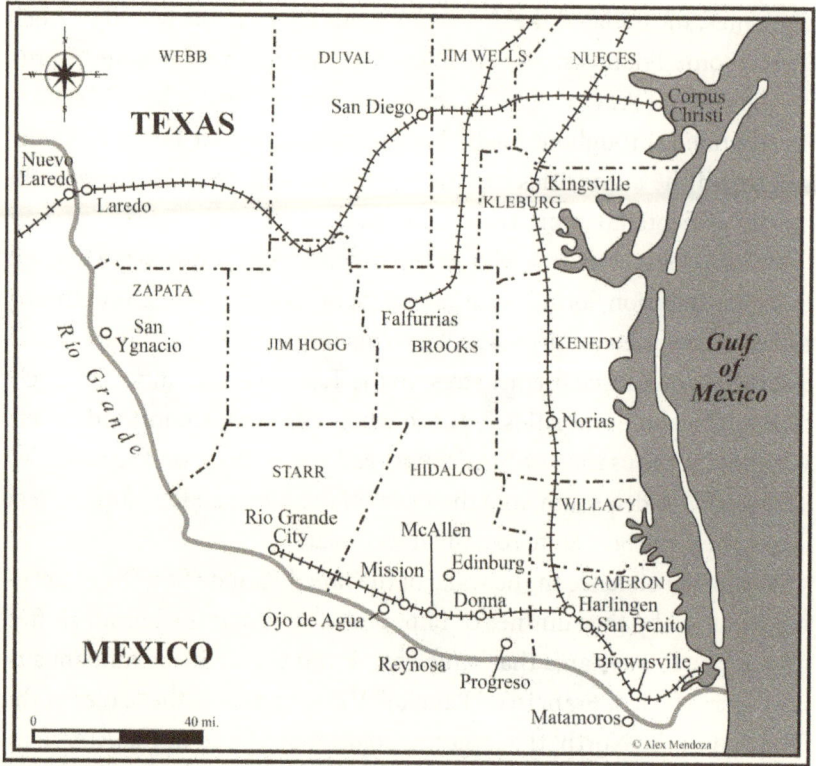

South Texas, 1910–20

Tejanos recoiled at the notion of being enemies of the state as they received scrutiny from federal troops, local law enforcement officials, and the Texas Rangers. Many chafed under the additional scrutiny.[33] The Spanish-language newspapers in Texas covered the militarization of the border with great vigilance, careful to adopt a neutral tone and support both the state authorities and the Mexican American community.[34] The contrast of Tejanos who supported the presence of additional troops and those who lamented the greater attention of the military and law enforcement served as an echo of eighty years before, when Tejanos fluctuated between supporting the Texas revolutionaries and those simply wanted to be left alone. Nevertheless, Tejanos continued to forge ahead and focus on jobs, wages, and education.[35]

By early 1917, the nation's attention shifted away from the Texas-Mexico border and the Mexican Revolution to the Great War in Europe. Since June 1914, the war between the so-called Central Powers of Germany, Austria-Hungary, and the Ottoman Empire and the Allied forces of Great Britain, France, and Russia had kept Americans on edge. At the onset of the war, Wilson maneuvered the country toward a policy of strict neutrality, hoping that he could instead focus on the national economy and trade. Though he campaigned for reelection in 1916 on a platform "He Kept Us Out of War," Wilson remained apprehensive of Germany and the Central Powers, particularly after a German U-Boat sank the *Lusitania* on May 15, 1915, killing over 1,000 civilians, including 128 Americans. After his reelection was secured in November 1916, the president shifted his attention from the Texas-Mexico border to efforts to end the war in Europe.[36]

Germany's increasingly desperate efforts to win the war created additional tension with the United States as unrestricted submarine warfare disrupted Wilson's efforts to remain neutral. Additionally, since 1914, Germany had hoped that Mexico would launch its own war against the United States to distract the Americans from events in Europe. In January 1917, German foreign secretary Arthur Zimmermann sent a telegram promising Mexico its lost territories in the American Southwest if it took up arms against the United States. Zimmermann's telegram was intercepted by the British and released to the public a few weeks later. The concept of unrestricted warfare may have seemed vague and nebulous to the American public, but the Zimmermann note was a tangible piece of evidence that Germany sought to attack the United States and harm the American people.[37] Sentiment about war had clearly shifted by the spring, and when Wilson asked for a declaration of war on April 2, Congress acquiesced. The United States declared war on Germany on April 6, with the Senate voting in favor, 82–6 and the House, 373–50.[38]

Wartime

President Wilson's April 2 address to Congress resonated with Americans.[39] True to his background as the son of a Presbyterian preacher, Wilson took the moral high ground and denounced Germany's submarine warfare as an attack against humanity. "Property can be paid for; the lives of peaceful and innocent people cannot be," he exclaimed. "It is a war against all nations," he argued.[40] With the Zimmermann telegram resonating in the background, the American press praised Wilson's call for war. Texas newspapers, too, fell in line and lauded the president's call to arms. The *Houston Post* urged all citizens to "manifest their loyalty" to the United States.[41] In West Texas, within days of Wilson's message, the *El Paso Morning Times* urged its residents to form volunteer companies and urged action against Germany agents in the United States.[42] Calls for patriotism were found on the front page of the *Cleburne Morning Review* as the North Texas town, approximately thirty miles south of Dallas, organized the raising of an extra-large version of the Stars and Stripes to demonstrate what it meant to "live in a country whose flag represents a real liberty and freedom unknown in many sections of Europe."[43] The *Austin Statesman* claimed that a twenty-thousand person "patriotic demonstration" at the capitol would "echo over all the country" as "emotions of patriotism were aroused and loyalty for the government expressed in the celebration of Loyalty Day." Although there were pockets of ambivalence about the war throughout the country and in Texas, the nation mobilized for war. The day after the United States declaration of war against Germany, Secretary of War Newton D. Baker proposed a bill for the creation of a million-man army through the draft.[44]

The Spanish-language press fell in line with the nation's call to arms and echoed the hyper-patriotism of most Texans. This was an about-face, considering that several Spanish-language newspapers had previously cast doubt on the motives of the federal government and state officials. Historian José Ramírez suggests that this reversal stemmed from a desire to overcome the perception of Tejanos as dissenters and subversives. The "Spanish-language press joined its English-language counterparts in supporting the Allied cause, though its conformity appears to have been, at least in part, a means of deflecting the charges of disloyalty and lawlessness that editorials" had long professed against the Mexican American community.[45] San Antonio's *La Prensa* newspaper, operated by Ignacio E.

Lozano, had railed against *Mexicano* injustices in the years prior to the war. Yet, by May 1917, the newspaper joined the English-language press in portraying Germans in a negative light and supporting the draft as the only option for the United States to raise the hundreds of thousands of men needed for the war.[46] Other Spanish-language papers followed suit, praising American patriotism and the nation's call to arms while at the same time suggesting that Germany had taken advantage of Mexico during the leadup to the war declaration. In Laredo, *La Cronica*, a newspaper which had long pushed for Tejano rights since the 1890s, used the war to propose a more amicable relationship between the United States and Mexico.[47]

The United States entered a war that had been grinding on for three years. Since 1914, the belligerent countries in the Great War had made repeated bloody frontal assaults in the face of entrenched positions, barbed wire, and machine guns. During the Verdun campaign of 1916, for instance, approximately one million French and German troops fell, as many as sixty thousand in less than half a day.

Even before 1917, the White House attempted to bolster the country's military forces. In 1916, the National Defense Act increased the Regular Army to 223,000 soldiers and the National Guard to 450,000 over a five-year period. The Naval Expansion Act created a three-year construction program for four dreadnoughts and eight cruisers. In addition, the Revenue Act raised the income tax from 6 percent to 15 percent to raise additional funding for the expanded military. It was an unprecedented peacetime military buildup. Yet, it was still short of what the US armed forces required as it entered the war.[48] The biggest shortfall remained the number of men needed to fight. The Europeans had instituted military conscription to restore their depleted ranks. For the United States, Secretary Baker's proposed conscription bill would prove to be the only way to build up the necessary troop strength in time. Passed on May 19, 1917, the Selective Service Act required all men between the ages of twenty-one and thirty-one register for the draft by June 5. Two additional registration drives would increase the range to men between eighteen and forty-five and ultimately register more than 24 million, 2.8 million of whom were inducted into service.[49]

US entry into the conflict in April 1917 once again thrust the Mexican Texan population into the maelstrom of an American war. While the Spanish-language press marched in lock step with the mainstream support for the war effort and Wilson's call to "make the world safe for democracy," most Mexican Texans would have wondered if democracy applied to them. Since 1900, state officials had made voting more difficult, and the Juan Crow laws of the era made segregation a profound reality for Tejanos. The *Matanza* in the wake of the Plan de San Diego had put Tejanos into the position of having to defend themselves from violence and outrageous charges while experiencing further losses of political and economic power.[50] During the First World War, Tejanos once more would have to make a choice: support the war effort or risk additional scrutiny similar to or worse than what they endured during 1914–15.

The Tejano community was never a homogeneous entity where everyone thought alike. The population was diverse and filled with different philosophical views and ideologies.[51] Tejanos who had lived in Texas for generations still supported the state and nation that had ostracized them from politics, schools, and society in general. Americanization had taken place, albeit unconsciously, over time. Yet, there remained a difference between urban and rural Tejanos of the era. Those who lived in cities (approximately 25 percent of Tejanos) adopted the fashions and ideas of mainstream America. Rural Mexican Texans, who still hoped for better conditions through cooperation, might have retained more cultural markers from their native Mexico. Yet, both urban and rural Tejanos generally supported the war effort.[52]

Accordingly, many Tejanos of all classes answered the nation's call to arms. Three registration efforts netted a total of twenty-four million citizens and non-citizens for the draft. In Texas, 5,000 of the 197,000 men who served in the armed forces had Spanish surnames. Individual reasons may have varied, but most cited similar motivations: patriotism and support for the United States. Other factors influenced the decisions of Tejanos, including a desire to escape the economic morass of poverty, ethnic pride inthe worthiness of the *Mexicano* people, and the hope for adventure in a foreign war.[53]

Compared to the recent war with Spain in 1898, Tejanos had new motivation for supporting the new conflict. Like African Americans, who had also been segregated and excluded from mainstream society, Tejanos sought to support the war and fight alongside their Anglo neighbors so as they could earn the right to vote and work without questions over loyalty.[54] In Laredo, Benjamin Ramos of *El Demócrata Fronterizo* urged his readers to support the war effort "for honor, for patriotism, for gratitude, for our own best interests" because "we have benefitted from her [the United States] liberties."[55] Laredoan Amador Sánchez, the former mayor who had been accused of disloyalty for not volunteering in the Spanish-American War, wrote an editorial for San Antonio's *La Prensa* on June 6, 1917, urging Tejanos to join the fight. The man who once emphasized that he was an American though his name was Spanish used the themes of liberty and justice to sway readers to support the war. He suggested that the Great War offered a way for Tejanos to support their nation, for history would not be kind to those who remained on the fence. "Who, in this time of need, at this hour of force and sacrifice, is not ready to support their flag, ready with arms and souls to fight in this struggle, will be castigated by justice in the future."[56]

Other civic leaders jumped at the chance to support the war by serving on local draft boards. The national draft law the president signed into law in May 1917 mobilized the registration of all men aged twenty-one to thirty through a series of national lotteries where registration numbers were called out. To provide a semblance of local control, draft boards would register the men and determine any exemptions. The service of husbands and fathers, as well as industrial workers, could be deferred. Later, two additional drives would increase the ages of those registered to any male between the ages of eighteen and forty-five. Under the direction of the Provost Marshal Enoch Crowder, more than 4,648 local draft boards sprang up practically overnight across the country. In Texas, 127,797 men were inducted into the US Army, 16,889 into the US Navy, and 2,073 into the Marine Corps.[57] Tejano leaders served on local draft boards, a compulsory service that was an unpaid position. In Laredo, attorney Juan V. Benavides, the son of Colonel Santos Benavides, served on the Webb County Draft Board. In Bexar, A. L. Hernández helmed the District one Board.[58] In El Paso, Bexar County, and the Río Grande valley, Mexican Texans served as registrants, clerks, and interpreters during the first registration process in June 1917.[59] The descendants of prominent Tejanos were used by newspapers to spur additional support for the draft. For instance, in San Antonio, José Antonio Navarro, the grandson of the famed *Bexareño*, resigned his position as the city auditor to enlist in the First Texas Infantry. The *San Antonio Express* applauded the patriotism of the "Scion of Famous Navarro Family."[60] Laredoan Amador Sánchez's prose may have influenced many readers of *La Prensa*, but his patriotism was hardly universal.

While thousands of Tejanos rallied to the Stars and Stripes, many others fled to Mexico to avoid conscription. Accordingly, Tejano enlistment likely could have been higher.[61] There is an explanation for this hesitation to adopt an American identity during the First World War. Until the first two decades of the twentieth century, many first-generation Mexican immigrants in Texas demonstrated a dual mentality, a bicultural identity. Even though ethnic Americans participated in the nation's society and economy, they still retained cultural aspects of their ancestral homeland. In his study of Mexican workers in Texas, historian Emilio Zamora describes this dual identity as it pertains to Tejanos. Zamora maintains that Mexican workers performed a circular migration across the Texas-Mexico border that shaped their "Mexicanist" identity as many Tejanos, particularly those in South Texas, felt a profound love and loyalty for Mexico.[62] As such, thousands left Texas, heading south to avoid this latest conflict. In December 1917, just eight months after the US declaration of war, *El Demócrata Fronterizo* reported on this exodus, pointing out *Mexicanos* were leaving the state with renewed vigor.[63] The total numbers of Mexicans and Mexican Texans who left the state are unknown, but they spiked during each of the three registration drives held for the draft.[64] Officials recognized the growing numbers at the main border crossing points from Brownsville to El Paso.[65] But Tejanos were not the only ones fleeing to Mexico to avoid the draft. Anglo draft dodgers also made their way across the Río Grande.[66]

The exodus of Mexican Texans in 1917 stemmed from a combination of factors, but it was mostly due to their unwillingness to fight. Some members of the Tejano community feared what Selective Service would mean to their people, including the notion that, as in Mexico, federal officials could simply seize citizens right off the street and impress them into military service.[67] These fears, stirred by German agents in Mexico and elements of the Mexican press, caused chaos and confusion among the ethnic Mexicans in the Lone Star State.[68] Others feared that a continued anti-Mexican backlash, like that which occurred just a few years earlier in the wake of the Plan de San Diego rebellion, could lead to further violence against Tejanos. The Texas Rangers, with their numbers bolstered after the border violence of 1915, once more factored into the mix as they drove Mexican laborers off the fields in Central Texas and continued to abuse and harass Tejanos.[69] Prompting the Rangers' added zeal in rounding up Tejanos was a $50 reward offered by the provost marshal general for rounding up deserters and slackers during the war.[70] The strain of being a prospective target for Texas law enforcement officials once again proved too great for the Tejano community. In one case, a Mexican citizen, Tomás Ramos, in Kyle, Texas, approximately twenty miles south of Austin, succumbed to the added pressure. On June 24, 1917, Ramos's dread of being drafted and separated from his family to fight a war that was not his own caused him to commit suicide.[71]

The frustrations that many ethnic Mexicans felt in leaving the state were not shared by all Tejanos. The middle class led the charge to get the Mexican American population to support the war. After all, they wanted to maintain their political and business ties to Anglo Texans and serve as a conduit to the masses. Accordingly, Spanish-language newspapers printed pamphlets and ran additional stories to convince the Tejano populace that the draft did not to kidnap Mexican Texans into military service and subject them to medical experiments or other nefarious circumstances.[72] In Laredo, officials made speeches and provided entertainment as they tried to allay fears about the draft.[73] Prominent Tejanos spoke to the masses to explain the process of the draft, its exceptions, and to emphasize the need for labor during wartime. Other educators, businessmen, and civic leaders banded together to implore the Tejano community to support the Stars and Stripes through a variety of means. Politicians like Congressman J. T. Canales from Cameron County championed support for the war effort.[74] Canales joined the Committee of Public Information's "Four-Minute Men," a cadre of 75,000 speakers from communities across the country who provided four-minute speeches to the public in support of the war.[75] The federal government's efforts to win the hearts and minds of the Tejano community did not end with speeches.[76] Federal authorities eased immigration restrictions until 1921.[77] In September 1918, the *Corpus Christi Caller* noted that the population of Mexicans in Texas had increased once again.[78]

Tejanos joined other Americans in showing loyalty to the United States. Right after the United States declared war on Germany, the *Laredo Weekly Times* published a story on the importance of flying the Stars and Stripes across the city. To be certain, the *Times* recognized Laredo's rich history as a bicultural community, but discouraged the customary use of the Mexican flag in parades and public areas. "There are several places in Laredo now displaying the Mexican flag as a decoration effect that are laying themselves liable to having the emblem removed," the paper proclaimed. The *Times* promised the city would make "taboo [the] old practice of carrying Mexican flag."[79] A year later, *La Prensa* in San Antonio echoed the Laredo effort, when it recounted a story from the border city of Del Rio, where the Mexican flag was flown during Mexican Independence Day festivities on September 15–16. The writers applauded Tejanos who protested the affront to the United States during wartime.[80] Border city authorities cracked down on any disrespect to the American flag. In April 1917, Francisco Aguilar and an accomplice were fined $20.00 for trampling on Old Glory in El Paso's "Mexican quarter" and causing a small riot.[81]

Newspapers in cities with a strong Mexican American presence urged *Mexicano* communities to rally behind the United States. In one headline, the *Houston Daily Post* proclaimed, "Texas Mexicans urged to remain," as it assuaged fears that the federal government would conscript Mexicans into the army.[82] *The San Antonio Express* did the same, urging Mexicans to remain in Texas.[83] *La Prensa* ran stories detailing work opportunities for Mexican women, proclaiming "the government needs thousands of employees." The *Laredo Weekly Times*, too, noted the need for Mexican laborers, particularly since state leaders feared a shortage of agricultural workers following the draft and the exodus of Mexican nationals. In July 1917, Laredo promised that the city would meet the requirements "demanded by the War Department."[84] The Tejano community could no longer demonstrate apathy or neutrality during an American war. Laredo's *Evolución* newspaper editorialized that "neutrality at this point could have, like the war itself, some disastrous consequences."[85]

Tejanos also offered their financial support. Mexican American community leaders came to the forefront to rally the community on behalf of Liberty Loans and War Savings Stamps in their respective cities. In Laredo, the Chamber of Commerce and its treasurer, G. B. Salinas, urged the Tejano community to be more actively engaged in fundraising for the war effort. Their publicity drives had an impact. Luis R. Ortiz, a *Mexicano* living in Laredo, purchased $30,000 in war bonds, the maximum amount an individual could buy, and the city far exceeded its quota.[86]

In past generations, Tejanos tried to remain neutral as the winds of war swirled around them. The Great War proved different as Mexican American communities contributed to the war effort in numerous ways. Beyond functioning as laborers and agricultural workers on the home front, they volunteered for local boards and participated in national campaigns. In Webb County, three of the five members of the Council of Descent were of Mexican descent. In Kleberg County, the local chairwoman of the National War Garden Commission noted that over ninety Tejanas participated in the project.[87] Partially due to pressure from the press and civic leaders, the American war effort had won over a sizable portion of the Tejano population. Yet, government officials continued to monitor Tejano loyalty and suspicious activities along the Texas-Mexico border.[88]

Military Service

While Tejanos supported the Great War with more enthusiasm than the Spanish-American War, some were still reluctant to serve the American cause. The struggle to win over the *Mexicano* population was noted by World War I veteran and civil rights activist José de la Luz Sáenz. In 1917, Sáenz, a native of Alice who had earned a teaching certificate in Comal County, blamed pro-German propaganda for confusing Mexican Texans. "We were divided when we should have stood together, like we are known to do when we have a clear understanding of our patriotic duty," Sáenz maintained in his memoir, the only firsthand account of a Tejano World War I soldier.[89] Sáenz might have not have fully understood the history of Mexican Texans and how patriotism and nationalism were not absolute in prior conflicts, but by the First World War, there was greater accultura-tion and assimilation than previous generations, and Tejanos did join the fight.[90] Juan Salorio of El Paso volunteered to fight because he felt loyal to the United States even though his Mexican identity remained strong. "I am a citizen of this country because I was born here and if there was a war of course I would have to defend this country because it is my homeland and I am a citizen in order to defend it."[91] In the South Texas community of Kingsville, during a Loyalty Day parade, more than one hundred Tejanos volunteered their services to the nation in April 1917.[92]

Other Mexican Texans in the Río Grande valley wrote the War Depart-ment to inquire about the possibility of organizing Spanish-speaking companies in the American military.[93] Jorge Villegas, a native of El Paso, joined the army to repay the debt he owed to the United States. In his correspondence with San Antonio's *La Prensa*, Villegas claimed that "even though he was Mexican, he recognized that he owed everything to this country: his skills, his education, and his character, were owed to the American culture and he wanted to believe it to be just to correspond . . . everything he and his family had received."[94] Another El Pasoan, Conrado Mendoza, tried to register on June 5, 1917, but officials turned him away because he was only seventeen years old. Undeterred, Mendoza went back to work at an airport in Riverside, California. He later saw his rejection as fate, since many of the men who enlisted that day died in a submarine attack on ship transporting them to Europe.[95] This newfound patriotism resonated in various accounts of the Tejano community. In San Antonio, the local press applauded the thirty Mexican Texans who joined a company in the US Army.[96]

Yet, a concern for many Tejanos remained the tinge of disloyalty left in the wake of the Plan de San Diego. Even Sáenz noted the importance of distinguishing between those who were confused and unable to understand the nation's call of duty as opposed to those who genuinely were afraid of combat. When he registered, he was asked if he was afraid to go fight in the trenches. "I do not have a reason to be afraid. I know I am expected to do this," Sáenz replied coldly.[97] Sáenz's resolute bravery notwithstanding, fear proved pervasive in the early stages of the war, and members of the Tejano community remained sensitive to charges of disloyalty. Newspapers such as *La Prensa* tried to convince Mexican Texans to remain resolute and fulfill one's duty to their new nation.[98] In a headline, the paper declared the "unfounded fear that Mexican Texans have with the new draft laws" needed to be overcome and that nothing "justified the abandonment of one's home and loss of dignity" in returning to Mexico to avoid military service.[99] A year later, *La Prensa* noted that Tejanos had answered the call of duty and though many deserved exemptions, their difficulty with the English language had led them to serve when they could have remained home to tend to their affairs.[100]

The Tejanos who joined the armed forces were no different from any of the other volunteers or draftees across the country. Despite instituting the draft, the federal government still hoped to inspire volunteerism. Yet this proved a difficult task among immigrant populations. Prior to the outbreak of war in 1914, many US residents demonstrated sympathy with their native land, such as Germany or Russia. Such divided loyalties forced Washington to declare neutrality, though its sympathies remained with the Allies. Many Americans doubted the government's sincerity, however. In 1915, the song "I Didn't Raise My Boy to Be a Soldier," proved to be the most popular song in the country, its verses demanding neutrality and peace.[101] As historian Geoffrey Wawro maintains, the Committee of Public Information, which was founded after the United States entered the war in 1917, remained steadfast in promoting loyalty within the many immigrant

Photograph of José de la Luz Sáenz from his 1933 memoir, *Los Mexico-Americanos en La Gran Guerra y Su Contingente en Pro de la Democracia, la Humanidad y La Justicia: Mi Diario Particular.*

communities in the country.[102] The country had no alternative, Wawro maintains, since about a quarter of the doughboys were foreign-born.[103] In his diary, Sáenz argued that Mexican Texans were unfairly perceived as disloyal, considering that many Anglo Americans also shirked military service.[104] Historian José A. Ramírez concurs, maintaining that Tejanos proved no better or worse than their ethnic counterparts as it pertained to evading military service.[105]

The nation's first draft produced 500,000 men. When these draftees and volunteers were funneled into the army in August 1917, they required preparation. First, they had to be housed, trained, and clothed. The War Department quickly built thirty-two training facilities across the country, and Texas, with its mild climate and open spaces, gained four new cantonments in San Antonio, Fort Worth, Houston, and Waco.[106] The army also expanded its air services installations in Texas.[107] Since cities served to gain economically from the War Department's cantonments, officials lobbied the authorities in Washington and made stringent efforts to clean up vice and immorality from their communities to secure federal support.[108] Some reformers believed the war could help drive social change at home. As such, efforts to drive out gambling and prostitution mixed well with the War Department's efforts to keep the soldiers focused on matters of training and discipline. Alcohol, too, became a target of federal and local government officials, who mobilized efforts to reduce vice near the new cantonments. In Laredo, *El Demócrata Fronterizo* described a "War against Bartenders." The paper reported that law enforcement officials targeted bars that served soldiers after hours or on Sundays. "Many bartenders have been arrested, and many more will still be arrested because they have yet to learn they cannot skirt the law," the paper warned.[109] In Dallas, county officials voted to stop the liquor trade, making it the largest city in the state to prohibit alcohol by local option.[110]

The War Department also launched an information campaign against venereal diseases. The army provided prophylactics to its men and proved lenient with those who became infected. Doctors, placards, and pamphlets provided the doughboys with their introduction to sex education.[111] Catchy slogans such as "how could you look the flag in the face, if you were dirty with gonorrhea" was designed to inspire both fear and patriotism.[112]

As soldiers arrived in camps, the army realized that many were uneducated and naive about the world around them. Some, in fact, had no idea how to play any recreational games. When they arrived at the partially built training facilities, they received a battery of tests, particularly psychological exams used to classify men by mental ability. Designed by Robert M. Yerkes, the president of the American Psychological Association, these intelligence tests were divided by "Alpha," for those who were deemed literate, and "Beta," a nonverbal test for those designated as illiterate. These tests alarmed some observers. The exams claimed, for instance, that as many as 25 percent of all inductees remained illiterate. The tests only reinforced pre-existing societal biases, as Mexican Texans and African American soldiers struggled to answer questions that reinforced cultural biases of the period.[113] The army doubted the tests' effectiveness and argued that intelligence tests did not indicate good soldiers and officers. Yet the impact of Yerkes and his colleagues would be picked up by white supremacists and eugenicists after the war to argue for the restriction of immigration and denial civil rights to African Americans.[114]

In the meantime, the army's Foreign Speaking Soldier Subsection urged military officials to organize non-English–speaking soldiers into language specific companies, headed by bilingual officers, and not discriminate against these soldiers. This so-called Camp Gordon Plan, according to one report, significantly increased the percentage of non-English–speaking soldiers' willingness to fight overseas.[115] At Camp Cody in Deming, New Mexico, army officials concentrated approximately six hundred Mexican soldiers for training, using the Camp Gordon model. Led by a cadre of Spanish-speaking officers, Camp Cody's experiment proved a success and served as an example to follow in the postwar period.[116]

As soldiers arrived in camp, training went beyond tactics and military drills. Before the men learned how to fight, they had to learn how to read and demonstrate good citizenship. The War Department approved community agencies, schools, and other volunteers to spearhead efforts to teach soldiers how to speak English. Thus, in addition to their normal military duties, these soldiers attended English classes daily for a period of up to three hours a day, usually for the duration of about four months.[117] Camp Travis, for instance, had 1,200 soldiers enrolled in its night-school program for learning English. The *Corpus Christi Caller* noted that the War Department gave every draftee a copy of *Home Reading Course for Citizen Soldiers*, a pamphlet designed to promote patriotism.[118] Christina Krysto of the Bureau of Immigrant Education, praised the soldiers of Mexican descent. "It is customary to believe that the Mexican is indifferent to learning English and the Italians eager for the opportunity, yet some of the finest pupils in Camp Kearny are Mexican," she wrote.[119] Tejanos and other immigrant soldiers also received courses in French, Bible study, stenography, and drawing.[120] The training and educational opportunities for soldiers allowed social reformers to impose middle-class values on the recruits, many of whom were accustomed to manual labor and limited educational opportunities.[121]

More than 95,000 men received training in a variety of basic trades in training camps across the country.[122]

Although biases and stereotypes against Tejanos might have been present as they entered training camp, the evidence suggests that discrimination proved to be fairly mild when compared to Black soldiers. In contrast with African American soldiers, officials did not segregate Tejanos based on race, and they served in military units with white Americans. Mexican Texans mostly received verbal insults or other forms of harassment that did not devolve into full-scale racial violence like the Camp Logan Riot of 1917, in which four Black soldiers and seventeen white men (including five police officers) were killed in a melee that stemmed from the indignities of Houston's Jim Crow laws and the Black troops' demand for equality.[123]

Though Tejanos did not experience any event as traumatic as the Camp Logan Riot, they remained keenly aware of potential discord. One enlistee, David Barkley Cantú, from Laredo, recognized this reality. Born in Laredo in 1899, to Josef Barkley, a career army soldier, and Antonia Cantú, a Tejana, David sought to conceal his ethnic heritage from army officials lest he be assigned mundane duties that would keep him from service on the front lines. The young Barkley Cantú even told his mother not to use his Spanish surname in their correspondence. He proved so adept at concealing his identity from authorities that they did not discover his ethnicity until the late twentieth century, decades after his death.[124] Sáenz put the matter of discrimination of Mexican Texans in perspective in his diary: "Our willingness to serve and to want to learn everything and to do it quickly, places us under scrutiny and subject to doubt, distrust, and suspicion." Prejudice might have played a role in the rejection of Sáenz's application for officer training.[125]

Instruction for all troops was guided by *Infantry Training*, a twenty-seven-page pamphlet by the army War College in 1917 that outlined a sixteen-week regimen. Following the advice of General John J. Pershing, the commander of the American Expeditionary Force (AEF), the Army demanded an emphasis on mobility exercises and rifle training, extending the program to eighteen weeks.[126] Pershing was convinced that the European powers had been in a stalemate because they did not have the

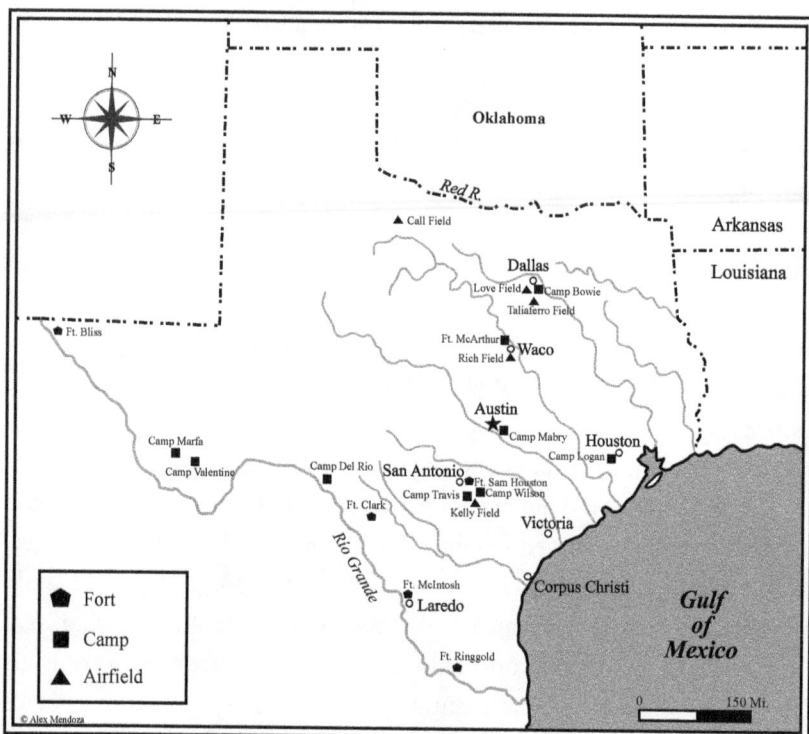

Military Installations in Texas During World War I

audacity to launch a war of mobility. He hoped to launch an assault, one that would break through the three-year-old defensive lines and advance all the way to Berlin. Pershing's ambitious plans notwithstanding, the American soldiers suffered from logistical and supply problems. Troops were forced to train with wooden rifles because there was not enough equipment to go around. In some cases, some artillery units did not fire a live shot until they reached Europe. The emphasis on the rifle and mobility meant that Americans did not receive instruction in trench warfare until they arrived in Europe.[127]

Mexican Texans did not mind training with wooden rifles. They were being fed, clothed, and exposed to a new world, earning money that often exceeded their normal earnings. Laredoan Higinio Valdez Jr., serving in the Fourteenth Cavalry, wrote to a hometown newspaper,

Evolución, explaining that he found the military "extremely agreeable." Valdez maintained that his fellow Tejano soldiers were treated well.[128] In his diary, Sáenz, who had been sent to San Antonio's Camp Travis for Basic Training, maintained that even though the military drills were dull and exhausting, soldiers appreciated routine activities and discipline. "We have much to be glad about in the military," Sáenz wrote. "Much of what is good comes from the strict adherence to orders. In civilian life we were free and sovereign but are now subject to the strictest of tyrannies."[129] Another Tejano at Camp Travis, Sergeant Joe Benavides of the 141st Infantry, concurred. He confessed that he enjoyed "army life" and that he and his fellow Tejanos were "eager for the time when they are ordered to prepare for the voyage that will take them to France."[130]

Texas's Spanish-language press kept readers apprised of training camp exploits and Tejano soldiers' efforts as they served for American democracy.[131] In most cases, Tejano doughboys were no different from their Anglo and African American counterparts as they experienced the mundane, repetitive drills and maneuvers necessary to make able soldiers. Like other recruits, Tejanos had no experience in firing weapons, driving cars, or even understanding simple sports. Yet, a few months after they arrived in camp, they were deemed ready soldiers.[132]

After basic training, American doughboys traveled by train to various ports, where they boarded ships and crossed the submarine-laden Atlantic Ocean to Europe. All units shared similar experiences: they suffered in crowded vessels and remained under close scrutiny by their superiors. The trips generally took a month. In June 1917, the First and Second Divisions reached Europe, the first American units to arrive.[133] When the Americans arrived in France, they were greeted by the solemn looks of tired Frenchmen as they marched to the front.[134]

Tejano soldiers stood in awe of the Old World's architecture and the art. Private Sáenz, of the 360th Infantry, said simply, "Seeing is believing."[135] Not everything that the Mexican Texan troops witnessed proved awe-inspiring. Tejanos were appalled by how the French welcomed the African American troops. "The only thing I can hold against the French people is they think too much of the Negroes," wrote Private Pablo González of

Brownsville. "Some of the French girls are married to negro soldiers," he claimed, "I guess tho[ough] it is only the lower class that pulls stunts like that."[136] González's racism was not unique among Tejanos, who lived in a segregated society in Texas. Many considered themselves or aspired to be considered white.[137] Even Sáenz, who wrote frequently on themes of racial equality and his contempt for discrimination against Mexican Texans, expressed disdain for interracial couples he witnessed in France.[138] Yet, Tejano soldiers did not have much time to scrutinize the European countryside and its people. Additional training and drills beckoned.

The first doughboys arrived in the wake of the failed Nivelle Offensive, an Allied effort to punch through the German lines in April and May 1917. The disastrous assault led to the loss of 187,000 French soldiers and a mutiny. General Philippe Pétain stopped the mutiny by promising to give the men leave and not subjecting them to more frontal assaults. The Allies needed reinforcements, and they desperately looked upon the Americans to buttress their lines.[139] The British and French commanders believed that the American troops should serve under European leadership and follow European strategy. Pershing and the Americans balked at this idea, insisting that American doughboys would refuse to be led by foreign officers. Moreover, Washington authorities insisted that an independent command be established lest they be left out of negotiations come peacetime. This so-called amalgamation controversy pitted a fight between Pershing and the Allied commanders. Pershing refused to yield. "I do not want to appear difficult," Pershing maintained, "but the American people and the American government expect that the American army shall act [independently] and shall not be dispersed here and there along the Western Front."[140] Pershing and the Allied commanders finally settled the matter in December 1917, but with a few reservations. Pershing acquiesced in letting US soldiers be assimilated into existing French and British units, but the Americans would follow orders of their own officers up to the division level. This way, the War Department reasoned, the Americans would gain additional training and seasoning under French and British Corps. Though this compromise proved to be an effective solution in the early battles, animosity would fester between the Allies for the remainder of the war.[141]

While the first American units arrived in Europe in the early summer of 1917, it took them nearly half a year to see any tangible frontline action against the Germans. By the second week of October, the French high command decided to include the Americans in a minor assault as part of their indoctrination to the European style of warfare. Four American battalions of the US First Division, under the supervision of the French Eighteenth Division, received instructions to bombard a portion of the line just north of Lúneville, near the town of Nancy, France. Though the action was inconclusive, the American troops saw their first fighting. Even if American involvement proved indecisive, the French desperately needed a show of support from the Yankees to boost sagging morale and depleted ranks.[142]

As 1917 faded to 1918, additional American units arrived. It would take months until American forces saw notable action. Until then, all US soldiers experienced the same fate: they were funneled into the lines, exposed to the trenches, and experienced life aside "no man's land" while receiving instructions that contradicted their mobility-focused training back in the United States. By the fall of 1918, Pershing assigned the Second Corps to serve with the British army. The Thirty-Sixth Division, with a large contingent of Texas and Oklahoma National Guard units, received orders to fight with the French. The Ninetieth Division, its ranks filled with Texas draftees, merged with the US First Army. These Texans would soon see action as the Allies prepared for the 1918 offensives to finally break the stalemate.[143]

The US Army may have hoped to train every soldier to the exacting standards of West Point, but that goal proved elusive. The War Department claimed that the average soldier received six months of training in the United States, two months of training in Europe, and one month of further instruction in quiet sectors along the Western Front. The doughboys received additional training with French weapons and the importance of artillery.[144]

Adding to the difficulties, the winter of 1917–18 was one of the harshest in recent memory. The Americans in France found themselves struggling without proper clothing and supplies as logistical shortfalls ran rampant during that miserable winter.[145] Sáenz did not reach France until June 1918. Being the prolific writer he was, he wrote home and described his joy at reaching the "cradle of democracy." Yet, he lamented that he was not allowed to write in Spanish due to censorship restrictions in the US military. Ever the optimist, he professed his desire to learn French due to its similarity to Spanish.[146]

No matter how much additional training the troops received, nothing compared to actual combat. On June 1, a German assault at Belleau Wood punched a hole in the French lines. The Americans scrambled to find their place as the fog of war caused confusion in the Allied units. But the German advance ultimately lost momentum, and the Americans held their own. A month later, the AEF and French forces launched a bloody counterattack at the Battle of Château-Thierry, less than fifty miles northeast of Paris, as the Allies sought to push back the German advances that sought to end the war with a climactic final offensive. Tejanos found themselves in the thick of both battles as the carnage of battle swirled around them. The Americans suffered more than ten thousand casualties in the two campaigns. Mexican Texan soldiers proved their worth in these engagements. El Pasoan Juan Salorio, a volunteer serving in the Second Division, fought at Belleau Wood. Born in the United States to Mexican parents, Salorio saw his service as an opportunity for adventure rather than patriotic duty. Surviving the whirlwind of combat, he later toured Europe and the rest of the world.[147] At Château-Thierry, San Antonian Refugio Serna was wounded in the campaign. Before he was shot in the foot, Serna helped several of his fellow soldiers escape capture as he shot at the advancing Germans with his machine gun.[148] By July 17, the great German advance had spent itself. The German population, which had placed great hopes in this last push to break the Allies, grew despondent in the wake of the failed offensive.

On July 18, the French high command ordered a massive advance against the Germans. The Americans, more than 100,000 strong, received orders to launch an attack on the right flank as the British thrust on the left and the French held the center. The Americans advanced more than a dozen miles in a week. But this assault did not come without cost. The Battle of Soissons, fought on a plateau marked with ravines and absent of trenches, quickly devolved into a back-and-forth slugfest, epitomizing the larger struggle of the German and Allied armies thus far. The fighting proved brutal and violent, and the Americans found themselves battling for their lives.[149] At Marne, a German artillery shell struck twenty-five-year-old Marcos Armijo, a mechanic from El Paso, causing him to lose both his legs. He survived for three days before succumbing to his injuries. According to *La Prensa*, Pershing recommended Armijo for the Distinguished Service Cross, which was granted posthumously in October 1918.[150] The Allies successfully pushed back the Germans, but at great sacrifice. The combined forces of the French, British, Americans, and Moroccans suffered more than 128,000 casualties in the campaign. But the war had shifted, and the Allies now held the advantage.[151]

After the Second Battle of the Marne, the Allies had stymied the German threat on Paris. The American engagements were designed to serve as a platform for an independent command, something that Pershing remained adamant about that July and August. On July 24, 1918, Pershing's headquarters issued General Order Number 120, to take effect on August 10, officially forming the American First Army. The three divisions from the British sector would soon be joined by the First, Second, Third, Fifth, Forty-Second, Eighty-Second, Eighty-Ninth, and Ninety-First. After an intense back-and-forth with the French high command, Pershing received approval to pit American forces against stalwart German veterans in difficult terrain. Moving their troops to the front of the line, the Americans planned to launch their first offensive and pierce the German lines on two separate fronts, flattening out the salient into a straight line. The soldiers trained on similar terrain, a significant improvement over earlier battles when troops possessed little knowledge of the area. After an artillery barrage on September 12, US troops pushed through the German defenses in brutal fighting that lasted four days. Though the Americans had accomplished their objectives, the German army remained intact.[152]

The horrors of war remained a constant presence. On September 14, Sáenz wrote that he and his colleagues came up to a grisly scene where Luis Rodríguez, a Tejano from Losoya, and a German soldier had impaled each other with bayonets. Though he wondered how the fight occurred, Sáenz recognized that each soldier merely tried to fulfill "the call of duty."[153] Ignacio Rodríguez from Laredo, a member of the 143rd Infantry, survived the campaign, but at a cost. He suffered a mustard gas attack by German forces, and while he remained in a prone position with his arms affixed to his gas mask, a German soldier attacked him with a bayonet, wounding his right arm and torso. Rodríguez wrote to his mother as he convalesced in a French hospital. The Laredo newspaper *Evolución* praised both the young Rodríguez and his mother for demonstrating "love and patriotism for the cause that Americans were bravely defending."[154] Other Mexican Texas soldiers were not as fortunate. Three Tejanos, Moisés Carrejo from Laredo, Canuto Farías from Beeville, and Cayetano González from Tuleta, along with two German American soldiers, suffered grisly deaths on September 20, shortly after the campaign. The five men had left their trenches to forage for grapes when a German artillery piece hit their position, leaving nothing but a "disgusting mass covered under dirt," according to an observer.[155]

St. Mihiel was part of the Hundred Days Offensive, a series of large-scale battles that took place in every sector of the Western Front. The French high command believed this strategy could employ fresh American manpower and force the war-weary Germans to surrender.[156] In late September, the Allies made one final push to destroy the enemy. In the ensuing Meuse-Argonne Offensive, the Thirty-Sixth and Ninetieth Divisions would see action alongside their British and French allies as they tried to break the German war machine once and for all. For forty-seven days, from September 26 to November 11, the Americans slugged it out with the Germans, fighting aggressively to end the war. One Tejano, Private Pablo Cortez, wrote briefly about the harrowing experience of combat. "When we went over the top when they gave us *escomecies* [sic] and then I started seeing that the Americans fell and also saw the Germans that fell. Further I turned around and no longer saw the corporal who I carried and so we headed for a sergeant of the same company."[157] Along the Champagne Sector of the Meuse-Argonne Offensive, Sergeant Miguel Barrera of Laredo was placed in charge of Company B with little experience under his belt. Barrera wrote:

> We were al [sic] green men and being the first time under fire, we didn't know what to do, but any how we took the front line, the G.I. can [name of German artillery shells due to being made of Galvanized Iron] were falling all along the line of course being my first night and there [sic] were falling about 2 & 300 yds away from where I was. I didn't pay much attention to the G.I. can, but my God when the G.I. cans begin to burst about 10 and 25 yds from where my Hole was, then I begin to get scared, and started to pray and I ask one of my men if he was afraid of the G.I. cans and he said, no, not much as long as they don't hit in my hole, so then I didn't have much chance to tell him I was afraid of the G.I. cans.[158]

Barrera wrote about his desire to go over the top and cross "no man's land." Encouraged and accompanied by a comrade, he crossed the dreaded killing zone. "I could hear and see the dust of the machine gun bullets hitting all around me and at the same time my comrades falling all around me, and when we reach our objective and we dug our holes and there where [were] only 8 men left of our bunch, we stayed in our holes all surrounded by machine guns and snippers [sic]," he later wrote.[159] Barrera later castigated himself for wanting to demonstrate his bravery when men were dying all around him. He survived, but the experience was not one he would forget. In the end, the Meuse-Argonne Offensive proved a success as the Allied armies pushed back the exhausted Germans more than twenty-miles before an armistice brought an end to the fighting.[160]

The Tejanos who experienced military combat would never forget what they saw. In his writings, Sáenz claimed that Mexican Texans held a warrior tradition that could be traced back to their Aztec roots. "The soldiers of my *raza* (race), the noble Aztec *raza*, do not falter," he maintained.[161] Certainly, Tejanos demonstrated a discernible martial spirit. Private Marcelino Serna, part of the Eighty-Ninth Division, Fourth Corps, First

US Army, received the Distinguished Service Cross for his bravery in the Meuse-Argonne. Serna, an El Paso native, single-handedly captured twenty-four German prisoners and prevented a fellow soldier from shooting them. Other Tejanos received awards for their actions on the field of battle. Private. Graviel García of Somerville, located about sixty miles east of Austin, earned the Distinguished Service Cross for his actions on October 16, 1918. García, fighting as part of Company C, 325th Infantry Regiment, 82nd Division, AEF, near St. Juvin, France, voluntarily went out into "no man's land" under heavy enemy fire and administered first aid to a wounded comrade. While making his way back with the man, García was himself wounded.[162]

While García's actions proved heroic, the Central Texas native did not receive the highest honors of Mexican American servicemen in the Great War. That distinction went to nineteen-year-old Private David Bennes Barkley (David Barkley Cantú) of the 356th Infantry. Barkley had remained careful not to reveal his ethnic heritage when he registered for military service because he feared that authorities would discriminate against him and give him menial duties. Growing up in San Antonio, Barkley Cantú was a good swimmer, making him an ideal choice to swim across a cold, icy river. On November 9, 1918, Barkley Cantú and a comrade received orders to infiltrate German lines to obtain information about the enemy's artillery and machine gun dispositions on the opposite side of the Meuse River. The two men succeeded in obtaining the necessary intelligence, making maps of the location of the enemy's artillery pieces. Upon returning to their units, the Americans ran into some trouble and were spotted by a German patrol. The two men jumped into the Meuse to swim back across. Barkley Cantú drowned but his companion made it back successfully, and the reconnaissance mission contributed to the success of one of the final Allied offensives prior to the armistice. For his actions, Barkley Cantú received the French Croix de Guerre, the Italian Croce al Merito di Guerra, and the Congressional Medal of Honor, the highest award for valor in the United States armed forces. Later, when his ethnic origins were discovered in 1989, he became the first Hispanic Medal of Honor recipient.[163]

David Barkley Cantú, Congressional Medal of Honor recipient. Undated US Army
photo, US Department of Defense, 180916-O-D0439-002.

Not every Tejano soldier was motivated by patriotism. In some cases,
acts of bravery from Tejano soldiers came from rage or resentment, like
in the case of Simón González, a day-laborer from the small Central
Texas town of Martindale, about ten miles east of San Marcos. González
was drafted into the 360th Infantry Regiment despite the fact that his
blind father, Maximiliano, protested his son's conscription due to his
dependency on him and the hardships his absence would cause. These
complaints to the local draft board and army officials went unheeded, and
Simón González left for Europe. González then transferred his hatred for
the German American–led draft board in his hometown to the enemy in
France. "I am here because of the Germans in Martindale!" he exclaimed
to his fellow soldiers. When German soldiers fell, González would laugh
to show his disdain. He fought the enemy fiercely, like a "caged lion,"
according to one observer. On November 1, 1918, in the last offensive push

before the armistice, González was killed in action, right outside the village of Villers-devant-Dun in northeastern France. González remained bitter against Germans until the end.[164]

After weeks of negotiations, the Great War came to an end on November 11, 1918. While the men initially expected that the fighting would resume, the next day rumors swirled that peace was at hand, and celebrations broke out among the Americans. Members of the Thirty-Sixth Division held a mock funeral for the German kaiser.[165] Sáenz was done with war. "I hope to God these are the last horrid scenes I will ever see," he wrote two days after the armistice. "The trenches are full of dead Germans who fought as the world's best soldiers but failed this time."[166] Americans lost approximately 117,000 men in the conflict, a significant amount, but low when compared to the millions of men lost by the other belligerent nations. Texas paid its own sum of fallen soldiers. More than five thousand Texas soldiers lost their lives in France. About one hundred Tejanos were killed in the war.

As the soldiers clamored to go home, the War Department had to figure out the logistics of returning more than 1,000,000 men back to the United States. The AEF ultimately decided to return the men in the order that they had arrived in Europe, meaning that the late arriving Texans would be among the last to leave, more than six months after the armistice. In the meantime, the army kept the men occupied with holiday celebrations, incessant drilling, and opportunities for sports and recreation. As soldiers returned home, they confronted the Great Influenza, which killed hundreds of thousands of Americans and millions of citizens worldwide. Approximately 800,000 American soldiers contracted the flu in the latter stages of the war. Forty-seven thousand died from the pandemic, almost as many men as died in battle. The situation proved so dire that Edward M. House, the advisor to President Wilson, refused to go to Europe to hear Pershing's views on the surrender lest he catch the flu.[167]

As the doughboys waited, they wrote to their families back home. Even illiterate Tejanos found fellow soldiers to write letters on their behalf. The soldiers were itching to let their families know they had made it through the war unscathed. A member of the 141st Regiment, Francisco Molina of Laredo, wrote to his parents, Secundino and Juanita, and told them he was in good health in France and joyous that the war had concluded. The *Evolución* printed a brief update as to Molina and the safety of a few other Laredoans.[168] Juan Benitos, from Corpus Christi, told his mother he was "having a good time" as he waited for Christmas.[169]

Spanish-language newspapers had printed excerpts of how Mexican Texans were doing during the war. Now that peace had been achieved, the papers wrote glowingly of the accomplishments of Tejano soldiers and their families.[170] However, not all updates proved positive. Tejano deaths made a somber storyline for these newspapers. The *Evolución* story "Muere en Campaña otro Laredense," argued that the death of Leonardo Díaz in the latter stages of the war was not in vain as he died defending his nation and his race.[171] San Antonio's *La Prensa* published an article on twenty-seven-year-old Polidoro Sosa, who died from his wounds on the battlefield on September 13, 1918. The paper praised Sosa, who had written his mother, María, shortly before his death, as a true hero who fought for "liberty and justice."[172] Ultimately, communities across Texas rallied to welcome back the returning soldiers. In June 1919, when a handful of veterans finally returned home to Laredo, the papers praised Tejano and Anglo soldiers alike, maintaining that they returned with glory for their service.[173] In Dallas, city leaders celebrated the soldiers of the Thirty-Sixth Infantry, Ninetieth Division, with a parade and mass picnic at Fair Park on June 14, 1919.[174] Whether large or small, each community welcomed their returning soldiers with open arms.

Conclusions

The Tejano soldiers who returned home after the Great War did not return to a world markedly different from the one they left in 1917. The war, for all its changes to the federal government, the economy, and the nation's place in world affairs, did not signify an end to the discrimination of Tejanos. Postwar elation soon gave way—again—to old-fashioned stereotypes and prejudice. Nevertheless, the First World War served as a turning point as Tejanos sought to stake a claim to the benefits of American citizenship.[175] During the interwar period, the burgeoning Tejano middle class founded an organization, the League of United Latin American Citizens (LULAC), which fought for the civil rights of Hispanics. LULAC believed that military service could bridge the gap between the American creed and practice. Accordingly, LULAC published José de la Luz Sáenz's wartime diary, *Los México-Americanos y La Gran Guerra y Su Contingente en Pro de la Democracia, la Humanidad y la Justicia: Mi Diario Particular*. The journal was the only published chronicle of a Mexican American soldier who fought in World War I and recounted Sáenz's experiences and his motivations in fighting for democracy, humanity, and justice. Throughout his diary, Sáenz argued that the ideals of democracy for which he fought could be applied to his fellow Mexican Americans in Texas in their struggle for civil rights. LULAC took up the fight that Sáenz and other Tejano soldiers waged on European battlefields.[176]

This fight for civil rights came as more Mexican Texans felt themselves to be American and adopted American traditions and values. As historian Carole Christian notes, World War I gave the Tejanos the first opportunity to consider themselves as Americans rather than marginal members of society. World War I Veterans such as Sáenz (Alice), Ben Garza (Corpus Christi), John C. Solís (San Antonio), and Manuel C. Gonzales (San Antonio), to name a few, focused their efforts on helping the Tejano community try to take advantage of the opportunities that American society could offer. During 1920s and '30s, Mexican Americans in Texas held a stronger sense of belonging to the United States than ever before.[177]

Tejano veterans generally returned to their prewar lives. Long-term military service was not a viable career for many Americans after the National Defense Act and subsequent legislation cut funding for the military. During the interwar years, the United States Army dwindled to about 130,000 men, a number that would remain below recommended strength until the late 1930s. During that time, the Texas National Guard numbered approximately between 6,600 and 8,200 men. It included disproportionately fewer Tejanos due to more stringent federal standards imposed by the National Defense Act. In the case of Company G, 143rd Infantry Regiment, 36th Division (the "Houston Light Guards"), the first Tejanos did not join until the 1930s. On the eve of World War II, Tejanos accounted for 9 percent of the members in the company. For Tejanos, National Guard service meant additional opportunities to stake a claim to the American dream.[178]

Yet, for government officials, the Texas National Guard provided an opportunity to further "Americanize" Tejanos in the wake of World War I. In El Paso, building upon the AEF's practice of segregating non-English–speaking soldiers, National Guard officials formed an infantry company made up mostly of Mexican Americans. In October 1923, officials organized Company E, 141st Regiment, 36th Division. The eighty-three men, mostly Tejanos, remained in service up until President Franklin D. Roosevelt mobilized National Guard units across the country.[179]

CHAPTER 5

"I THINK NOBODY IS MORE AMERICAN THAN I AM"

Mexican Texans and World War II

The world for Mexican Texans had changed dramatically after the First World War. In the years following the war, Tejano servicemen enjoyed the acclaim and respect that military service brought them. They returned to their prewar lives and took pride in having made the world safer for democracy. In Corpus Christi, ads in the local newspaper read "Welcome Home Boys," and "We Welcome You Home."[1] Other ads, such as one from Reed Automobile Company, echoed the talking points of the Wilson administration by highlighting these returning veterans as the bastions of liberty across the globe.[2]

Some veterans took advantage of this newfound goodwill and used their military service to gain valuable employment that might have been unavailable to them prior to the war. In El Paso, Pete Leyva, a former newspaper delivery boy who volunteered for the navy in 1918, used his war service to land a job as a truck driver with the city. In his later years, Leyva recalled that the mayor was a supporter of World War I veterans and gave Leyva a job. "I saw him on the street one day," Leyva described, "and he says, 'Pete, what are you doing?' I says [*sic*] nothing. He says, 'Come on, I give you a job. I'm the Mayor of the city.'"[3] Other veterans followed suit, and when possible they parlayed their military service into jobs.[4] "When we came back, we got preference for all the jobs," Leyva recalled. But as he noted, not every veteran who returned to the United States was able to work: many of them suffered from various health issues brought on by poison gas and other injuries. "Of course, some of the boys couldn't work; wounded, sick from swamps over there." After his truck-driving stint for the city, Leyva found employment as a deputy sheriff by drawing again on his veteran status.[5]

For many Tejanos, the initial postwar euphoria meant more than jobs. With the end of the Mexican Revolution in the early 1920s, anxiety over the border seemed to ease in the Lone Star State. For the next two decades, Mexican Texans navigated the challenges of the post–World War I world, the Great Depression, and continued discrimination. Tejanos continued to fight for social justice as deportations and repatriation during the 1930s hindered their goal of integration into the American mainstream. Tejano military veterans of World War I and other community leaders emphasized integration while fighting for equality during the 1930s. During the interwar years, Mexican Americans in Texas had a stronger sense of belonging to the United States than ever before.[6] But as the nation headed toward another world conflict, Tejanos navigated the world around them with great care.

Pearl Harbor

During the Great Depression years, the United States adopted a policy of isolationism as Asia and Europe erupted into war between 1933 to 1939. Still, war came to American shores. On December 7, 1941, the Japanese attacked Pearl Harbor. President Franklin D. Roosevelt called it a "day which will live in infamy," and the United States declared war the following day.[7] On December 11, Germany declared war on the United States. The US entry into World War II once again thrust the Tejano community into another conflict.

Yet, unlike past wars, Tejanos responded to the nation's call to arms with the same patriotic fervor as their Anglo-American neighbors. As many as 750,000 Texans served in the armed forces during the war, a proportionally larger percentage than any other state. Perhaps more than 250,000 of them were Tejanos; Precise figures remain unknown because the military listed Mexican Americans as "white."[8] The Mexican Texan origins of men like Laredo's John Valls, whose father was white and whose mother was a Tejana, could easily be overlooked.[9]

Historians often refer to World War II as a watershed moment for Mexican Americans and their quest for social and political equality. As Arnoldo De León maintains, Tejanos found themselves in a new position within the state and nation. What De León dubs the Mexican American Generation of the 1920s and 1930s "became increasingly insistent on their right to enjoy the privileges guaranteed them under the United States Constitution."[10] As a new world conflict began in the early 1940s, the Tejano community sought to become genuine Americans and prove themselves in battle while the family sacrificed for the war effort at home. Like the previous world war, Tejanos viewed service in the military as a means to achievement and recognition that Mexican Texans found unattainable in everyday life. While socioeconomic opportunities and the desire to enter mainstream American society were significant motives behind Tejano military service, patriotism and nationalism also proved important.[11] Luis Leyva, an undocumented migrant born in Mexico but a longtime resident of Laredo, was not drafted, but he volunteered almost immediately. "I know no other country," he explained. "This is my country; this is where I live."[12] By 1941, Tejanos identified with American ideology more than ever before. Although El Paso's Company E was composed mostly of Mexican Americans, it adopted the slogan "Remember the Alamo."[13]

Large numbers of Mexican Americans answered the country's call to arms, and their stories of serving in the US armed forces or supporting the war at home had rich meaning for the Tejano community. The ambivalence and hesitation with which Tejanos greeted previous wars disappeared with the war against the Axis powers in 1941. Despite the deportation movements and continued ethnic prejudice of the prior decade, the Tejano community rallied behind the Stars and Stripes, despite some naivete about national affairs. Laredoan Arnulfo D. Azios, who would later become Harris County's first Hispanic judge, was embarrassed to admit that he did not understand what Pearl Harbor meant in 1941. "Frankly, I didn't know what Pearl Harbor was," said Azios.[14]

Scholars suggest a variety of reasons for Mexican American enthusiasm and support of the war. The traditional motives of economic self-interest and desire for citizenship stood at the forefront behind enlistment, but Tejanos also joined the ranks of the armed forces to pursue a path toward naturalization. "I couldn't find a good job because I was an alien," El Pasoan Randel Fernández said. "At the time, joining the armed forces was the fastest way to become a citizen."[15] Like Marcelino Serna in World War I, some Tejanos opted for military service in the 1940s to secure citizenship status.

Other Mexican Americans enlisted to prove their self-worth. In some ways, this "warrior tradition" served as a way for them to demonstrate their distinctive brand of patriotism, which followed the Mexican cultural emphasis on masculine valor.[16] Scholar George Mariscal argues that *Mexicano* "warrior patriotism," emphasizes bravery and the "readiness to die for *la patria* [the homeland]."[17] Alvino Mendoza, for example, recalled that he "wanted to see how much machismo" was in his character when he enlisted in the US Navy.[18]

Discussions of the motives behind the enlistment of Tejanos can obscure the thousands of different personal reasons that led men toward war. For instance, Reynaldo B. Rendon of Corpus Christi joined the military to get out of jail. In his later years, Rendon recollected that he had been picking cotton in Mississippi. In 1942, when he returned to Texas, an immigration officer boarded his bus and learned that Rendon was born in Mexico and was not a legal citizen of the United States. Law enforcement officials took him to jail. While he was in prison, he met some military police officers, who suggested he should enlist in the army to obtain his freedom. Figuring the military would "beat imprisonment," Rendon took up their offer and enlisted. "I volunteered to get out of jail," said Rendon and "not to become an American citizen." He later served in Europe with Company E as a truck driver.[19]

In contrast to Rendon's hardheaded realism, Bob Sánchez of Laredo enlisted in the navy in 1945, because he thought service would be a "bit romantic." Though he recognized his responsibilities as a loyal American citizen, it took him a while to get used to the idea of being a military man.

Private Enrique Ochotorena, Company E, World War II, on the left, with three of his comrades. Photo courtesy of the Contreras Family, El Paso.

In time, though, he gained more self-confidence.[20] Charlotte, Texas, native, Ramón Martín Rivas, stuck to a traditional motive for enlisting. He earned only eighteen dollars a month with the Works Progress Administration when he decided to enlist in April 1941. Afterward, he recognized that the war changed his life. "I think nobody is more American than I am," Rivas said. "I was born in this country, and I spent 4 ½ years of my life to fight the war."[21] While men like Rivas and Rendon spoke glowingly of answering the call to arms, others did not feel strongly about the war. Laredo's Noé Sandoval recalled his friends and family telling him to flee to Mexico when he received his draft notice at the age of eighteen. Sandoval laughed at them. "I'll never regret it," Sandoval said. "I thought it was an obligation to join the service in World War II."[22]Others, like Natividad Campos, simply sought adventure and an escape from the doldrums of his hometown. "There was not much to do in the town I grew [up] in," Campos later recollected. "Besides[,] I was at the age when you look for adventure."[23]

Other Tejanos shirked duty for reasons that varied just as much as the motives to enlist. For instance, in 1942, in Falfurrias, a small town in South Texas, approximately eighty-miles east of Laredo, the local newspaper reported that the local draft board was seeking information on Luis García and Gilberto Alcántar, two Mexican Texans who were believed to have fled to Mexico to avoid service. The paper noted that García gave the fake identity of Roque Cantú to draft board officials, provided his last known whereabouts, and detailed his supposed employment in nearby Kingsville. Alcántar was born in Falfurrias according to the newspaper. But he registered in Mississippi before he disappeared. In the case of both men, the newspaper urged "friends or family" to contact officials so these men could be inducted into the military as the draft board intended.[24]

Though there is no record as to the reasons behind García's and Alcántar's draft evasion, Selective Service regulations allowed for deferments or reclassification and for conscientious objectors to seek exemption or noncombatant work. Farmers and farm laborers were among those who could seek deferments as essential workers. Most conscientious objectors in World War II offered religious reasons as their rationales for exemption. Draft boards were supposed to accommodate enlistees' religious beliefs, particularly those who were Jehovah's Witnesses, Quakers, Brethrens, and Mennonites. Even Corpus Christi's Reynaldo Rendon was asked if he felt comfortable with killing due to his Catholic faith. Conscientious objectors could find noncombatant work to serve the war effort, including duty as a medic or chaplain or remaining behind the lines to contribute to public works projects. Ethnic Americans pointed out, however, that draft boards rarely sympathized with their reasons for avoiding military service. African Americans, Native Americans, and Mexican Americans all complained that few, if any, of their fellows ever made it onto local draft boards. "The boards were loaded with Spanish names in their files, and very few were ever exempted, reclassified, or found too essential to not be drafted"[25]

As Tejano soldiers prepared to depart for various training camps across the country, many felt a certain amount of trepidation venturing into the unknown. The US Army set up over thirty camps across the country to train the men in weapons handling, basic drill orders, military discipline, and command structure, among other things. As the soldiers nervously reached their respective reception centers, they were shipped out to their assigned training camp, usually the next day. Soldiers guessed that if they shipped out in the morning, they would be sticking close to home. If they received orders to travel overnight, then they would be sent hundreds of miles away.[26] Company E left the Lone Star State to train at Camp Blanding, Florida.[27] In Texas, enlistees could be sent to any of the dozen camps spread throughout the state: Fort Bliss, Fort Hood, Fort Sam Houston, Camp Fannin, Camp Hood, Camp Travis, Camp Bullis, Camp Wallace, Camp Swift, Camp Maxey, Camp Hulen, Camp Howze, and Camp Wolters. The US Navy and the US Army Air Force also had installations in Corpus Christi, San Antonio, and West Texas for the duration of the war. Border towns like Harlingen and Laredo, with their temperate climates and clear skies, welcomed gunnery schools, while the Naval Air Station in Corpus Christi trained naval aviators.[28] The lessons gleaned from World War I and the budgetary constraints of the 1930s made World War II camps more efficient than those of previous generations.[29]

For many Mexican Texans, the training camps were unlike anything they had ever seen. Georgia's Fort Benning, for instance, which specialized in infantry training, lay on a site that covered more than 197,000 acres and could accommodate more than 95,000 personnel. It had its own fire department, sewage, and transportation system. For many Tejano soldiers, this camp was larger than their hometowns. Texas's biggest camp, Fort Hood, had a capacity for 68,000 men, larger than all but seven Texas cities.[30] Regardless of where they were sent, all the enlistees came to recognize the reality of life in the military and the doldrums of uniformity. Most camps looked the same, a constant maze of rectangles and monochromatic colors. Often, soldiers got lost going to and from their barracks.

Compared to those of the World War I era, the training programs of the 1940s military took a more basic approach to preparing the men to fight a war. The first phase of basic training lay with converting these civilians into soldiers. This included learning the elements of drill and physical conditioning.[31] The second phase taught soldiers the concept of developing their specialty and cooperating with others. That meant engaging in team or unit training. William R. Ornelas of Brownwood received his basic training at Camp Grant in Rockford, Illinois, before volunteering for the 101st Airborne, the "Screaming Eagles," in 1943. At Fort Benning's jump school, he along with other paratroopers learned about unit building. Ornelas believed that his life as a farm laborer made basic training easier. "I was used to hard work so I went through it real easy," he recounted. "We used to go march 30 miles a day with a full pack," Ornelas said. "It's hard on people that never did things like that."[32]

As Mexican Texans entered these training camps, they were more confident of their place as Americans. Unlike the fear and anxiety many felt during World War I, over the previous twenty years Tejanos had become familiar with the workings of government and were thus not as apprehensive as before. Thanks to the efforts of pro-assimilation groups like LULAC, many Mexican Americans viewed military service in a far more positive light than in prior generations. Solidifying assimilationist efforts, when the 1940 US Census classified Mexican Americans as "white," it opened up a world of possibilities. To be sure, soldiers of Mexican descent were still socially discriminated against, but the legal classification of being deemed white allowed them to train alongside their Anglo counterparts in the service.[33]

The US military strove not to distinguish between ethnic groups or national backgrounds at the institutional level. While training together might have broken some of the barriers of intolerance, government officials made efforts to create a sense of togetherness and belonging. Using the media, radio programs like *Your Army* and films such the Frank Capra–produced *Why We Fight* series, the army portrayed the Allies as the defenders of religion and traditions against the Axis powers. Capra's films, "showed Americans of diverse religious, class, ethnic, and regional backgrounds putting aside differences and disagreements in their embrace of nation."[34]

Like other marginalized Americans, many Mexican Texans entered training camps expecting poor treatment or harassment. Yet, the bulk of Tejano accounts reveals a complexity of experiences. Some Tejanos found that their fellow GIs were willing to help them translate things they did not understand or direct them to perform a task properly. Porfirio Martínez of Round Rock believed that there was less discrimination at his training camp in Galveston than he experienced growing up and working in the rock quarries of Central Texas.[35]

Still, differences like language and physical appearance could elicit taunts and jeers from other soldiers. Joe Villa of Yorktown, Texas, claimed he never felt discrimination when he was drafted. He recognized, however, that several men received promotions above him but blamed it on his own "broken English."[36] Language could still be a barrier. Yet many Tejano, relished being able to speak Spanish with their peers. Corpus Christi native Raymond Muñiz recalled how "any time he came across another Latino, from anywhere, he was happy to hear the Spanish tongue." Muñiz recalled thinking: "Well hey, you're talking my language!"[37] Natividad Campos of West Texas agreed. "When [Latinos] got together, we would automatically carry a conversation in Spanish, not in English, because we weren't very professional in English," Campos recalled. "So [the white soldiers] would give us hell and say, 'you're in the American Army, speak

English.' So I spoke English."[38] Some sergeants berated the men when they spoke Spanish, but Mexican American troops reverted back to their native language whenever possible.

Other types of harassment that Mexican American soldiers experienced in camp generally revolved around cultural differences that were exacerbated when men from varied backgrounds came together. Soldiers admitted that they teased each other about their ethnicity, their home states, or religion, but they never meant harm. "It was all in fun and never any hard feelings," noted Jerry Davis of the Eleventh Airborne. This type of back-and-forth often marked these exchanges from soldiers of similar rank.[39] One soldier suggested Mexican American soldiers were disliked by their peers for their behavior related to eating, historian Thomas Bruscino noted. The joking could be rough, and some enlistees were offended, but soldiers generally understood it did not come with "bad intentions."[40] The armed forces continued to train the men to think that their lives depended on one another, regardless of ethnicity or religion. El Pasoan Albert Caballero, who served in the Thirty-Sixth Infantry Division during the war, affirms this notion. "When the combat started, we learned [*sic*] how to respect each other," he recalled.[41]

While some Tejanos remembered unity and camaraderie, other Mexican Texans felt the ostracism and discrimination from the onset of basic training. Laredoan Virgilio Roel, a private in the Eighty-Fourth US Army Infantry, noticed discrimination right away. "I found a lot of prejudice, mainly resentment from white soldiers, especially if a Mexican American soldier got a better assignment because of his intellect. There was also crude discrimination by both commissioned officers and high-rank enlisted men in cases where the Mexican Americans were of a darker complexion," Roel said. Río Grande valley native Private Juan Martínez of the First Cavalry Division also noted the racial friction within the ranks of the US Army, noting that one Anglo soldier in his own squad wanted nothing to do with him. "He hated me and didn't want to take orders from me," Martínez remembered.[42]

One of the biggest changes to World War II training compared to World War I came in the diversity of combat training required for the

American GIs. During the Great War, the doughboys only had to learn how to fight in the trenches of Europe. In World War II, the army had to train soldiers to prepare for the deserts of North Africa and the jungles of the Pacific. Soldiers also had to be ready for combat in open ground or mountain ranges, depending on their individual units. One way army leaders dealt with this variety was to avoid any specialized approach for the sake of efficiency and brevity. Instead, they established a basic training program after which troops went on for specialized instruction. For instance, soldiers who were to work on amphibious operations went to the California-Arizona Maneuvers Area after basic training, and paratroopers reported to Fort Benning. If additional training was needed, soldiers continued to receive instruction overseas.[43] Weapons training with standard firearms dominated the routine. "Part of the training was shooting rifles and combat; it was nothing special at all," claimed Isidro Ramos of Martindale.[44]

Tejano soldiers experienced a rigorous six-day a week training camp alongside their fellow soldiers. Each week could also include sixteen-hour days, which might include combat training, mail call, cleaning details, housekeeping chores, showering, and, of course, mealtimes. Physical training could be an ordeal with countless hikes and drills on obstacle courses that varied depending on the location. The culmination of the training regimen required soldiers to navigate a 1,500-foot obstacle course with a rifle and thirty-pound pack in three and a half minutes. "It was a lot of marching, walking, and drilling," noted Calixto Rangel from Falfurrias.[45] Many of the soldiers stationed in Texas complained about the hot and dusty conditions. The men of Company E complained that mosquitoes were their biggest foe while receiving training in South Carolina in the summer of 1942.[46] Others chimed in to complain about a litany of other issues, ranging from uniforms to boredom. But for the most part, training kept the men busy. Other than Sundays, the GIs had little free time. Some men broke under the strain, but most did not.[47]

Tejano soldiers who came into this world of strict discipline and harsh conditions recounted that they were up to the challenge since most of them experienced poverty prior to training. Lauro Castillo, a native of

Bishop, Texas, laughed at how well he had it in training camp. "I loved it," Castillo said. "At home at the time, I didn't have water, light, gas, refrigerator—nothing. When I went into the service, I felt like a rich man—good food, hot water, no leak in the roof." He joked that he probably gained thirty-pounds in camp since he was finally getting three square meals a day.[48] José R. Navarro from Asherton concurred and felt that camp was better than his home in South Texas. "Lots of the soldiers really disliked the place and said so. But for me, it was lots better than Asherton: It had electricity and [indoor] sanitary facilities," claimed Navarro.[49]

Following basic training, the men began the Process of Overseas Movement, a brief period before they made their way overseas for combat. This proved a nerve-racking time for many men; many had never left their home counties, much less the United States. The authorities in Washington began sending troops across the Atlantic as early as January 1942. For many, this was probably the most stressful time of their nascent military careers.[50] Eighteen-year-old draftee Joe Villa, from Yorktown, Texas, recognized he might not be ready for war when he faced leaving the country for the first time. Villa admitted he had never left his hometown before he received his draft notice and "feared he would not know what to do in a different country."[51] Others recognized that same anxiety in a variety of ways. Jesse Acuña's way to deal with the change was to just grin and bear it. "They took us to a reception center and then they put us on a train to New Jersey," said Acuña, a native of Trent, Texas. "We stayed there a couple of weeks. It seems like you're just there, all at once. You'd just get on a train or a boat. I was just hoping I could get back."[52]

The Spanish-language press in Texas had undergone significant decline since the First World War, a victim of the Americanization and assimilation movements across the state. Yet, local newspapers in predominantly Tejano areas continued to cover the men who left to fight. The *Laredo Times* carried a Spanish-language section in its Sunday edition in 1942. On February 22, the *Times* noted how one of the city's own, Raúl Aguilar, nineteen years old, volunteered to join the army after Pearl Harbor. The paper claimed that Aguilar was "happy and content" in his new military life at Camp Roberts, California, following a short stint at

Fort Sam Houston. As he waited for further orders, the *Times* noted that his parents, Pablo and María, lived in the Colonia de Guadalupe, Laredo's first public housing, which opened in 1941.[53]

As troops reached their ships, a perilous trip awaited, an arduous three-week voyage crossing the Atlantic. The men had to overcome crowded conditions, a paucity of fresh water, and poor food. One Mexican American soldier, Eliud Acevedo, recalled the fury of the seas. "It was a hell of a trip," Acevedo recalled. "I couldn't stand the waves—seasickness."[54] Making matters worse, the threat of U-boat attacks kept the men on edge for the duration of the voyage.[55] Adding to the foreboding before departure were the blackouts instituted along the East Coast to avert German attacks. "I remember when we left it was real dark and the lights were dim," recalled José Adame of El Paso, of the day he left the United States.[56]

Europe

Unlike African American soldiers, who remained segregated until 1948, Tejanos were integrated in every branch. The bulk of them, however, served in the army. According to historian Arnoldo De León, these Mexican Texans "differed in stages of Americanization, and perhaps even class standing."[57] Some were well-to-do, others not; some had a solid education, most did not. Regardless of their background, their training led them to the first major operation of the war, where decisions were made far above their paygrade.[58]

The first land operation in the European Theater of Operations (ETO) lasted about a week, in North Africa, where more than 170,000 troops arrived as part of Operation Torch. [59] Tejanos experienced their first combat in Operation Torch. Fort Worth native Fred Gómez of the Forty-Fifth Division, remembered being one of the few Mexican Americans in his unit. After training in Illinois, Arkansas, and Pennsylvania, Gómez took almost two weeks to cross the Atlantic before reaching the ETO. He noted that facing the Germans proved sobering. "They caught us off guard; they had been preparing since 1936," Gómez said. Nevertheless, he put on a positive spin on the North African experience, remembering that he actually liked the food while stationed there.[60] El Paso native Santiago Craver

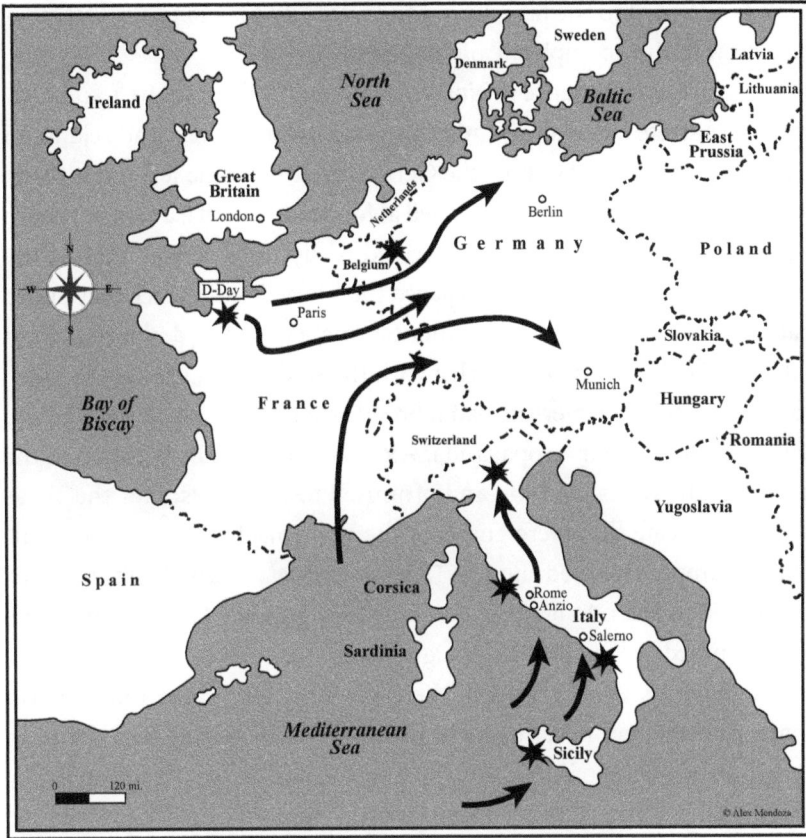

The European Theater, World War II, 1943–45

served in the medical corps in North Africa. The second of four children raised by a single mother who died when he was seventeen, Craver felt that he had an affinity for caregiving. He recalled how wounded soldiers stared at him as he flew around the battlefield in his ambulance. In one case, it became personal as one of his El Paso friends had been wounded, his fingers cut completely off.[61] Excelling in a different role, Richard Ortiz was good with his hands. As a graduate of San Antonio's Vocational Technical School in 1941, Ortiz maintained aircraft for the North African Campaign Air Transport Command. He claimed he was one of the few

Texans assigned to the task during the war.[62] By May 1943, the Germans had been pushed completely out of North Africa.[63]

The combat experience in North Africa changed the soldiers and their officers; naivete faded away amid the harsh reality of war. The Tejanos of Company E got wind of how the German war machine felt about them, and all Americans, when they arrived at Magenta, Algeria, a former French Foreign Legion post. The men arrived ready to wage war against the Germans but instead they first engaged the Vichy French. Later, they had to battle the heat and the aftereffects of Atabrine, a new drug designed to ward off malaria. As the men struggled with the side effects, they got to listen to "Axis Sally," an American radio broadcaster employed by the Nazis to disseminate German propaganda. Axis Sally reportedly mentioned the Thirty-Sixth Texas Division and promised to drop passes for the Texas boys to indicate they were guests of the Wehrmacht. The boys of Company E simply assumed she was "*llena de mierda*" (full of shit) but they continued to listen to her broadcasts as they guarded German prisoners and prepared for the next campaign.[64]

The Tejanos who arrived in the ETO after 1942 came into a world many of them had never thought possible. While testing had begun in July 1940, Operation Torch saw the first combat use of paratroopers, by the 509th Infantry Regiment in Algeria. [65] Eduardo Peniche joined the paratroopers when he learned that his dreams of flying airplanes proved impossible, as he could not pass the written exams due to his language deficiencies. When presented with the opportunity to apply for airborne training, Peniche jumped at the chance. "So they say . . . 'You jump out of airplanes, and you get $50 a month jump pay.' Well, $50 a month jump pay and you wear a suit like that. I go for it," Peniche recalled.[66] Other Tejanos like Alfred Flores and William Ornelas joined the paratroopers and learned valuable lessons. Ornelas later maintained that the military taught him to accept responsibility, regardless of the situation.[67]

During the campaigns for Sicily and the rest of Italy of 1943–44, the American GIs demonstrated improved combat and logistics operations.[68] These campaigns seemed to have solidified the bonds of camaraderie for the American GIs. Mexican American soldiers, too, felt a deeper affinity

Tejano GIs in North Africa, World War II. American troops in North Africa sample the wares of a fruit vendor. Left to right: Sergeant Hardy Patillo of Austin, Texas; Captain Louis Dubcak of Lexington, Texas; Sergeant Adan Garza of Laredo, Texas; and Private First Class Herbert Lipsey of Dade City, Florida. During the Second World War, Tejano soldiers found themselves fighting alongside fellow Americans who might have once discriminated against them in schools or other occasions. Photo courtesy of Library of Congress, Prints and Photographs Division, Washington, DC, LC-USW33-000797-ZC.

for the men in their units as the test of battle forged stronger bonds. The Sicily and Italian offensives cost the Allies heavy casualties, but the shared trials of combat bred kinship among the men. Roberto Vásquez of Laredo claimed to view his fellow soldiers as family. "We acted like brothers," he said. "Once we got into battle, we had no differences; we just protected each other."[69] Other GIs—Tejano and Anglo alike—seemed to concur with Vásquez. Company E's Sergeant Gabriel Navarrete received a head wound in the Salerno landings. Upon his return to his unit, Navarrete received a battlefield promotion to second lieutenant. Military policy dictated that he be transferred to another unit. Navarrete, who was born in El Paso, had come to see the company, made up of lifelong friends, as family. He turned down the battlefield commission to remain with his company.[70] Friendship and camaraderie expanded beyond combat. Guadalupe Conde, a member of Company F, had been assigned as a cook in the Second Battalion. As the only Tejano in his unit, the men in his company fondly referred to him as "My Mexican." When Conde received an offer to join Company E—the all-Mexican unit—he declined because he was so attached to the men in his company.[71]

World War II soldiers of Mexican descent shared much in common with their peers. Generally, like the other GIs, they demonstrated no overt patriotism and did not embrace flag waving or heroics. Most of them simply wanted to do a good job at whatever task they were assigned. They just wanted to survive the war and go home to their families. Ultimately, these men simply saw themselves as warriors doing their duty.[72] José R. Navarro from Asherton, Texas, fighting in the Ninety-Ninth Infantry Division of the US Army, summed it up. "You were not looking to do outstanding, heroic things. You did what you needed to do, what you were trained to do: fight and win," he said.[73]

As the Italian campaign continued its stalemate into 1944, Allied planners shifted their attention to an invasion of France across the English Channel.[74] When D-Day finally came, on June 6, 1944, it had taken months of preparation and more than a year of planning. More than 100,000 Allied troops came ashore on the beaches of Normandy. Through perseverance, the Americans pushed the Germans back from their murderous defenses and gained a foothold on French soil. South Texas native Emilio Portales, one of the men who fought at Utah Beach, recalled: "We got off the landing craft and the Germans were up on hills shooting at us. So we kept running and trying to dodge bullets and shrapnel." "We just kept going and going and going until we broke the lines," he emphasized.[75]

Combat proved the ultimate experience for the World War II soldier. Ricardo Martínez Bustos, a Tejano infantryman from the town of Gulf, was in awe of the fighting to secure the beaches. "All [you] could hear were guns," Bustos said. "You could see a lot of soldiers on that beach. It was really bad."[76] The worst of the fighting took place on Omaha Beach. The memory of the assault and the ferocity of combat left an indelible mark on the participants. For San Antonio native Francisco R. Vega, the brutality of D-Day began even before they got in range of the German guns. "Many men didn't make it to the beach. They would [fall] off the nets and be smashed between the ships" and the landing craft, Vega recalled. Then, once they landed on the beaches, the horrors of war were almost overwhelming. "When I finally made it to the beach, I was lying in the sand and the body of another soldier bumped alongside me and said, '*ese* [that] guy.' I was surprised to hear Spanish and as I turned around to see this soldier next to me, I heard a dull, metal sound and there was a hole in his helmet. He was still and I never saw his face," Vega reminisced. "We referred to Omaha Beach as 'Bloody Omaha' . . . to me[,] it was as close to being in the killing floor of a slaughter house here in the states."[77] The ferocity of the Omaha Beach landings was not lost on the rank and file. Johnnie Marino of El Paso got the message loud and clear. "They told us, 'If you see someone hit or is laying there, don't stop. If you stop, you're going to be with him,'" he remembered. "We were like sitting ducks."[78]

Operation Overlord had achieved its objective, landing Allied forces on the European mainland. As additional reinforcements poured across the English Channel, the Allies needed to break out of the Normandy beaches and advance into the interior of France. The memory of the brutal fighting at Utah and Omaha weighed heavily with some men, even years later. "I don't want to remember," reminisced Mike Silva, a rifleman in the Ninetieth Division.[79] Eduardo Peniche, a native of Progreso, in the Río Grande valley, landed in Normandy on D-Day +3 (June 9). This was Peniche's first exposure to combat. And that's when he saw the first dead Germans, he recalled, "but then I also, I saw an American soldier, young soldier, big, big guy, probably over 6 foot, had a neck wound, and he had bled to death." The imagery of death and the carnage of war proved palpable to Peniche. "That was very scary," he said. "I saw dead Germans, 11 of them. I saw cows, bloated, horses, a lot of this stuff. You knew you were in combat."

New GIs arrived on the front lines, new to combat. Ernesto Pedregón Martínez of El Paso enlisted in the army in September 1944. A few months later, he entered combat but did not immediately recognize the sound of gunfire. "We were so innocent at the time, we thought it was a rainstorm," Martínez said.[80] In December, a German counterassault in the Ardennes Forest broke through the Allied front. This last gasp of the Germans pierced a fifty-mile-wide column through the American First Army. The so-called Battle of the Bulge wreaked havoc on American forces. But through fierce defensive fighting at Bastogne and St. Vith, the Allies succeeded in halting the German advance.[81]

As the final German offensive sputtered to a halt, the Americans began to think of the end of the war and returning home safely. Despite the hardships of campaigning in Europe, the American GI passed the time writing letters to friends and family during their idle moments. The soldiers notified the recipients of their health, the weather, and sometimes offered descriptions of the world around them. The armed forces recognized the connection between morale and the mail to and from home.[82] "In the letters I sent my mother, I asked her to pray day and night for me and I know that it helped," a Tejano soldier recollected.[83] Even though overseas mail delivery became erratic near the front lines, a connection to home proved important. Sometimes military censors screened the correspondence. Abelardo García, a native of Beeville, located about forty-miles northeast of Corpus Christi, found out about the screening process when he received a letter from his girlfriend with X's and O's at the bottom, signifying hearts and kisses. "The military scratched it off because they thought it was some kind of code," García recalled.[84]

A theme among many of the soldiers' letters was the fear of death on the field of battle. As the armies marched closer to Berlin in 1945, the Tejano GIs noted the reality of death as it surrounded them at every turn. Twenty-year-old Corpus Christi native Alfonso L. Dávila was struck by shrapnel in Germany. His comrades dragged his wounded body into a big foxhole, where he lay next to dead soldiers for five hours while waiting for treatment. He remembered, "It was the first time I ever saw so many dead soldiers."[85] Even though soldiers recognized fear was always present, many felt they had no time to dwell on those feelings lest they or their comrades suffer the consequences. "In all sincerity, you don't have time to fear. You assume . . . that you will not be hit. But somebody else will. But it's terrifying . . . cause you know it's a false self-assurance," Peniche remembered.[86] "There were times when there were bullets going by six inches from my head. I was just happy to be alive," recalled Randal Zepeda Fernández.[87] The general consensus was to do their jobs so they could return to their friends and family back in the United States. "All I wanted to do was come home. Get it over with and get back," recalled William Ornelas of Brownwood, Texas.[88]

The race to Berlin in the spring of 1945 saw the Soviets pressing from the east and the British and Americans from the west. Hitler committed suicide a day later. By May 7, the Third Reich surrendered to the Allies. In the midst of that final push to Berlin, the Allies made a horrific discovery as they came across the concentration camps that the Nazis had used to conduct their final solution of exterminating millions of Jews and other "undesirables."[89] El Paso native Johnnie Marino was one of the first Tejano soldiers to come across the camps in 1945. Entering the camps in Hadamar and Belsen, which Marino said were dubbed "the Murder Factory," he saw a deep ravine, approximately one hundred feet long, filled with dead bodies piled on top of one another. "The Germans were in such a hurry to leave they didn't have time to cover them," Marino noted. Later, when he came across additional concentration camps, he noticed dust flakes on their uniforms and atop their jeeps. Marino and his fellow soldiers were flabbergasted when they learned that the dust was, in fact, ash coming from a tall chimney nearby that had burned Jewish prisoners.[90] Fellow El Paso native Joe Lerma was in shock, too. "The sight and smell of human death is terrible," he said. Lerma's assignment was to inform the camp survivors that the war had ended, and the Allies had liberated the camps. "The people were afraid to come out," Lerma recalled, describing the difficulty in convincing the men and women that conditions were safe for them.[91] One Tejano, Ernest Quiroga of Dallas, had a brush with the horrors of the Holocaust in a different capacity. Quiroga was a musician with the US Army who received a somber assignment—to entertain the people liberated from concentration camps. "I entertained persons that were in concentration camps and I always wondered why they were always in a daze." Quiroga recalls playing his accordion, trying to aid their recovery. "I was playing my accordion and one number that I played was a typical Mexican song—*Besame Mucho* (Kiss Me Much)," Quiroga said, but "they were still in a daze."

The Pacific

For Americans, the war against Japan took a backseat to the European theater after Pearl Harbor, but the Philippines, Guam, Wake Island, the Gilbert Islands, and Hong Kong all fell to the Japanese by the end of 1941.[92] Though the "Germany first" approach was politically and diplomatically expedient, the Joint Chiefs of Staff always kept an eye on the Pacific, deploying enough US Army, Army Air Force, Navy, and Marines personnel to launch advances against the growing Japanese presence. Plus, the American public demanded retribution in the wake of Pearl Harbor. In fact, many Tejanos joined the service because of the Japanese attack in Hawaii. José Eriberto Adame of El Paso heard about the Pearl Harbor attack on the radio when he was nineteen years old. He joined the army soon thereafter and served for the duration of the war.[93] Aaron Mendoza heard about the attack while he was still in high school. Though he wanted to join the US Army Air Force at the time, he had to wait to enlist, ultimately joining the navy in 1943.[94] Juan Medina Sánchez, another young Tejano who answered the call to arms in the wake of Pearl Harbor, called Corpus Christi home. When his mother died at a young age, his father remarried, and the boy left his father to live with his aunts or wherever he could find shelter. He spent time with his cousins committing petty crimes in order to survive, but when the country went to war, Sánchez traveled to San Antonio to enlist. Like other Mexican American young men in the 1940s, Sánchez felt it was his duty.[95] Emiliano Gimeno shares a similar story. The twenty-year-old El Paso native had just gotten married in the summer of 1941. He and his wife were expecting their first child when news of Pearl Harbor reached the Gimeno household. Gimeno joined the navy right away, believing it was his "duty" to participate in the war. "In a way, I did not want to go because of my wife and kids, but I had to go to defend my country," Gimeno recalled.[96]

Animosity and hatred also colored their war experiences against the Japanese, however, and spurred feelings of revenge. Racism informed the war against Japan, flowing from the highest levels of government to the rank-and-file soldiers as songs, media, and official documents indicated the Japanese were a subhuman species that demanded little mercy. Anti-Japanese sentiment peaked in the months following Pearl Harbor, culminating in Executive Order 9066 which resulted in the incarceration of tens of thousands of Japanese Americans in internment camps as purported threats to national security despite the lack of evidence of widespread subversive activity.[97] The *Los Angeles Times* wrote, "our Japanese-Americans, citizens by the accident of birth, but who are Japanese nevertheless" should not be trusted.[98] Anti-Japanese sentiment clouded many soldiers' judgments during and after the war. One Tejano veteran, Moises Sánchez, who lived in El Paso before joining the army and fighting in the Pacific, swore he came across Japanese subversives in California before the war. He was living in a Mexican barrio at the time and recalls that several Japanese men who lived in the neighborhood held mysterious meetings in the back room of a grocery store. He insisted these men fled to Mexico and were later confirmed to be spies.[99] The hysteria over Japanese subversive activities influenced views on the home front, and soldiers and sailors brought them to war in the Pacific.[100]

American servicemen sometimes bent the rules of war when facing the Japanese. Scholars argue this willingness to "fight dirty" can be attributed to the fact that American troops believed that the Japanese did not conduct themselves honorably in war. The surprise attack on Pearl Harbor, the emergence of the details of the Bataan Death March, and the execution of US airmen following the Doolittle Raid of 1942, among other events, all colored the sentiments of American troops. A stark example of the contrast between the two major theaters of operation was reflected in the treatment of missing soldiers. In Europe, if a soldier was wounded or went missing after a patrol or battle, his comrades hoped that in a few weeks they would receive notice that he was in a German prisoner-of-war camp, where he would suffer but likely survive the war. In contrast, if a soldier was wounded or went missing in the Pacific, he was considered as good as dead since the Japanese were notorious for killing wounded Americans.[101] Most Americans did not fully understand the Japanese view of war, in which their life belonged to their emperor and dying in combat was an honorable end. These views made the Japanese troops a formidable foe, to say the least.

The fear of what could happen to them if they were wounded weighed heavily on servicemen fighting in the Pacific. One Tejano Marine from Vinton, Andrew Aguirre, noted just how callous the war had made many of his fellow "leathernecks." Aguirre lived a humble life picking grapes and making wooden crates prior to the war. When he turned eighteen in 1943, he joined the US Marine Corps and went to the frontlines at Guadalcanal. Never having traveled far from home prior to his time in the military, Aguirre recalls one incident that made him take notice. One morning, as Aguirre was admiring how beautiful the scenery looked, he was startled by a fellow marine's response: "It's a beautiful day for killing."[102]

By any measure, the fighting in the Pacific was fierce. The unofficial motto for the soldiers fighting in the Southwest Pacific was "Kill the bastards," a grim worldview that reflected the cruelty of war. Some American units did not take prisoners in the Pacific and justified their policy by citing Japanese atrocities. Japanese soldiers were often shot whether armed or not. Many wounded Japanese troops were summarily shot, much to the chagrin of intelligence officers who hoped to glean information from captured soldiers. Gonzalo Garza, a marine from New Braunfels, remembered the difficulty of fighting the Japanese in island strongholds. At times, Garza was part of a force sent to distract the Japanese in feinting maneuvers while the main American force attacked from the opposite side. Garza drew the somber task of cave patrol on Saipan. "My job was to . . . go out and search all the caves around the beaches because most of the Japanese soldiers that had remained and not surrendered, or had not been killed, were hiding in the caves of Saipan," Garza recalled.[103]

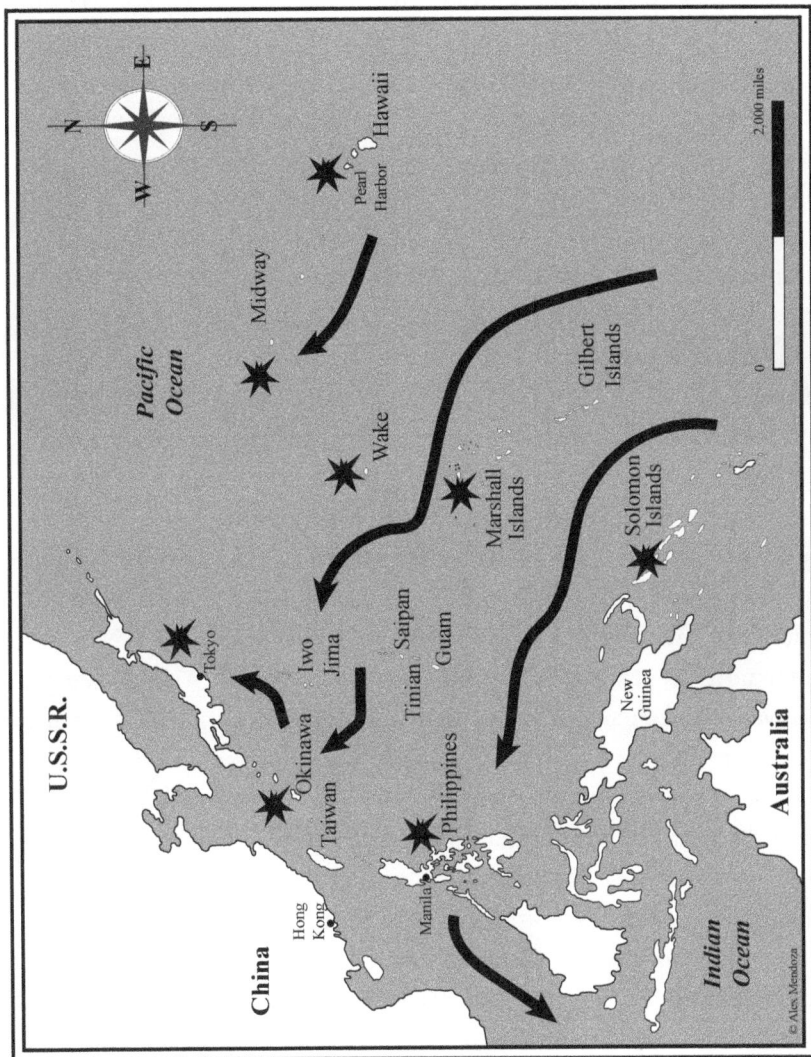

The US Military in the Pacific, World War II, 1942–45

Memories of the ferocity of combat in the Pacific remained strong years after the war. Laredoan Benigno Gaytán was only seventeen years old and working as a stock boy in his hometown when war broke out. He joined the navy and was assigned to the Pacific theater, where he witnessed bloody Japanese kamikaze assaults on US ships. Gaytán served on the USS *Telfair*, a Haskell-class attack transport, at Okinawa in the spring of 1945. He recalled a fellow soldier telling him, "You're going to see action today, Tony." Sure enough, on April 2, at about 5:00 a.m., a Japanese plane rammed into the starboard side of the ship. Gaytán was only one hundred feet away. "I could have got killed right there," he recalled, wincing at the memory of his injured right knee. "Still I can hear those bullets," he added, making whooshing sounds, "hitting right at us."[104] A few weeks later, a fellow South Texas Tejano, Genovevo Bargas, also had a close call with a kamikaze plane that rammed into his ship, the USS *Comfort*. The kamikaze missed the ship's smokestack, but still damaged the vessel and inflicted dozens of casualties. "We only saw one part of the Japanese [pilot's] body," said Bargas, motioning from the neck up, "the rest was nothing." Bargas survived, but the close call remained fixed to his memory years later. "We lost a lot of people, but I don't remember how many. That was the worst of my close calls," Bargas recollected.[105] Servicemen who survived kamikaze attacks continued to note the harrowing experience years later.[106]

Alvino Mendoza, a seaman from Austin serving on the USS *St. George*, a seaplane tender, remembered his experience surviving a kamikaze attack during the Okinawa campaign of 1945 more than half a century later. "We got hit by a suicide plane, and it was early in the morning," Mendoza recalled. When the Japanese kamikaze hit his ship's crane and exploded, he grabbed ahold of a hatch and hoped to hit the water rather than perish under twisted steel. "I was afraid I would land on one of the decks below, which was solid steel. And so I am looking, and I'm grabbing. It took a matter of seconds [in] your mind," Mendoza said. The enemy plane killed several pilots and caused enough damage to temporarily disable the ship, but Mendoza survived the ordeal with the memory of his close call. The memory of those suicide planes certainly left a mark. "Immediately, when we arrived, we were constantly under attack, mostly by the kamikaze planes. And I could look at the stern of a ship and see destroyer escorts that were on patrol duty, in the cove, get hit and split right in half," he noted.[107]

Other survivors noted the horrors of World War II in various ways. Sergeant Homero Martínez of Laredo, serving in the 36th Infantry, 131st Field Artillery, 2nd Battalion, had been captured by the Japanese on the island of Java on March 8, 1942. After eluding the enemy for days, Martínez and others ultimately surrendered to the Japanese. Martínez endured more than three years of imprisonment. In his later years, he could not understand how cruelly his captors had treated him and his fellow prisoners whom they forced to work on railroad construction in Burma: "Some things were beyond my comprehension." Hesitant to recall most of his experiences as a prisoner of war in a 1998 interview, Martínez nevertheless noted that even after half a century after the war, he struggled to forget. He said he still feared hunger and thirst, noting that he weighed 188 pounds when he was taken prisoner, but weighed only 93 when freed. After the war, he remained thankful for his hometown and his community, which took care of his parents while he was "lost" in the war. In 1949, he served as a pallbearer for the funeral of a fellow Tejano, Luis Guerra, who died at a slave-labor coal mine in Osaka, Japan, on September 28, 1944.[108]

The reality of death created a somber mood among those in the Pacific, even if they were in noncombat positions toward the rear. San Antonian Felipe de Ortego y Gasca served as airplane mechanic with the US Marine Corps. Though he worked far from the fighting, he still recalled the anxiety of battle. "Many of us could hear the fighting, the battles going on," he said. "I think there were times when we didn't know what was going to happen." Ortego y Gasca emphasized the rollercoaster of emotions. "In some instances, it was exhilarating, and in some instances, it was fearful," he said. "There was always the threat of lurking danger."[109]

Like their counterparts in the ETO, Tejano servicemen in the Pacific remembered the friendship and camaraderie forged through the combat experience. No soldier was ready for battle, no matter how much they claimed they wanted to see fighting. And those who did see combat hoped to make it out alive and return to their families. Action near the front lines brought forth a flood of emotions: fear, anxiety, loss, and anger, just to name a few. The testimonials of the veterans demonstrate many different feelings. One marine, Raúl Muñoz Escobar, noted that the best way to describe his initial experience in combat was to call it "hell—can't describe it any better." Escobar was barely eighteen years old when he first saw action in 1944. He complained of having flashbacks from his war experiences into his eighties, particularly of him witnessing a fellow marine getting shot in the head. Escobar recalled he took an additional edge of anger going into combat. At Iwo Jima, he earned the nickname "Crazy Escobar" because of his recklessness on the battlefield. Escobar blamed his rage on receiving a letter from his wife telling him she was obtaining a divorce since she did not think he would survive the war. After that he was angry and he claimed, "I didn't fear danger." Yet, despite that bravado, the memories and flashbacks remained for the rest of his life.[110]

Fellow marine Andrew Aguirre noted the profound sadness witnessing friends die in battle. "Part of you dies with them," a somber Aguirre recalled years later.[111] Ricardo García, another El Pasoan who joined the Marines also remembered how hard it was to lose a friend in battle. A member of the Fifth Division, which saw action at Iwo Jima and Okinawa, García survived some of the fiercest fighting of the war. "Some of my buddies, they were gone there," he recalled. "I tried to help them, but some of them couldn't be helped." At Okinawa, García almost died, suffering a wound that placed him at the bottom of a pile of bodies, unable to speak. His comrades assumed the worst. Finally, able to move his hands, he received help from medics. García lost the use of his left eye and suffered post-traumatic stress disorder, but he remained appreciative of his life.[112]

The harrowing experience of battle in the Pacific left many Mexican American soldiers thinking about the world they left behind. Isidro Ramos of Martindale grew up in humble origins in Central Texas, one of seven children of Mexican immigrants. He knew poverty from a young age and struggled along with his family during the Great Depression. During the war, Ramos joined the army and was deployed to the Pacific, where he first saw action near the Philippines in 1944. His first exposure to combat was a dogfight between Japanese Zeros and American P-38 Lightnings. "That's the first thing I remember seeing, and I'll never forget it." Ramos said. "It was horrible." For Ramos, he claimed that he and his fellow soldiers tried not to think too much about what was going on around them. They simply just tried to survive. "We were just going to fight, and some[times] we didn't come in contact with the enemy for weeks," he claimed. Ramos recalled he suffered many nightmares after the war, usually about being unprepared for battle. He was glad that they eventually stopped.[113]

Post-traumatic stress disorder was not something that World War II veterans recognized at the time. Yet, in later years, they came to accept and realize that the horrors of war did not end in 1945. Laredoan John Valls, who served in the Fifty-Second Armored Infantry Battalion in Europe, claimed he suffered headaches and nightmares more than seventy years after the war. After he was discharged he ran track and field for Baylor University and returned to Laredo to teach and serve as a leader in the community. The memories of the war stuck with Valls. "The thing that bothers me most is that I killed people. They're not coming home, but I'm home," Valls said in a postwar account. "They're dead because of me." Sometimes these recollections had a physical effect. "I'd have these awful headaches and lose my peripheral vision," Valls recounted. "I dreamt I was in my own funeral procession."[114] Other veterans returned to their families and tried to reintegrate into society. Yet, their families knew that it was best to leave them alone and not talk about the war. El Paso's Enrique Ochotorena, a sergeant in Company E, returned to the United States in 1944 after being wounded. In his later years, his family knew that he did not want to speak about his experiences in the war and that he despised the Germans. "That's all we knew, that he hated the Germans," said his nephew, Gilbert Contreras. "He only spoke about the war to his brother and his [Ochotorena] youngest son. No one else."[115]

President Truman's decision to drop the atomic bombs on Hiroshima and Nagasaki in August 1945 came at a an immense cost of life and led a long-standing debate over whether dropping the bombs was necessary to win the war.[116] The surrender of Japan to the United States took place on September 2, 1945, when Japanese leaders signed the formal Instrument of Surrender aboard the USS *Missouri* to General Douglas MacArthur.

President Truman designated that day as V-J Day for victory over Japan, and the nation rejoiced. Mexican American sailor Raymond Vega recalled both V-J Day and V-E Day (for victory in Europe), which had occurred a few months earlier: "Everyone was dancing; everyone was singing. Everyone was asking, 'When can I go home?'"[117] Sam Casarez of Austin was stationed in San Francisco when news of the Japanese surrender reached the United States. He noted the relief and joy across the nation as people celebrated the end of the war. "Those were huge parties," he recalled. US Navy veteran Elias Guajardo of Austin was on board his ship near Sabu (possibly Cebu) when news reached of the Japanese surrender. "We were anchored out in the bay and you could see the thousands and thousands of Japanese coming down from the mountains with flags, surrendered," Guajardo noted.[118] Every serviceman, no matter where he served in the Pacific, had only one thing on his mind by that point: going home.

On the Homefront

On July 4, 1941, months before Pearl Harbor, several *Mexicano* residents of Lockhart, Texas, a town about thirty miles southeast of Austin, were enjoying an outdoor celebration in honor of Independence Day. The main streets of the town were crowded as residents gathered to dance and celebrate. Late into the evening, the orchestra announcer interrupted the dancing to make a formal announcement: "I have been asked to make this announcement: that all Spanish people gathered here must leave the block, since this is an American celebration." The Fourth of July was for "white people only." As several Mexican American families left the celebration, not wanting to create a disruption to the celebratory mood of the townsfolk, the incident revealed that in for many Anglo Texans, people of Mexican ancestry were not Americans nor capable of becoming Americans.[119] The incident was a stark reminder to the Mexican Americans of Lockhart: they were still regarded as second-class citizens and outsiders in American society.

The Tejano community was not deterred, however, by doubts or overt acts of discrimination. They had come to appreciate the American dream. The interwar years had created a shifting consciousness within Tejanos, which moved them closer to a Mexican American identity. The deportation of many Mexicans and reduced numbers of immigrants during the 1930s had altered the cultural make-up of Mexican Texans as they embraced Americanization. M. C. González, the president of LULAC during the 1930s, urged Tejanos to accept American ideals and values.

Military service and support of the military were key markers of Americanization. In 1930, when the American Legion in Edinburg, in the Río Grande valley, recognized the city's fallen soldiers, the Tejano community jumped in to remind everyone that among those who sacrificed for their nation were two Mexican Americans. In newspaper editorials, Tejanos railed against segregation of soldiers at the local cemetery, insisting that there was no "greater disrespect" than to "grow a hedge between them and the comrades with they fought on foreign soil for the preservation of American ideals and principles."[120] The Tejano community made sure no one doubted their loyalty and patriotism during the Second World War. The surveillance of Mexican Americans, as had occurred in the First World War, was not repeated in this new conflict.

From the onset, unlike World War I, no widespread resistance to the draft took place. After the initial moments of panic in December 1941, people on the home front mobilized to support the war financially and emotionally, and they sacrificed their comfort during the government's period of rationing wartime goods. Tejano men who were not in the military acted quickly, moving to urban areas to seek work as factories re-tooled. The logistical behemoth of the federal government required manual laborers. Tejanos found skilled-labor positions in Texas cities, as well as opportunities in menial and unskilled jobs throughout the state.

Through the creation of the Fair Employment Practices Commission (FEPC) by Executive Order 8802, people of color suffered less discrimination in employment at defense industries and government jobs. Though imperfect, the FEPC seemingly relaxed the tensions present over Tejano labor during the Great Depression.[121] Mexican American women found jobs and volunteered for the military and served in the Army Nurse Corps or the Women's Auxiliary Army Corps.[122] Some Tejanas, like Rafaela Muñiz Esquivel of San Antonio, served with the 242nd General Hospital in France. "Mother never seemed to worry too much about me," Esquivel remembered years later. "She knew [that] I knew what to do. . . . I think she was more concerned about [my brothers]. She knew they would be at the front."[123] Those who could not help on the warfront helped on the home front. Tejanas joined the Office of Civilian Defense, which undertook preparations for an Axis assault on the American mainland. These women served in Texas cities that had air bases, such as Laredo, Big Spring, and San Antonio. [124]

Tejanas on the home front also made the sacrifices that the federal government asked from its citizenry. The government's War Production Board (WPB) designated a number of raw resources, including steel, aluminum, and rubber as essential for the war effort. Through propaganda campaigns spearheaded by the Office of War Information, the WPB told civilians about the importance of recycling scrap metals and other materials.[125] In South Texas, the town of Falfurrias rallied behind the state's representative of the WPB, Thomas L. Mullican, who urged Texans to organize scrap metal drives and work with the federal government to overcome the shortage of prized metals. The Tejano community in the South Texas town jumped on board, helping local defense guards collect scrap metals. Though not all these scrap metals made a tangible difference for the War Department, this example of the Tejano community working alongside their Anglo neighbors seemed to galvanize the Texas home front. Each group felt like it was doing its part to support the war effort.[126] The government also rationed other products, including gasoline and certain foods. Like many Americans, Mexican Texans grew their own food and collected needed materials to support the war.

Tejano communities across the state appeared much like any other community, blending culture and patriotism to fully embrace Americanization as the citizenry prepared to defend the homeland from the enemy. In December 1941, El Paso city leaders mobilized quickly as volunteers stepped forward to serve as watchmen to keep the city safe. The chief of police requested men past the draft age as the department was flooded with requests to volunteer. Mayor J. E. Anderson urged the city to come together when he wrote, "Now we can unite, stop all our silly dissension and get down to the serious business of seeing that our country wins the war."

The city organized quickly, creating the El Paso Civil Defense Council, with about 2,300 members who "swung into action," the *El Paso Times* noted. The organization included fire and rescue personnel, Red Cross, "utility divisions, intelligence department and recruiting divisions."[127] Hundreds of miles to the southeast, Laredo officials followed suit, setting up a civil defense organization to protect the city and the state from foreign adversaries. Like residents of other US cities, Laredoans organized a "Bomb the Japs Club." In February 1942, Governor Coke Stevenson visited the city and remarked, "They have a detailed program that is clicking perfectly." It unquestionably is one of the finest in the state."[128] In Corpus Christi, reports of U-boat periscopes sent shock waves across the state and rallied Tejanos and Anglos to join the Coast Guard to watch the waterways and ensure safe passage of Texas oil in the Gulf.[129]

During the war, labor shortages in agriculture in the Southwest proved acute. In 1942, pressure from farm owners and diplomatic leaders prompted government officials to pass legislation that created the Bracero Program, which would allow laborers from Mexico to work seasonally in the American Southwest. More than 300,000 agricultural workers came to the United States per year legally, while many others entered without documentation as the Good Neighbor Policy and the war effort made the hysteria of the deportation drives of the 1930s a thing of the past. Marcelino Ramírez Bautista lost his job in the United States during the 1930s. He moved back to Mexico and started a family in Zacatecas. But, when the Bracero Program got underway, Bautista returned to work for various railroads. When the war was over, he settled permanently in the United States.[130]

Mexican American–civil rights leaders such as M. C. González, George Sánchez, José de la Luz Sáenz of LULAC, among others agitated for greater civil rights for Tejanos during the war. This cadre of middle-class community leaders argued that Mexican American participation in the war gave credence to their demands for equality. Yet, LULAC leadership was quick to note their battle for equality applied only to those Tejanos who embraced their definition of American values. These Tejano civil rights leaders embraced the concept of trying to obtain "white rights for some, rather than equal rights for all" due to a pragmatic view of what they could accomplish.[131] Their efforts, along with pressure from the Mexican government and Texas farm owners desperate for laborers, resulted in the state legislature ratifying Governor Coke Stevenson's Caucasian Race Resolution, which theoretically granted "all persons of the Caucasian Race"(including, theoretically, Mexican Americans) the same "equal accommodations."[132] Additionally, the Texas Good Neighbor Commission aimed to be more respectful of the rights of Hispanics.[133] Though segregationist policies and racism of continued to mark the Lone Star State into the postwar era, the foundation laid down during the Second World War served the Tejano community well during the battles for civil rights in the decades ahead.

Despite their ongoing battles for civil rights, Mexican Texans continued to demonstrate patriotism and support for the nation. In the wake of Pearl Harbor, some communities paused civic celebrations and other public diversions. In 1942 Falfurrias, for instance, the local paper reported that R. L. Schultz, the general chair of the rodeo association, canceled that summer's rodeo in "deference to the tire and gasoline rationing program" of the Roosevelt administration. With popular entertainment needed as a diversion, however, the rodeo returned the following year.[134]

In Laredo, city leaders would not be swayed to cancel its signature patriotic events, the George Washington Birthday Celebration and Parade in February. A recent addition to the festivities was the inclusion of a track meet dubbed the Border Olympics, which saw participants from the University of Texas at Austin and Texas A&M University come to the border city during the war. Later, in March 1942, a mere three months after the Japanese attack on Pearl Harbor, the Border Olympics carried on its tenth annual track meet.[135] In 1943 and 1944, meet organizers offered an added twist on the event: military service men would compete to demonstrate the importance of supporting the armed forces in athletic endeavors. In a novelty event, members of the armed forces from Laredo's military bases donned gas masks and raced one another. Also, there was a "machine gun" relay in which competitors assembled a machine gun and then ran to a certain point. City leaders argued that the track meet would benefit the country at war since "army and navy officers have expressed the wish that physical fitness programs in colleges and high schools be continued."[136] The Border Olympics, then, filled an important role for a nation embroiled in the "Good War."[137] The fact that Laredo, where more than 95 percent of the population was of Mexican descent, carried on its Border Olympics throughout the war, while the 1940 and 1944 International Olympic Games were canceled, speaks volumes about the determination to carry on such amusements.[138]

In Brownsville, more than two hundred miles to the southeast of Laredo, the city carried on its celebration of Charro Days, when both American and Mexican heritages were celebrated with parades and other festivities. Residents from Brownsville and Matamoros, Tamaulipas, just across the Río Grande, attended the cultural festival and recognized the unique culture of the Texas-Mexico border.

While civic celebrations and other public events highlighted patriotism and love of country, there were countless other ways that the Tejano community demonstrated their national pride. Newspapers proclaimed that the eyes of the "Democratic World were upon" Texas; national pride and support of the war became paramount.[139] Local high schools such as Laredo High (later Martin High) used their extracurricular activities to support the war effort. Like Americans elsewhere, the student body bought war bonds. Martin High's "Cadet Corps" carried out the typical functions of flag duty and organized speeches in support of the war throughout 1943 and 1944. At football games, the Martin High School band, under the direction of Elmo Low, performed the "V . . . for Victory" stunt to wild applause, according to contemporary accounts. The band even played in the Civilian Defense parade. Students created "Victory Gardens," not only to reduce reliance on the nation's food supply, but also to serve as a morale booster in a time of war. Patriotic mobilization affected practically every member of the Tejano community, young or old.[140]

Postwar

When World War II came to an end, the Tejano community celebrated along with the rest of the country as the veterans returned home. As in previous conflicts, Tejanos performed bravely on the field of battle. Of the thirty-three Texans to receive the Medal of Honor in the Second World War, five were of Mexican descent, Lucian Adams of Port Arthur, Macario García of Sugar Land, José M. López of Brownsville, Silvestre S. Herrera of El Paso, and Cleto L. Rodríguez of San Antonio. This figure is especially notable considering that out of the thirteen Medals of Honor awarded to the nation's Hispanics in World War II, almost half came from Texas. The Texas Division, the Thirty-sixth, also received great acclaim as fourteen of its soldiers received the Medal of Honor. Company E's Silvestre Herrera was awarded one for his service in France in 1945.[141]

Formal recognition and honors for their military service meant a great deal to these Tejanos, particularly in the postwar era. For instance, Private First Class, Manuel D. Martínez, a member of the 359th Infantry Regiment from Laredo, participated in the D-Day invasion, receiving the Bronze Star for his "heroic" actions in taking over an assault after his squad leader had been wounded. Fifty years after the war, Martínez received another honor, the Jubilee of Liberty Medal from the French government in recognition for his participation in the liberation of France. Martínez was ecstatic upon receiving that award, proudly displaying his new medal for the local newspaper. He acknowledged that it was a great honor on behalf of American veterans.[142] Another Laredoan, Valentín Aguilar of the Eighty-Fourth Division, received a Purple Heart, the European Theater Operations Medal, the Good Conduct Medal, the Combat Badge, and the Bronze Star. Aguilar was particularly proud of his Bronze Star. "They pinned that medal, [Senator] Phil Gramm congratulated me, and from that day on, I felt very proud and I felt like I did the right thing for this country," Aguilar said.[143]

Decades later, San Antonio native, Manuel C. Vara, who served in the Pacific, reflected on his reasons for joining the fight:

> I was eager to get into the war. I may not have understood it, but I saw it as someone attacking our country, and our response was that the proper thing to do was to fight back. We understood that [joining the military] was the patriotic thing to do, and for me

Private Daniel M. Martínez, Laredo, Texas. Martínez, of the 359th Infantry Regiment, served honorably in the European theater of World War II. He received the Bronze Star for his heroism in battle and, later, the Jubilee of Liberty Medal from the French government in recognition of his participation in the D-Day invasion of Normandy. Photo courtesy of Magda Martínez.

at least, it was not a question of trying to get revenge against Japan, but simply that they needed to be stopped or else who knows where it would end if [Japan] was not stopped on their side of the Pacific.[144]

The feelings of Vara epitomized how many Tejanos felt. While some enlisted for the sake of romantic adventurism, to get out of jail, or to seek financial opportunities, most Mexican Texans were much like their Anglo-American comrades, joining the military for the sake of patriotism and the defense of the country they loved.[145]

At the same time, ties to their ancestral homeland remained intact. Medal of Honor recipient José Mendoza López of Brownsville was also awarded the Condecoración del Mérito Militar, Mexico's highest military honor. The Oaxaca native had moved to Texas as a young boy after his mother's death. He later dropped out of school and struggled to make ends meet until the onset of the war. He joined the army in 1942 and received orders to go to Europe. During the Battle of the Bulge, López saved his company from a German assault by single-handedly carrying a heavy machine gun and defending their flanks while they retreated. For his bravery, he was recognized by both countries.[146]

Conclusions

The Second World War witnessed Tejanos contributing to the task of defeating the enemy. Mexican Texans served in both the European and Pacific theaters, in every branch of the armed forces, distinguished themselves on the fields of battle, won a disproportionate number of honors and recognition from military leaders, and placed themselves in positions of leadership. Certainly, many of those who enlisted to fight did so for the sake of economic advancement and self-preservation, similar to Tejanos who fought in the First World War. But the vast majority volunteered for the sake of duty and love of their country. On the battlefield, these Mexican Texans simply wanted to prove their worth and get through the war to return to their families. They represented the broad trends found among servicemen of any ethnicity. Simply put, they were like their peers who wanted to do good for their fellow soldiers. The experience of traveling to Europe and the Pacific exposed these Tejanos to a world they thought they would never experience, especially those who came from humble origins in the far reaches of the Lone Star State. Their newfound confidence would inform their fight for greater recognition and civil rights when they returned to the United States.

One example of this assertiveness came from Ernest Eguia from Lockhart, who remained in occupied Germany after the war and helped rebuild German infrastructure and held various logistical duties while in the army. When he came home, Eguia used his wartime experience to earn a job with Warren Petroleum Company, employing his military skills as a civilian to build a pipeline across Texas. Yet, for all his success, Eguia remained disenchanted with the discrimination that remained present even in the postwar period. At one point he was driving in downtown Houston when police officers swerved in front of him and stopped his car with guns drawn. When the arresting officer realized Eguia was a veteran, he released him but called him a "smart Mexican" as he left. Eguia. "I thought that coming back to Texas, things would have changed," an exasperated Eguia noted.[147]

The Tejano community fought for those changes and for civil rights during the Second World War. While not as articulate as the "Double V" campaign that marked the African American war effort, Mexican Texans were keenly aware that the war against authoritarian dictatorships served to bolster their struggle for social and political equality at home. Regardless, LULAC had been fighting for those rights and promoting Americanization since the 1930s. The war only increased the desire of the Tejano community to demand a better place in society. Organizations like LULAC, founded in 1929, and the American GI Forum, organized in Corpus Christi in 1948 by Dr. Héctor P. García, galvanized support for Mexican Americans across the country.

The postwar era opened opportunities for education and financial security previously unavailable to Tejano veterans. The GI Bill, which expanded educational and economic opportunities for Mexican American veterans, gave many Tejano servicemen the hope that racial discrimination would remain in the past as they viewed themselves as Americans rather than Mexicans.[148] Albert Z. Caballero from El Paso had an interesting take. Caballero shirked the usual ethnic designations of his era. Instead, he considered himself an "American of Mexican descent, not a Mexican American."[149] The complexity of how Tejanos identified themselves would persist into the postwar era and the Cold War of the late twentieth century.

CHAPTER 6

"YO QUERÍA SER AMERICANO"

Tejanos and the Korean War

The Tejano GIs who returned to the United States following the end of the Second World War paid little attention to the geopolitical implications of the Cold War that began soon after the surrender of Germany and Japan. The soldiers who fought for Uncle Sam resumed their lives, proud of what they had accomplished and hopeful for a better future. Yet, they came back to a world that had hardly changed at all.

Despite proving themselves in combat, Tejanos were still haunted by discrimination as they made the transition to peacetime. In one outlandish case, Fort Bend County native Macario García, who had received the Medal of Honor along with twenty-seven other soldiers at a White House ceremony in August 1945, was denied service at a Richmond, Texas, restaurant the following month. An outraged García fought with the owner and was arrested by police soon thereafter. LULAC and groups such as the Comité Patriótico Mexicanos (Committee of Patriotic Mexicans) rallied to his defense. After the legal case sputtered to a halt and charges were dropped, García returned to his life and became a symbol of the discrimination that Mexican American soldiers continued to endure. Undeterred, García became a US citizen and graduated from high school after the ordeal. García dedicated himself to supporting his fellow veterans, finding work as a counselor for the Veterans' Administration (VA).[1]

García's experience was not an isolated incident. Other Tejano veterans noted that the Juan Crow world they left behind to fight totalitarianism abroad remained intact when they returned home. Sometimes the experience proved sobering. In the case of Beeville native Martín Sánchez, it remained outright baffling. After returning from the war, Sánchez heard that he would be welcomed anywhere if he wore his military uniform. He was not. When Sánchez went to a local store wearing his uniform, the shop owner said, "We don't serve no Mexicans here." Despite Sánchez's service in the armed forces, it did not matter to this particular proprietor. "You gotta go up by the railroad track there," Sánchez recalled the shop owner saying.[2] Joseph Alcoser, a Central Texan who volunteered in Dallas, agreed that the war brought no changes to the plight of Mexican Americans. "I volunteered because I felt it was the only way out. My dad always said that men had an obligation to defend their country. I felt that if I went and came back things would be different. I thought there would be less discrimination," he recalled. "Three years later, things were exactly the same."[3] West Texas native Estanislado "Stanley" Reyna suffered his own indignities, too. After being discharged in 1945, Reyna traveled to Lubbock for a checkup at the VA clinic. While in town he went to a barbershop to get a haircut. After sitting down in the chair, he was asked what his origins were. Reyna replied, "American." The barber said, "No, I mean, what's your [ethnic] origin?" Later, Reyna was given a meal voucher to use at local restaurants in Lubbock. But after visiting a few establishments, it became clear he was not going to be served. A dejected Reyna returned his unused meal ticket and went home.[4]

In some cases, discrimination against the former servicemen turned violent. In one of the most egregious incidents of racial violence against Tejano servicemen, Private Benigno Aguirre of San Angelo was beaten unconscious by a group of a dozen Anglo teens. On September 1, 1945, the teenage boys had been drinking before deciding to visit the "Mexican" side of town to "beat up some Mexicans." They piled into a pickup truck and had made two unsuccessful attempts before coming across twenty-year-old Aguirre and two of his friends, Pete González and Rudy Salazar. "There are three Mexicans!" González recalled hearing. González and Salazar got away, but Aguirre was unlucky. Standing at a mere five feet nine and weighing 115 pounds, he stood no chance against the drunk teens. According to newspaper reports, Aguirre was beaten unconscious and remained in critical condition at the local hospital for months. The Tejano community was incensed by the failure of local law enforcement to fully investigate the matter due to the boys' affluence and political connections. Despite pressure from the Mexican American community, most of the teens received slaps on the wrist with probated sentences. Only one received a fine of $125. No serious charges were levied against the boys.[5]

Negative feelings against Mexican Texans continued to persist across the Lone Star State, such as in the case of Private Felix Z. Longoria of Three Rivers, Texas, approximately seventy miles west of Corpus Christi. Longoria had been killed in action in the Pacific, his body buried in Luzon. In 1948, his remains were supposed to be sent to his family for burial in Three Rivers. However, the local mortician refused to have a wake for a "Mexican" in their place of business, despite Longoria's honorable service record, which included commendations for bravery and a Purple Heart. The resulting imbroglio prompted the family to reach out to Dr. Héctor P. García of nearby Corpus Christi and the founder of the American GI Forum, a civil rights organization created in 1948 to ensure that Mexican Americans received proper care under the GI Bill. García reached out to the funeral director and received the same response as the Longoria family. Undeterred, García mobilized a publicity campaign to highlight the injustices of the Longoria affair. In 1949, the resulting exposure captured the attention of US Senator Lyndon B. Johnson. Through the intervention of Senator Johnson and the American GI Forum, Longoria's body eventually came to rest at Arlington National Cemetery.[6]

The Longoria affair and other incidents notwithstanding, Tejanos refused to acquiesce to the social, economic, and racial subjugation of past generations. Even though the Second World War and military service had not provided the results many veterans envisioned, the war did open opportunities for education and financial security previously unavailable to them. The war and the subsequent GI Bill, which expanded educational and economic opportunities for Mexican American veterans, had given many Tejano servicemen the hope that racial discrimination would remain in the past. The Second World War opened additional opportunities for returning Mexican American veterans in the realm of education and medical care. The battles for civil rights and equal treatment, led by LULAC and the American GI Forum, which was more open to opposing the political structure of the Lone Star State, resonated in the Tejano community during the postwar era. Later, the two Texas organizations would see their influence reach across state lines in the struggle for Mexican American equality.[7]

The need for organizations like LULAC and the American GI Forum was imperative. The good will and the modest gains made by the FEPC and the Texas Good Neighbor Commission soon evaporated in the postwar period, and Mexican Texans had to face the reality that they were still political outsiders. The poll tax and the boss system, which manipulated the Mexican Texan vote through economic coercion, prevented Tejanos from making any significant gains at the ballot box. In the social realm, de facto segregation kept Mexican Texans in dire straits as most Texas cities still maintained separate housing for Anglos and Tejanos. In 1945, LULAC cofounder and working lawyer Alonso S. Perales compiled letters, affidavits, articles and testimony that gave evidence to the mistreatment of Mexican Americans in Texas in his book, *Are We Good Neighbors?* (1948). The LULAC lawyer maintained that 150 Texas towns refused to provide equal services to people of Mexican descent. Mexican Americans "whether in uniform or in civilian attire, are not allowed in public places, cannot buy food or clothes in certain designated areas, cannot secure employment in any industry except as common or unskilled labor, cannot receive the same wages as other Americans in the same area," Perales wrote.[8]

While discrimination remained stubbornly unchanged, World War II undeniably altered the landscape of Texas. The modernization and urbanization ushered in by the war industries showed no signs of abating in the postwar era. Agriculture, long the economic backbone of the Lone Star State, shifted from individual ownership and tenant farmers to corporate ownership and a significant drop in tenants. At the same time, mechanization replaced manual labor with machines. Mexican Texan laborers contributed to the growth of Texas cities when they left the farms to find work. The number of farms and people who dwelled in rural areas in Texas both witnessed significant drops from the previous decade. These changes to the traditional order of the Lone Star State fit right in with the desire of Tejanos to reach the American dream. World War II had taught Mexican Texans the advantages of integrating into American society, and as they moved to the cities to work and prosper, they demanded their rights as American citizens.[9]

The Cold War Military

While Mexican Texans dealt with discrimination and inequality in their home state, the beginning of the Cold War altered the normal pattern of demobilization and retrenchment found after previous American wars. While military tribunals sought justice for the victims of Japanese and German atrocities, the efforts to create a collective global security organization, as imagined by Franklin Roosevelt, forged ahead after his passing. In the summer of 1945, delegates from fifty nations met in San Francisco to craft the charter for what would come to be called the United Nations (UN). Modeled after the 1920 League of Nations, the UN was to be an international body designed to prevent another world war. Organized with two legislative bodies, a larger General Assembly, which gave equal representation to each nation in the world, and a smaller Security Council, which bestowed permanent seats to the five founding power countries, the United States, the Soviet Union, the United Kingdom, France, and China. The UN Security Council held the power to decide when world peace was threatened, and each of the five permanent members held veto power.[10]

Although the UN came into existence with a peacekeeping mandate, US armed forces remained on occupation duty in Germany and Japan. In Europe, the alliance that yielded victory over Nazi Germany faltered. In Germany, the Soviets established a zone in the eastern half of the country, including partitioning the eastern part of the capital of Berlin. The Americans, the British, and the French divided the western half of the country in what would ultimately become the Federal Republic of Germany (West Germany). A political and ideological demarcation took place in Europe as the remaining "Superpowers," the United States and the Soviet Union, vied for influence over world affairs. Prime

Minister Winston Churchill noted the rising unease when he gave his "iron curtain" speech on March 5, 1946, which intensified Americans' long-standing fears of communism. In Asia, the United States assumed the primary role in reconstructing Japan. President Harry S. Truman appointed General MacArthur to serve as supreme commander and oversee Japan's occupation, which lasted until April 1952. After 1947, the two superpowers jockeyed for influence in a new type of conflict called the Cold War to describe the proxy conflict that took place in lieu of direct military action. When communists took control of China and the Soviets detonated their own atomic bomb in 1949, America's postwar world seemed full of peril.[11]

While authorities in Washington fretted over the geopolitical chess of the Cold War, US armed forces demobilized and worked to return the citizen soldiers and sailors back home. The military had expanded to employ more than fifteen million people and feature a budget of ninety-one billion dollars by 1945. As it had after previous conflicts, the rush to demobilize in the return to a peacetime force practically debilitated the armed forces, but the men in uniform were eager to return home and to their prewar lives as quickly as possible. The scale of how quickly the troops returned home made heads spin. Within three years of the defeat of the Axis powers, the United States Army shrank from 8,267,000 to 554,000 personnel. The navy went from 3,400,000 to a little over 400,000 in the same time span. By 1950, the US armed forces had just 1,460,000 men and women in uniform. Demobilization coincided with congressional efforts to cut military spending. The cost-cutting measures did not stop at personnel as arms and equipment were also struck from budgets, leaving the armed forces with dilapidated weapons. Political leaders seemed to have forgotten that it took longer than a year to properly train, fit, and deploy troops during the two world wars.[12]

The rapid demobilization of the armed forces placed the United States in a precarious situation. On the one hand, American leaders were determined to stave off the threats of communism and Soviet expansion. But on the other hand, President Truman and other political leaders urged fiscal restraint with the military during peacetime. This parsimony made the goal of centralizing the nation's armed forces through efforts such as the universal military training program more challenging. The National Security Act of 1947 served as a compromise of sorts, creating the new Department of Defense and establishing the Air Force as a separate branch. The following year, Congress repudiated the idea of mandatory military service and determined that a newly passed Selective Service Act, requiring all men over the age of eighteen to register for service, buttressed by the National Guard and Reserves, could provide necessary manpower. In the meantime, the Truman administration and the military focused on atomic weapons and other advanced technologies to deter the spread of communism.[13]

Despite the budgetary restraints of the postwar era, Tejanos still vied to serve in the armed forces in the late 1940s. For many, military service still proved to be the best option to improve their economic circumstances. Dallas native George Castañeda joined the Eleventh Airborne, US Army, to escape the poverty he had known all his life. Born in 1927, Castañeda worked as a migrant farm worker shuffling back-and-forth between Texas and Michigan in his adolescence. At the beginning of World War II, he was too young to join the war effort, so he continued to toil in the fields, picking fruits and vegetables and earning as much as thirty-five cents an hour. Though factory workers during the war era earned more money than that, Castañeda lamented that he was still too young for an industrial position. His dream had been to work at a factory like the other "*Mexicanos* in Michigan" who landed work with "General Motors, Ford, and Chrysler." But in 1948, with the encouragement of his older brother, Castañeda decided to enlist, a decision he believed changed his life forever. Though his fellow soldiers could not pronounce his name, calling him "Sergeant Castanita," he felt fortunate that a career in the army saved him from life as a farm worker.[14] José F. Páez of Laredo joined the army under similar circumstances. Born in 1929, in the barrio La Guadalupe, just northeast of downtown, he quit school at a young age to help support the family, which consisted of four sisters and one brother. Any money he earned he gave to his mother. At the age of nineteen, Páez decided he would enlist in the US Army to serve his country and help provide for his family.

José F. Paéz (left), Private First Class, US Army. Paéz, who died in 1982, served for seven years in the army. Photo courtesy of the Paéz family.

On August 31, 1948, he enlisted as a private and looked at his service proudly. An enlisted man could earn as much as sixty dollars a month if he had no dependents, a far cry from the farm wages and manual labor salaries available during that era. Mexican Americans in the Lone Star State might have still been regarded as second-class citizens in the late 1940s, but they certainly recognized that one avenue to escape poverty was through military service.[15]

The armed forces that Tejanos joined in the post–World War II era did not resemble the military of their predecessors, as it was also undergoing sweeping changes to its social makeup. In December 1946, President Truman established a Committee on Civil Rights to investigate the status of civil rights in the United States and to propose measures to improve conditions for Americans. Looking for ways to give America an advantage in the Cold War, Truman hoped the nation would escape vestiges of its past. A year later, the committee stated its findings in a 178-page report and pointed to a disturbing pattern of racial discrimination across the country. Among the recommendations made by the committee would be the elimination of poll taxes, a permanent FEPC, and a litany of other measures that shook the very core of Truman's Democratic Party. Truman felt he had to act in the areas he could control as commander in chief. First, he passed the Women's Armed Service Integration Act on June 12, 1948, a step toward gender equality in the armed forces by granting women regular status in the US military. Then, a month later, the president signed Executive Orders 9980 and 9981. The former ordered the desegregation of the federal workforce while the latter desegregated the armed forces. Though desegregation of the armed forces would lurch forward slowly until the middle of the next decade due to the vacillation and obstruction of obstinate military and political leaders, it proved to be a watershed for the social makeup of the armed forces.[16]

Korea

In the midst of President Truman's efforts to introduce gender and racial equity to the armed forces, communism continued to be a matter of concern for Washington officials. By 1947, the Truman administration viewed communism as a monolithic force that was destined to take over the world and that every Soviet threat had to be countered. Truman's containment policy was premised on making equivalent responses to communist actions in threatened areas. It was unclear if the nation could meet its military demands under current conditions. A 1950 report by the National Security Council, NSC 68, called for a rebuilding of a conventional military force to provide various options beyond nuclear war. This proposal departed from the American military tradition of not keeping large standing armies in peacetime. NSC 68 recommended increasing the defense budget from

$13.5 billion to $50 billion as the Soviet threat loomed. Truman, though, remained convinced that the American people would not accept the increased spending NSC 68 proposed and did nothing. Little did the president realize that events halfway across the globe, in northeast Asia, would force him to reassess within a few months.[17]

In the postwar era, Korea did not receive close scrutiny from the US State Department. The nation had been occupied by the Japanese in the early twentieth century, and since 1945 it had been divided at the thirty-eighth parallel into two occupation zones, with the Soviet Union holding the North and the United States in the South. They had planned to hold elections to unify the country sometime in the future. The North, led by Premier Kim Il Sung, wanted to unify the country under communist control, while the South, led by President Syngman Rhee, had other ideas.

US attention remained fixed elsewhere. Secretary of State Dean Acheson had not even mentioned Korea as an area of interest in a 1950 speech. Thus, when the North Koreans crossed the thirty-eighth parallel on June 25, 1950, with two infantry divisions amounting to more than 150,000 troops and one tank brigade, it came as a total surprise for American military and civilian leaders. Both the Soviet Union and China approved of Kim's attack because they assumed the United States would not intervene. President Truman, however, determined that Korea had to be saved. The United States went to the United Nations for support in stopping the North Korean attack, which had moved at lightning speed through South Korea. On June 27, the UN voted to stop the invasion, taking advantage of the fact that the Soviets had boycotted the Security Council and could not oppose the American position. On June 30, Truman pledged American troops to support South Korea. He did so without congressional authorization or a congressional declaration of war. Because of the Korean invasion, Truman came around to supporting NSC 68.[18]

While US officials scurried to react to the North Korean invasion, the boots on the ground were no match for the rapid advance of the North Korean People's Army (NKPA) and its T-34 tanks. Korea had been ignored by American policymakers, and the neglect clearly showed in the summer of 1950. The South Korean Army (ROK) numbered approximately 95,000 men, but were ill-prepared and trained to deal with guerrilla warfare, not the conventional army movements of late June and early July 1950. The American military advisors assigned to the sector, the American Korean Military Advisory Group (AKMAG), knew the ROK would be no match for any opposing force. One Tejano, Sergeant Arnoldo Gutiérrez from Laredo, was part of the five hundred-man AKMAG, a unit responsible for training the ROK with modern weapons. In an ironic twist, considering the social status of Mexican-born Texans and how their Anglo neighbors viewed them, Gutiérrez and his unit, which included several other Tejanos, were charged with "Americanizing" the South Koreans. "We worked under the 8th Army, and we were there to train the South Koreans . . . and instruct them on the American way of life, including the responsibilities of freedom and democracy," Gutiérrez noted. The consensus remained that the ROK would be unable to fight effectively in battle.[19]

Adding insult to injury, the United States had provided a paltry $10.2 million of equipment to its South Korean allies in 1950, and few of those pieces had arrived by that summer. Within days, the North Koreans had threaded their way through the mountainous terrain south of the thirty-eighth parallel in six columns, capturing the capital of Seoul and the port city of Incheon while setting their eyes on the southern coast. In contrast, the ROK fell back in disarray. As expected, within a week after the initial advance, the North Koreans had pushed the ROK back to near the city of Pusan (also spelled Busan) at the southeastern tip of the country. The US Army's closest unit was the Twenty-Fourth Infantry of the Eighth US Army in Japan. As a result of the budgetary constraints of the previous five years, the unit was understrength and equipped with dilapidated weapons. But with Truman's approval, General MacArthur ordered General Walton Walker to get the Twenty-Fourth ready to move. But the first unit to make its way to Korea was the 525-man First Battalion, Twenty-First Infantry Regiment, otherwise known as Task Force Smith, named for its commander, Lieutenant Colonel Charles B. Smith. Smith's unit loaded into six C-54 transport planes and headed to South Korea while additional troops followed by sea. Smith's force arrived in the first week of July and immediately stepped into battle. Suffering heavy casualties,

Smith's force delayed the numerically superior NKPA enough to allow American reinforcements to pour in and establish a perimeter around Pusan. By the end of July, Walker was able to stabilize the UN lines around Pusan and with the North Koreans' supply overextended, the American reinforcements had stabilized the defensive perimeter at heavy cost.[20]

As MacArthur and Truman planned the next move in the fall of 1950, shortages of men and matériel had to be dealt with. Simply put, the army was undermanned and not ready for large-scale combat operations when the North Koreans poured over the thirty-eighth parallel. On the eve of the invasion, US Army strength was 630,201 troops, of whom 360,063 were stationed in the continental United States and 108,550 in the Far East Command. The National Guard and Organized Reserve Corps could field an additional 500,000 men, and 185,000 students were available in the Reserve Officers' Training Corps (ROTC) programs. Truman urged the passage of the Selective Service Extension Act of June 30, 1950, which focused on the National Guard and other reserve units. By the end of the year, additional men were needed, and 200,000 draftees were soon called upon. (Since the United States did not enter the war alone, as US armed forces participated in the conflict alongside seventeen other countries that were part of the United Nations peacekeeping force, a full-scale American mobilization was thought to be unnecessary in the summer of 1950.)[21]

In some respects, the patriotic fervor that marked enlistment in World War II was absent in the Korean War even though nearly 148,000 Hispanics from across the country served in the military during the conflict. For Mexican Texans, the rationales for enlisting in the military remained the same as in past conflicts: support for the nation, defense of one's home, and the desire to escape poverty. After 1945, Tejanos displayed more American nationalism and patriotism than they had in previous decades. Soldiers and sailors spoke passionately about the need to fight to defend one's country. In Laredo, for instance, the once recalcitrant border town embraced the martial spirit brought forth by the Second World War. By 1951, the local high school, Martin High, boasted five companies of cadets in the ROTC, which hoped to "develop excellent leaders" in military science. The school also had an ROTC band and held military reviews throughout the year, including participation in the coveted Washington's Birthday Parade and Celebration. Members of the ROTC wore their uniforms in the school yearbook, *La Pitahaya*, nominated a queen for homecoming court, and drilled incessantly at the nearby football stadium, Shirley Field. In fact, they had more pages in the school yearbook than the 4–6 Tiger football team that year.[22] In the following year, 1952, students dedicated the yearbook to the school's ROTC commander, Major August O. Hein, for "expanding the ROTC and developing a liking for it among boys."[23] Many Mexican American teenagers in South Texas understood the martial expectations of the post–World War II era. Gabriel García of Mercedes, Texas, saw what his older brother had done for himself through military service and was "an inspiration for him to enlist For some Tejanos, pride and patriotism ran deep.[24]

The extension of the draft after 1950 brought in additional recruits. Just as in previous wars, fear of combat and the unknown inspired some potential draftees to run away. In South Texas, twenty-year-old Laredoan Horacio Vela received his draft notice soon after the onset of the Korean War and was tempted to flee to Mexico, something that several of his fellow Tejanos had done during the two previous world wars. Yet he resisted the urge to run away and instead leaned into a sense of personal honor that he held dear. According to his son, Ricardo, Horacio was an honorable man, brave almost to a fault. Though he later confessed his anxiety to his family, he revealed that he wanted to support his country's call to arms. So, with a noble regard for the United States government that had provided him a lifetime full of memories, Vela reported for duty. He was ultimately assigned to the Seventh Division as a sharpshooter in Korea. Vela's military service record indicates he earned two medals, a United Nations Service Medal and a Korean Service Medal with three bronze stars, for his service.[25]

The memory of World War II and how Mexican American soldiers had achieved respect and upward mobility through service to their country also loomed large during the Cold War era, despite the setbacks and disillusionment that came upon returning to the United States. Recollections of the patriotic duty exemplified by previous Mexican American

Horacio Vela. When Vela received his draft notice, he was tempted to flee into Mexico, something that many Tejanos had done during the two world wars. But he chose to fight. Vela was assigned to the Seventh Armored Division as a sharpshooter. At the conclusion of the war, Vela's DD214 (military service record) indicated he had been awarded two medals, a United Nations Service Medal and a Korean Service Medal with three bronze stars. Photo courtesy of Ricardo Vela and family.

generations who had fought in the previous two world wars influenced how some Tejanos viewed their service during the Korean conflict, and some of those veterans led by example.[26] Congressional Medal of Honor recipient Cleto Rodríguez of El Paso, for instance, continued to train troops in Texas as an advisor for the National Guard.[27] Veteran Ernesto González recalled, "We didn't have much knowledge in Duval County about the Korean War. The only reason I went was because my brother had been drafted . . . and my family would cry every night . . . and so I told my father, 'As soon as I'm old enough I'm going to join the army so I can help my brother win the war, so that he can come back.'"[28] In the Río Grande valley, Rolando Hinojosa echoed González's sentiments. As a young boy, Hinojosa was deeply moved by Pearl Harbor as patriotic sentiment gripped the nation in the wake of the surprise Japanese attack.

Unable to enlist because of his age, Hinojosa heard the nation's call to arms until he was old enough to enlist. He hoped to serve his country and gain an education under the GI Bill. "There was a lot of propaganda, movies and everything," he remembered of the patriotic entertainment after 1941. His two older brothers joined the armed forces, something that the younger Hinojosa was finally able to do in 1946, when he turned seventeen. By the onset of the Korean War in 1950, Hinojosa was called to active duty. He related his military service to both patriotism and familial obligation as he recalled how his older brothers had served in the army and navy during World War II.[29]

Other Tejanos desired to improve their socioeconomic standing and escape poverty through access to the economic benefits of programs like the GI Bill. They knew there were few alternatives. And if they could obtain additional benefits beyond a paycheck, all the better. Harlingen native Felipe Soliz, one of six children born to Mexican immigrants who moved to the Río Grande valley, registered for the draft at eighteen. His mother had died when he was in the fifth grade, and he had bounced around living with different family members after his father died seven years later. When he passed his physical, Soliz proclaimed, "I found a home in the Army."[30] Luis Landin joined the army under similar circumstances. Growing up in abject poverty, he saw few options. "I used to shine shoes and sell newspapers, but I never felt comfortable doing those jobs," Landin later recalled. "It wasn't for me, so I joined the Army."[31] San Antonio native Carlos R. Quijano grew up in the Alazán Apache Courts, a housing project on the city's West Side. At the age of eighteen, he enlisted in the Marines Corps in 1951, right out of high school. It was his opportunity to escape his upbringing, and he forged a military career that spanned more than twenty years.[32]

Just American-born Tejanos signed on, Mexican immigrants in Texas, also joined the ranks of the military, and they were influenced by similar notions of socioeconomic improvement. The nation's naturalization laws, coupled with the military's need for more soldiers, proved to be a perfect mix for Mexican immigrants during the years leading up to Korea. In 1918, Congress had modified its naturalization laws in order to make it easier for immigrants serving in the military to become United States citizens. By the 1940s, the federal government had continued to support the streamlined naturalization process of soldiers born in a foreign country. Pete Castillo, a Tejano from Austin who was drafted into the army in 1952, noted the number of *Mexicanos* in the ranks. "[The government] had drafted many *Mejicanos* from the Valley that were there with me," Castillo recalled. "They took these guys out of the field; they'd never gone to school. One Anglo made a remark while he was in the front of the [shower] line and said, 'I don't know why all these Mexicans are here instead of [in the line for African Americans].'"[33] Corporal Raúl M. Chavarría, a native of Tamaulipas, Mexico, was one of those men who saw military service as an that opportunity for a better life as he found himself thrust into war Originally arriving in Texas to search for work, the twenty-four-year-old menial laborer eventually made his way to Chicago, where he received a summons to return to Texas and to report for military service. "Para ser sincero, yo quería la ciudadanía. Yo quería ser Americano" (To be honest, I wanted citizenship. I wanted to be an American), Chavarría remembered. After training in El Paso, Chavarría left the Lone Star State bound for New York, but then he was sent to Germany, much to his chagrin. "Yo pedí ir a Corea, pero me mandaron a Alemania"(I asked to go to Korea, but they sent me to Germany), he remembered with a chuckle. Chavarría became a US citizen in 1954, one year after the United States and North Korea signed an armistice. He appreciated the opportunity that military service gave him toward citizenship and kept his uniform for more than half a century.[34]

Combat

The Mexican American soldiers who made their way to the Korean peninsula did not have the luxury of a long training camp. Regular soldiers were the first to meet the exigent circumstances before any draftees would make their way to the Asian theater. The US Army of 1950 was a shell of its World War II self, and it showed from the start. Rolando Hinojosa was one of the soldiers who were part of Task Force Smith, which landed in Korea on the Fourth of July. The next day, this unit was obliterated by

Raúl M. Chavarría. Some Mexican nationals used US military service to gain citizenship during the twentieth century. In the case of Corporal Raúl M. Chavarría, born in the Mexican state of Tamaulipas, he joined the ranks of the US Army while en route to work in Chicago from San Antonio, serving in the Fifth Division during the Cold War. Photo courtesy of Raúl Perez and the Chavarría family.

the NKPA, suffering 30 percent casualties at the Battle of Osan. Hinojosa described the chaos:

> This was the very first battle for all of us, except for the old sergeants and for the officers [who] were World War II vets. Now, a lot of [our] guys cut and ran . . . They fought as well as they could, then they ran because even though there was no infantry of the NKPA, [the] North Korean People's Army, they had tanks. And a lot of [our] guys . . . wound up in the rice paddies . . . They abandoned their uniforms. Some lost their boots [and were] walking around and running around in shorts . . . We had to go around driving in trucks . . . picking up the guys and driving 'em out of there. It was pretty bad.[35]

The troops who first arrived in Korea had been pulled off occupation duty in Japan and were poorly prepared to meet the buzzsaw of the North Korean forces. But the Americans fought back fiercely, and additional reinforcements allowed them to hold on to the Pusan Perimeter until the fall. Yet, the memories of the Osan onslaught remained.[36]

The Korean War unfolded differently than World War II as the Truman administration sought a limited war, remaining careful not to escalate the conflict and draw in the Soviets. The president wanted to keep the violence contained to the Korean peninsula, make sure the war remained a coalition effort of the United Nations and NATO, and maintain the ability to rearm and refit US forces and their allies. That fall, MacArthur suggested the best way to achieve the president's goals was for the Americans to launch an amphibious invasion of Incheon, on South Korea's west coast, well to the rear of the NKPA, so they could retake Seoul and cut off the enemy's supply lines. On September 15–16, 1950, MacArthur succeeded in cobbling together enough troops to fill out the US Army's Seventh Infantry and the Marine's First Division. With minimal losses, the UN forces overwhelmed the North Koreans. Meanwhile, General Walton Walker's force broke out of the Pusan Perimeter and started advancing northward. The NKPA, suffering heavy losses, retreated across the thirty-eighth parallel. The temptation to cross the thirty-eighth in pursuit proved

too great for MacArthur, who believed that the unification of Korea was
within grasp. Despite warnings from the Chinese and the Soviets to not
cross the parallel, MacArthur, buoyed by his success at Incheon, ignored
those warnings, and Truman granted permission to advance into North
Korea. On October 19, the Eighth and Tenth Armies marched north, and
the UN passed a resolution allowing troops to follow the Americans. By
November, UN forces had reached the Yalu River on the North Korean
border with China. At first, sporadic fighting broke out between the
Allies and the Chinese. MacArthur remained convinced he would win
by Christmas. However, on November 25, approximately 300,000 soldiers
of the Chinese People's Liberation Army poured across the Yalu, forcing
the Americans into a full retreat. Truman's worst fears about escalations
had just come to pass.

The men who found themselves in this harrowing position in the winter
of 1950 were regulars and reservists, men who joined the military for the
opportunity to obtain a better life. But they were now faced with equipment
shortages in an area with harsh terrain and a brutal climate. Mexican
American soldiers who were there recalled the arduous conditions. South
Texas native Eliseo Cremar, who was born on a ranch near the town of
Freer, was a member of the Second Infantry Division, Thirty-Seventh
Field Artillery Battalion that reached the Manchurian border. He recalled
that the conditions were so frigid that his toenails came off along with
his socks when he took off his boots. The men in his unit were warned
to not put warm water on their frostbitten feet or faces; still, several of
them lost their ears and noses to frostbite during the campaign. Cremar
was close to losing his feet to frostbite, but the care of a fellow Texan, a
doctor, saved them. "Sometimes I don't want to remember," Cremar noted
about his war experience.[37]

Rolando Hinojosa had been assigned to a tank reconnaissance force
after the defeat of Task Force Smith. He, too, recalled the brutal winter,
calling it "one of the coldest winters [Korea] had that century." It proved
so memorable that Hinojosa, who later used his GI Bill benefits to earn a
PhD in literature, wrote a poem about his first six months in Korea. The
winter of 1950–51 were encapsulated by this stanza:

Drive North. Encounter With
the Chinese. The Rush South.
Caught in the Pass. Defeat of
the Eighth Army.[38]

Austin native Carlos Quijano remembered his arrival at Incheon years later, recalling that his ship was covered in ice and that he and his fellow marines received gloves, wool caps, and coats, as well as heavy insulated footwear to keep their feet warm in 1952. Quijano commanded about a dozen men in a machine-gun unit.[39] Nicolas Náñez, a mine-sweeper from Laredo, also remembered the harsh winter temperatures, which ranged between thirty and forty degrees below freezing, more than half a century later. "We had a hard time [that winter] but I'm proud to have served my country," Náñez said to a local newspaper reporter at an event.[40]

After Yalu, the allied forces retreated back to the thirty-eighth parallel with the Chinese and North Koreans in pursuit. By February 1951, the lines had stabilized, and the war shifted from large-scale offensive operations to a stalemate, each side facing one another across the thirty-eighth parallel, with sporadic attacks that stretched the lines across the Korean peninsula. The fact that the war remained limited in scope frustrated MacArthur, and he openly griped about Truman's policies. By April 1951, the bombastic general penned a letter to Republicans in Congress openly criticizing the president's directives. The tension between the commander in chief and his key lieutenant had always been tense, particularly since the Chinese intervention, but this was the last straw. Truman removed MacArthur from command and promoted General Matthew Ridgeway in his place. Ridgeway helped stabilize the lines along the thirty-eighth, and his forces were now facing more than 700,000 Chinese and North Korean troops. The Americans bent but did not break, holding firm despite repeated assaults. Fighting was vicious, as armies fought for a few miles simply to claim a strategic point or gain an advantage by seizing the high ground. Both sides built fortifications that resembled the trenches of World War I and the fighting remained limited, without the use of nuclear weapons. From June 1951 to July 1953, fighting continued in this manner, with each side suffering heavy casualties.

Like World War II, the Tejano combat experience in Korea was marked by personal bravery and esprit de corps. The loss of life of comrades proved the most devastating to most soldiers. South Texas native Ernesto Sánchez recalled that he requested to go to the front lines in 1951. The twenty-three-year-old corporal, a member of the 40th Infantry Division, 223rd Regiment, knew the dangers. He wrote his girlfriend back in Laredo about the risks of combat in Korea, but he lied to his mother, telling her that he was still in Japan. But Sánchez witnessed the brutality of combat in every part of his war service, as he saw combat in the battles of No Name Hill, the Iron Triangle, and Heartbreak Ridge. He saw three of his company's commanders killed in action, one of them shot between the eyes. Yet, none of these was the most harrowing experience for him. The incident that affected him most was when several of his fellow soldiers died in a friendly fire incident, something that he still got emotional about in an interview almost sixty years later. Sánchez also remembered that killing other men proved devastating. At one point, he caught a small group of Chinese soldiers sneaking up to his camp and he opened fire, killing them. He was so shaken by the event that he went to speak to a priest who told him he had no choice, "it was you or them." Sánchez replied, "They were someone's sons." Looking back at his Korean War service, Sánchez believes he suffered from post-PTSD after every battle.[41]

Many of the Tejano Korean War veterans chose to ignore the emotional trauma and mental health struggles that the war brought on. José Luis Cantú from Laredo was drafted into the army in 1950. He and a large group of Laredo Tejanos departed the city on November 17 of that year. Cantú received an assignment with the Army Corps of Engineers at the rank of private. In Korea he served admirably, until 1952, when he was wounded, later receiving a Purple Heart for his actions in combat. Once he returned home, Cantú chose to follow a common path for the era. He was the archetype of the strong, silent type who remained resolute and stoic in the face of personal challenges and adversity. Personified by Hollywood actors like Gary Cooper and John Wayne, the idea that strong men should

José Luis Cantú Photo. Private Cantú along with numerous draftees, departed from
Laredo on November 17, 1950. Afterward, he was assigned to the Army Corps of
Engineers. While serving, Cantú was awarded a Purple Heart, but he never discussed
how he earned it with his family. Photo courtesy of the Cantú family.

be self-reliant and masculine ran deep in America's culture during the
1950s and '60s. The US Army's failures to understand the trauma of combat
and fully reject the stigma of mental illness impacted many veterans of
the war. Many of them chose to not talk about the war with anyone.[42]
According to Cantú's daughter, Sara, he had plenty of photos of his time
in the army, including a photo of the two dozen men who left Laredo in

buses after enlisting. Yet, her father never spoke about his war service after he took a job with the Texas Department of Transportation. She shrugged it off when she was growing up. Only later, when she inherited his memorabilia after his passing, did she wonder more about his service. "He never shared information regarding the acquisition of this medal," Sara Cantú noted.[43]

Carlos Quijano remembered the battlefield tension. "At night [the North Koreans] used to shoot rockets at us, and we would shoot back at them," Quijano said. "Every morning there was a sniper up on a hill. We would come up to wash our faces, and he would be waiting for us."[44] José Luis Muñoz, a mortar man and machine gunner with the Nineteenth Infantry Regiment, described the chaos of combat as an avalanche of chaos on young men. "I was eighteen years old," Muñoz remembered. "It was like a beer hall brawl during the first months of the war. The fighting was so crowded. Sometimes we would wound our own guys." Ultimately, the more salient memories stemmed from the hand-to-hand combat he experienced on the front lines at the end of 1950. "There was a Korean kid, maybe seventeen or eighteen years old. He came at me with his rifle and fixed bayonet. I tried to fight him off," Muñoz recalled. "We were both scared." Muñoz killed the enemy soldier.[45]

Tejanos held ambivalent views about their service in Korea. To some, they remained frustrated with their senior officers, whom they felt were ill-prepared to lead them to battle. Others criticized Truman's decision to remove MacArthur. Neftalí Zendejas, an Air Force mechanic from El Paso, recalled how "disappointed" he was when he heard that Truman relieved MacArthur. He was convinced that the commander in chief had made a significant mistake. The United States "would not succeed in the 'police action' in Korea after this decision," Zendejas said.[46] In contrast, his fellow El Pasoan, Arnold B. Peinado, held a positive view of his experience after easing back into civilian life and becoming a successful business owner. "We didn't face any financial or ethnicity problems," Peinado maintained. After the war, he became a successful architect.[47] Others focused on trying to make a little extra money to make ends meet so they could return home safely to their families. Eliseo Cremar earned extra cash in Korea by loaning money to his fellow soldiers during poker and gambling nights and recouped more than twice what he loaned out. He also became rather adept at doing additional work to supplement his income. Every week, for instance, he continued a moneymaking practice he started at basic training: doing his fellow soldiers' laundry for a quarter a load.[48] Sergeant Richard Moya of Austin had a more philosophical view of his service, calling his stint as the man in charge of ration breakdowns the "best job in Korea." "Everybody loves you 'cause you have the rations, their food!," Moya rationalized.[49]

The Tejanos who saw service in Korea were no different from the many Anglo and African American troops who found themselves in East Asia fighting a war they did not quite understand. Certainly, most of them saw themselves as the vanguards against communism, which seemed to be coming to knock on their front doors back in Texas. Government policy and press coverage during the Cold War certainly painted a grim image of the purported communist plan to take over the world. Laredo's Ernesto Sánchez saw his service through this prism. Sánchez was not particularly patriotic or enthusiastic about the military. He was not destitute, nor did he come from a hardscrabble background along the Texas-Mexico border. At the onset of the war, he was a college student working on his degree at Texas College of Arts and Industries in Kingsville, and he loved South Texas, and he never wanted to leave his family. Yet, all that changed when he learned of the North Korean advance across the thirty-eighth parallel. He said to himself, "Well, someone has to stop them." At that point Sánchez decided to step up and join the army.[50]

The Korean War ended with a whimper, with an armistice signed on July 27, 1953, after some sporadic fighting along the front. The stalled talks for months, the election of President Dwight D. Eisenhower and his veiled threats at escalation, as well as Stalin's death in 1953, brought both sides to the table once more. The key sticking point involved the repatriation of prisoners and whether they should be forced to return if they did not want to go back to their homeland. Ultimately, the treaty partners agreed that prisoners could stay where they were if they chose to. The war resulted in more than 33,741 Americans killed in combat and an additional 103,284 wounded. The South Koreans suffered, too, amassing nearly 600,000 casualties. Korea was divided with a demilitarized zone at the thirty-eighth parallel. Though observers were not happy with the outcome, which essentially reverted Korea to status quo antebellum, American diplomats considered the war a success because South Korea did not fall to communism.

Just as they had in the previous wars, Mexican Texans performed well, earning awards and accolades for their bravery in combat. Thirteen Latino soldiers received the Medal of Honor for their acts of bravery on the battlefield during the Korean War. Of these, four medals went to Tejanos: US Marine Corps Sergeant Ambrosio Guillén of El Paso; US Army Sergeants Victor H. Espinoza, also from El Paso, Mike C. Peña of Corpus Christi; and US Army Corporal Benito Martínez of Fort Hancock, about forty-miles from El Paso. Guillén distinguished himself by helping fend off an enemy assault near Songuch-on and forcing the enemy to retreat before he was mortally wounded. On July 25, 1953, he was fighting with his unit near the front lines. Quickly, his unit was pinned down by enemy fire and attacked by enemy battalions and mortar fire. Guillén remained steadfast as he gathered his men in the face of withering enemy fire to defend their positions and evacuate the wounded. His platoon rallied and engaged the enemy in hand-to-hand combat until the Americans forced them to retreat. In the process, Guillén received mortal wounds and died within hours. His parents were given his medal posthumously. Espinoza was a one-man battering ram against the enemy, in 1952, as he singlehandedly silenced a machine-gun crew, destroyed an enemy tunnel, and took out two enemy bunkers, allowing his unit to gain a stronghold near Chowan, Korea. He returned to El Paso after the war, and his family received his medal posthumously, in 2014. Peña earned his commendation at the Battle of Tabu-dong when he manned a machine-gun to cover his unit's withdrawal. The sergeant succeeded in holding off the enemy until the following morning, when he was killed in combat. His actions allowed his men to retreat. Just like Espinoza, he received his medal posthumously in 2014, when the White House ordered a review of overlooked army veterans from the Korean War.[51] Upon that same review, Martínez received his

Medal of Honor for fending off an enemy assault on his outpost position before being mortally wounded. Realizing that an enemy encirclement was imminent, he decided to remain at his outpost alone to delay the enemy's advance. Armed with only an automatic rifle and a pistol, Martínez delayed the enemy by about six hours, allowing his unit to withdraw.[52]

Conclusions

The Korean War, which came a mere five years after World War II, forced the Tejano community to reckon with the discrimination and the regression that marked the late 1940s. As soldiers returned from the "Good War," many felt that their state and nation ignored their sacrifice. World War II Navy veteran Joseph Alcoser, from Melvin, gave voice to that displeasure:

> I volunteered because I felt it was the only way out. My dad always said that men had an obligation to defend their country. I felt that if I went and came back things would be different. I thought there would be less discrimination. Three years later, things were exactly the same.[53]

These feelings were echoed by others who felt betrayed by the nation they fought for. Twenty-five-year old Martín Sánchez from Beeville concurred. He returned to the United States after his tour of duty in the army only to find out he was still a second-class citizen. At first, Sánchez was appreciative of the opportunities afforded by the GI Bill, which allowed him to go to barber college. He set up a small barber shop in his hometown. But Sánchez chafed at the continued discrimination. On the eve of the Korean War, he and three of his friends visited a bar in Oklahoma and recalled a waiter denying him service until he confirmed he wasn't a Native American. "There was a lot of discrimination," lamented Sánchez. He noted, too, that the Cold War and the accompanying age of conformity influenced Mexican Americans to shy away from holding from the Spanish language and Mexican culture.[54]

The discrimination did not deter Tejanos from military service in Korea. Their motives mirrored the previous twentieth century wars: patriotism, economic opportunities, pride, and, in some cases, securing a path to citizenship. Korean veterans, too, grew disenchanted with the continued discrimination of the 1950s, particularly after the Eisenhower administration's large-scale deportations of Mexican immigrants rounded up more than an estimated 1.3 million people in 1954 and set the Mexican American community on edge. The immigration roundups were well-received by the public as anti-Mexican sentiment and racial stereotypes ran rampant during the decade. Korean veteran Raúl Chavarría, who had enlisted in the army to obtain citizenship, recalled feeling nervous and apprehensive about the deportations. "En aquellos tiempos yo no viajaba muy lejos de la frontera," he said. "Le tenía miedo a la migra" (In those days, I didn't travel too far from the border. I was afraid of the Border Patrol). After the anti-immigrant hysteria weakened, Chavarría made a strong effort to learn English and assimilate.[55]

The Korean War era also inspired more stringent efforts by the Mexican American community to demonstrate patriotism and civic pride. The Cold War rivalry with the Soviet Union influenced Americans to pursue conformity with greater fervor than ever before. Many Americans adapted to mainstream culture and avoided expressing any semblance of discontent in order to uphold traditional values. The Tejano community embraced these values, particularly since they mirrored the Mexican cultural mores. The leading Mexican American civil rights organizations, LULAC and the American GI Forum, embraced these ideals that emphasized Americaniza-tion and assimilation. As they maneuvered to obtain greater rights and privileges for Mexican Americans, they were consistent in their approach that military service could carve the path to guaranteed rights under the US Constitution. Military service would, in fact, demonstrate that Mexican Americans are proud citizens who are willing to serve, fight, and die for their country. While some veterans were disenchanted by neglect and discrimination, they stood ready to answer the nation's call if needed.

CHAPTER 7

"WE PROMISED TO GET
EACH OTHER THROUGH"

The Vietnam War and Tejano Military Service

By the time the Korean War ended in 1953, the US armed forces were experiencing a massive transformation to their social, structural, and strategic makeup. Desegregation of the military under President Truman proved just the beginning of a social reckoning a long time coming, as women entered the military in the Cold War era.[1] Also, the Pentagon streamlined the draft in the wake of the Korean War, allowing for men between the ages of eighteen and thirty-five to serve and ending paternity deferments for married men. If conscripted, men would serve in the armed forces for a period of twenty-four months and an additional six-years in the reserves.[2]

With the advent of the atomic age, weapons technology assumed paramount importance. As such, the armed forces put more emphasis on finding and cultivating the brightest minds than they had in earlier conflicts, such as when semi-literate volunteers and draftees served in the World War I era. To cultivate the minds of the rank and file, the Department of Defense turned the military into a bastion of educational opportunities. The list of offerings was impressive, ranging from basic literacy to university-level classes.[3] As the military planned to fight wars with atomic weapons, missiles, helicopters, jets, and a slew of other modern technologies, the traditional soldier, enlisted for a lifetime, would be replaced by short-term volunteers and draftees who would learn new skills before reentering the civilian life.[4]

By the time of the Eisenhower administration, the US armed forces hewed to his "New Look" strategy of containing communism. The Pentagon looked to the potential use of nuclear weapons to counter Soviet-led threats across the globe while reorganizing the military and relying more on espionage and covert operations. The conventional forces of the US military would have to do more with less, as President Eisenhower believed that a large military would overburden the American economy. Expenditures for the armed forces saw a rapid decline after the Korean War armistice in 1954, when annual spending was approximately $43.4 billion. The following year, budget cuts saw spending reduced to $30.4 billion, although it inched back up to $40 billion by the end of the decade.[5] The army bore the brunt of these cutbacks in its personnel. In 1945, the US Army numbered 8.3 million soldiers. That figure dipped to 555,000 in 1948, rose to 1.6 million, in 1953, but fell back down to 500,000 in 1955.[6] To prevent another debacle like the early days of the Korean War, when troops were initially not well prepared, the army instituted Basic Combat Training, an eight-week course designed to promote physical fitness, combat skills, and socialization. The new army would see new recruits and draftees of various backgrounds, from Ivy Leaguers to the uneducated. The US military of the 1950s needed to transform its personnel to deal with the threats of nuclear war and limited conflicts with conventional forces during this trying decade.[7]

While the American military struggled with new missions and redefined war aims, the Tejano population continued to navigate the changing political, social, and economic landscape of the Lone Star State. The decade following the Korean War saw continued prejudice and discrimination. Sometimes, Tejano veterans refused to accept these vestiges of the past. World War II and Korean War veteran Armando Sánchez from El Paso recalled one time that he and an Anglo soldier went to a Texas restaurant in East Texas. They placed their orders, but the server told Sánchez he would have to eat his meal by the back door because "We don't serve Mexicans here." Sánchez's friend was incensed. "Listen, he is as much American as you are. He is U.S. Army. If you don't feed both of us, we are going to shoot up this place," as he pulled out his .45-caliber revolver. Sánchez pulled out his .45, too, and placed it on the counter. The restaurant staff immediately served both men but later called the police. "They couldn't prove anything," Sánchez recalled.[8] The foremost Mexican American civil rights organizations of the era, LULAC and the American GI Forum, railed against the remaining vestiges of discrimination and segregation during the 1950s and 1960s.

Though prejudice and discrimination remained entrenched in the state, Tejanos saw glimmers of hope. Thanks to the gains of the World War II generation and the GI Bill, more Tejanos saw hope in gaining an education. A high school diploma was now attainable, and college was no longer an impossible goal in the fifties. More Tejanos became white collar professionals such as educators, attorneys, and doctors, to name a few. Yet, access to new opportunities came at some loss for Mexican Texans, as *mutualistas* (mutual-aid societies) and Spanish-language newspapers disappeared with the advent of acculturation and assimilation. By 1960, more than 86 percent of Tejanos were born in the United States. One way Americanization was discernible was in how Mexican American civil liberty groups argued against illegal immigration from Mexico and for deportation of Mexican nationals during the federal government's so-called Operation Wetback, launched in 1954.[9] In the midst of these changes, the Tejano community continued to view military service as a way out of poverty and as a demonstration of national pride and bravery. As historian Arnoldo De León maintains, the Mexican American "GI generation" of this era was pro-democracy, pro-capitalist and committed to the American fight against communism.[10]

Border communities reflected the continuing Tejano commitment to the military. In 1949, the Truman administration created Armed Forces Day, which was to be celebrated on May 20 of the following year, to pay tribute "to all the individuals who are in the service of their country all over the world."[11] In Laredo, residents welcomed the opportunity to "honor all of America's armed forces," while in Del Rio, a hundred miles away, city leaders planned to offer public tours of Laughlin Air Force Base and to celebrate the military with picnics, parades, and luncheons.[12] In San Antonio, home to bases for the US Army and Air Force, city leaders pulled no stops as they launched a massive celebration, which included an open-house event at Randolph Air Force Base; a parade featuring the soldiers from Fort Sam Houston, veterans of past wars, civic organizations, and ROTC groups; and a jump from paratroopers of the Eleventh Airborne Division. The city, which drew great pride in its military heritage dating back to the Spanish colonial era, recognized the significance of Armed Forces Day. As photographers snapped pictures of children sitting inside airplanes, the celebrations reinforced patriotic sentiment and identification with the military.[13]

During the post–Korean War period, Tejanos' draw to the military endured. The events of the Armed Forces Day celebrations across the country only underscored the gravitational pull that military service had for Mexican Americans. As World War II and the Korean War had demonstrated, military service offered economic opportunities and functioned as a tool of Americanization. Driving the point home, Hollywood canonized the armed forces with its war movies. Actors like John Wayne and Audie Murphy, to name a few, became a de facto propaganda arm for the US armed forces in films such as *They Were Expendable* (1945) and *To Hell and Back* (1955), where they portrayed heroic soldiers fighting against evil. These 1950s films had an impact on young Mexican Americans coming of age in the post–World War II period. Jim Acevedo, a young Mexican American farm worker from Nebraska, argued that movies influenced his desire to enlist in the Marine Corps at the age of eighteen. Acevedo recollected:

> At that time, it was Mom's apple pie and the American flag. It was the thing to do. Everybody spent a tour in the military. It was all based on nationalism. It was based on the movies that we went to as a kid, your John Wayne movies . . . You see all these things, and you just kind of feel obligated to pull a tour for your country.[14]

Laredo's Mercurio Martínez shared similar memories. He was a child during World War II, but he recalled watching movies about the war. When he went to the movies during the Korean War, he remembered the impact that the newsreel war reports before the feature presentations had on him. When the Korean veterans returned home, he recalls feeling "impressed" by their accomplishments.[15]

A significant factor in influencing Mexican Americans to gravitate toward the military was family. As historian and veteran Steven Rosales demonstrates, a "generational transfer of memories during the Cold War often produced a chain reaction within Mexican American families compelled to follow in the footsteps of relatives who had served in World War II and Korea."[16] Victor Ramírez, from Del Rio, recalled that his brother's service inspired a childhood dream to enlist. "I wanted to follow my brother," Ramírez noted, "[He] instilled a lot of pride in me."[17] A family history of military service drew some men to the uniform. One Mexican American veteran, George Mariscal, of Los Angeles, illustrated this reality in a postwar interview:

[The military] was a presence, always in my family, because all my uncles had served, and my father was a World War II vet, a Marine Corps vet, and that was very important to him. We had in our garage growing up . . . two samurai swords and a Japanese flag, a blood-splattered Japanese flag, and an old M-1 rifle . . . and he always had very exotic stories about Japan . . . So it was a big thing for him and there were a lot of stories.[18]

Accordingly, Mexican American men viewed military service during the mid-twentieth century as a way of not only defending their country and gaining an opportunity for a better living, but also of upholding their family honor.

Vietnam

As the Eisenhower administration set the nation's new defense policy during the 1950s, the struggle to contain communism under the auspices of the "Domino Theory" would be put to the test. In French Indochina, reoccupied by France after nationalist leader Ho Chi Minh declared an independent Vietnam in August 1945. Eisenhower was leery of getting involved in another conflict in Asia once French efforts to gain the upper hand led to a full-scale insurgency. Yet, Eisenhower poured money into the efforts of the French government to subdue Ho Chi Minh's forces lest he be accused of being soft on communism. In 1954, when the French suffered a disastrous defeat at Dien Bien Phu and decided to abandon Vietnam, the Eisenhower administration rallied behind the South Vietnamese leader, Ngo Dinh Diem, and his efforts to resist the communists in the North. Two years later, in 1956, Diem refused to participate in a nationwide election to determine the future course for the country, which had been divided at the seventeenth parallel. When another insurgency broke out following Diem's actions, the United States felt it had little recourse but to continue to provide aid and support to the South Vietnamese government and its Army of the Republic of Vietnam (ARVN). Through the infusion of money, weapons, and military advisors to train the ARVN army, the Americans hoped this experiment in nation building would reap fruitful results.[19]

By the time President John F. Kennedy took the oath of office in January 1961, the nation continued to face various threats across the globe. To counter these communist challenges, Kennedy opted to replace Eisenhower's "New Look" with his own "Flexible Response" policy. Kennedy's idea was to counter Soviet threats proportionately. If the Soviets threatened to use nuclear weapons, the United States would counter with weapons of its own. If the communists used military troops to launch an invasion, the Americans would respond with its own conventional forces. In the case of revolution, the United States would respond with counterinsurgency forces and financial support to the endangered nation. Crises in Germany and Cuba marked the first year of the Kennedy administration, but Vietnam continued to draw attention. Kennedy sent more than 16,000 military advisors by 1963, a figure that dwarfed Eisenhower's 900 advisors. The Americans chafed at Diem's increasingly undemocratic and repressive means of holding onto power, but they remained steadfast in supporting the anticommunist leader until a military coup ousted and assassinated Diem. Kennedy's own assassination a few weeks later overshadowed the regime change and the deteriorating situation in Vietnam.[20]

After Kennedy's death, the new president, Texan Lyndon Baines Johnson, inherited a quagmire in Vietnam that countered his own domestic goals. Yet, he held firm to his predecessors' security ideas, committing aid to South Vietnam to deflect charges that he was soft on communism. As

Johnson prepared to run for election on his own right in November 1964, he continued to support covert operations against North Vietnam. On one mission, on August 2, the USS *Maddox* reportedly received fire from North Vietnamese gunboats in the Gulf of Tonkin. In response, on August 10, Congress passed the Gulf of Tonkin Resolution, which authorized the president to use conventional military forces to defend South Vietnam. The policy of containing communism opened the door to air strikes, more covert operations, and combat soldiers. By the following spring, American troops poured in. As casualties mounted, the calls for additional soldiers grew louder as US and South Vietnamese forces struggled to defeat the insurgents and the North Vietnamese Army. The president was hesitant, however, to launch such a massive ground operation and risk Chinese and Soviet intervention. Consequently, he attempted to defeat the communists by launching massive air operations against the North and a simultaneous pacification program in the South to win the hearts and minds of civilians with economic aid and support. Meanwhile, ground troops continued to arrive. By the end of 1965, the Pentagon had ordered approximately 179,000 troops to Vietnam. Without a formal declaration of war and without NATO countries willing to send troops to Southeast Asia, the Johnson administration had to shoulder the burden of war alone. The president relied on the draft to fill the ranks, hoping that a spirit of volunteerism would develop in the meantime. Foregoing the use of its trained reserve forces, the Vietnam military would rely on the conscription of young men.[21]

Service

As the war continued to escalate, Mexican Texans once more faced the choice of military service. The brothers, sons, and cousins of the World War II generation had witnessed the benefits that serving in the armed forces could bring, even if that service hadn't brought complete social equality. The main reasons Tejanos decided to sign on remained the same: patriotism, citizenship, and escape from poverty. The latter, of course, remained predominant in 1960s Texas. Castroville native Raymond García dropped out of school and enlisted in the army in 1969 because he needed to support himself economically. "My mom couldn't really support me," García said. "I was the only one left in the house, and I wanted to support her, instead of the other way around."[22] Plácido Salazar, from the Río Grande valley, echoed García's plight when he enlisted. "There was a middle class, a lower class and then there was us right below the poor people," he recalled. Recognizing the opportunity that military service could provide, he dropped out of high school a few credits shy of graduation and enlisted in the Air Force.[23] El Paso native Fernando Rodríguez, the son of two Mexican immigrants, grew up in similar circumstances As a young boy growing up on the Texas-Mexico border, he did not recognize how poor his family was. As he grew older, he came to realize his family was poorer than those of his friends. "We didn't have all the luxuries that a lot of other people used to have," Rodríguez recalled. He enlisted in the Air Force. "I didn't have any options. I knew I wasn't going to go to college because there was no money," Rodríguez pointed out.[24]

Along with these economic motives, the warrior tradition, described above by George Mariscal, still resonated. For some Mexican Texans, risking one's life for the nation and exhibiting bravery in battle proved an individual's manhood. World War II Congressional Medal of Honor recipient Silvestre Herrera, an army private who was raised in El Paso, put it bluntly: "I am a Mexican-American and we have a tradition. We're supposed to be men, not sissies." Herrera was not alone in thinking about the martial spirit of Mexican Americans. Career army veteran Humberto González later maintained that Mexican Americans had an affinity for bravery in battle. "Every platoon, every rifle [squad] had a Rodríguez or Martínez [who] was an outstanding soldier. . . . There was something about this fighting business that we ate up! Perhaps we welcomed the chance to show this nation that we were loyal, faithful, and could be depended upon given the opportunity." [25] Charley Trujillo, a sergeant in the 196th Light Infantry Brigade, confessed that there was a propensity for the "Raza" to demonstrate their manliness by walking point or carrying a large M60 machine gun.[26] Tejano Eduardo Teniente of Laredo noted that he enlisted in the Army on May 10, 1966 because of his love for the United States. Growing up in the barrio known as El Puente Blanco [the White Bridge],

Eduardo Teniente. Teniente served in the 173rd Airborne Brigade from November 24, 1966, to December 1, 1967. Photo courtesy of the Teniente family.

he and his brothers "loved the military" as they played soldier in addition to Cowboys and Indians. Years later, after graduating from Martin High School, he felt that his "country needed him to fight Communism in Southeast Asia." Not content with a regular army appointment, he felt he needed to do more. "I wanted to get into something that would test my courage," Teniente recalled, "so I asked to be an airborne paratrooper," arguably one of the most respected units in the Vietnam War.[27]

Sometimes family history and the warrior tradition were connected. Brownsville native Richard Brito had been raised in a middle-class family. His father was a prominent businessman in the city who served on the board of directors at the Brownsville First National Bank and the local school board. He also grew up in a family of veterans, including his father's cousin, who was a pilot in Mexico's 201st Fighter Squadron flying a P-47 in the Pacific theater of World War II. "In 1964, there were conversations about Vietnam, whether the likelihood of having to serve," Brito recalled. "When [President Lyndon] Johnson announced the buildup in 1965, building up Vietnam [by sending] a lot of troops over there, I remember coming home telling my wife I have to go [into] the Army. I [couldn't] be the only brother not to serve."[28] Another South Texan, José Antonio "Tony" Dodier, "didn't think twice about joining the Army" based on his father and grandfather serving in the military during World War I and World War II. When Tony enrolled at Texas A&M University, he enrolled in the Corps of Cadets and participated in the ROTC. Upon graduating, the twenty-one-year-old Dodier received a commission as a second lieutenant and became a platoon leader in the 198th Brigade, 23rd Infantry Division.[29] George Sáenz also hailed from a military family. His father was a World War II veteran and he "grew up in the VFW halls of El Paso." When he graduated from high school, he joined the Navy. "It had nothing to do with money," Sáenz explained about his reason to enlist. "I just didn't worry about that."[30] Family tradition proved important for Tejanos who joined the military during the Vietnam War era. They were the heirs of the "greatest generation," descendants of men who were forged by the trials of the Great Depression and World War II.

While the pressures of family history might weigh on the decision of individual soldiers to enlist, it was far from the only reason Mexican Texans joined the military during the Vietnam era. Like in previous conflicts, their motives remained complex. Each soldier had his own individual story behind his motives for enlisting. For instance, Corpus Christi native Nestor Rodríguez pointed to neighborhood tensions after a recent breakup with his fiancée as a motive to enlist. In 1966, shortly out of high school, he got engaged to a girl from his neighborhood. According to Rodríguez, when he called off the engagement, the situation got tense. "The neighborhood had become mobilized around the wedding," Rodríguez recalled. "People took sides, like, 'He should have married her,' or, 'No he shouldn't have.'" With his home life uncomfortable, he chose to join the army to escape.[31] Similar to Rodríguez, Houston native John Reyes enlisted in the marines to escape a recent breakup with his girlfriend. He dropped out of high school, much to the chagrin of his father, which

José M. Soto. Soto (left) served in the US Marine Corps during the Vietnam War, enlisting before he could be drafted. Photo courtesy of Javier Soto and the Soto family.

Reyes recognized was a "cowardly" way of dealing with the problems of his youth.[32] Like soldiers in previous wars, revenge also served as a catalyst for enlisting. Felipe Ramírez of Laredo had a friend killed in Vietnam in 1969; consequently, Ramírez enlisted in the army. "I wanted to go kill a couple of Vietnamese," Ramírez explained. "Back then, that was how I was thinking about war."[33] Richard Pérez of Houston opted to enlist in the Marine Corps to be able to pick his own service and go "with the best."[34] This reasoning was echoed by José M. Soto of Laredo, who chose to enlist rather than be drafted. He picked the marines "because of all the propaganda that they only take the best," recalled Soto. "I felt that I was a good candidate. I was in very good shape and I was very good in sports so I felt strong."[35] Others succumbed to the Hollywood romantic portrayal of military service and joined the armed forces to demonstrate their patriotism based on what they had seen on the silver screen.[36]

Regardless of the catalyst behind individual motives, the new recruits needed to be turned into citizen soldiers, following the traditional path of American military service since the Revolution. Draftees and volunteers alike would serve for a period of about a year in most branches (the term was thirteen months for the Marine Corps). Upon arrival, the soldiers would undergo an intense physical training regimen designed to prepare them for combat. Basic training took approximately eight weeks before troops went to Advanced Individual Training for another eight weeks. San Antonio native Raymond "Ray" Saucedo went through the army's eight-week basic training course and felt it did not prepare him for combat. He complained about training with obsolete equipment and shaky preparation. Saucedo felt "physically fit" but remained doubtful that his field training, which consisted of taking three steps and stabbing a dummy, would prepare him for actual combat in Vietnam. "They're teaching you how to kill, but that wasn't the way it was in Vietnam," he said. "You don't really see the person coming at you."[37] Veterans recalled the mundane tasks of preparing for combat while donning full gear. Soldiers ran in combat boots with rifles in hand and trained in water to prepare for jungle warfare. Laredoan Felipe Ramírez acknowledged that the training was difficult, but he had an advantage. "I was young and in shape from football. A lot of them were not in shape," he said. "Training was still tough, but I had to do it."[38]

Basic training sought to strip a soldier's civilian identity and eliminate all semblance of individualism. Yelling, hazing, sleep deprivation, and mundane tasks all marked the training camp experience.[39] For some Tejano soldiers, particularly those from the border, there was also the initial culture shock of being thrust together with people from varied backgrounds. El Paso native Adam Nieto recollected how different his basic training camp life was. "Well, being from El Paso, being around—I thought the whole world was Mexican. So when I went to basic training, I look around and said, Where's the Mexican guys?," he chuckled.[40] Others were just happy to escape the poverty that they were accustomed to. "I didn't know you were supposed to eat three meals a day," said Adán Daniel Arrellano, joking about his lower-class upbringing near Austin.[41] Army recruit Nestor Rodríguez, recalled the difficulties of training camp, but he came out stronger. "I was terrified. Maybe I cried. I was scared. But slowly we kind of bonded in basic training," Rodríguez said.[42]

The Ground War

After training camp, the troops traveled to Southeast Asia to engage the insurgent communist forces that threatened to topple South Vietnam. Since 1965, Johnson and his advisors had tried to balance a gradual increase of American military pressure on the enemy while making strong efforts to not alienate Western allies and or bring on Chinese or Soviet intervention. While American airstrikes increased in intensity as part of this gradualist approach to the war, ground troops continued to pour into the country. Through this strategy, Washington hoped to bring the North Vietnamese to the negotiating table. To that end, in 1966, American military manpower in Vietnam had increased to approximately 385,000 men. The following year, troop levels reached 485,000. Despite these significant increases, Johnson's military advisors wanted additional men and suggested mobilizing the National Guard and the Reserves, an action that the president saw as a bridge too far. The army and the marines would just have to win this war with their overstretched manpower.[43]

The Marine Corps used various pacification programs, such as the Combined Actions Program, while in South Vietnam. The US Army, on the other hand, favored large-scale operations to find and kill enemy forces. These so-called search-and-destroy operations were designed to demonstrate American superiority in weapons and technology to exact ghastly death tolls on the enemy and win the war by attrition. From 1965 to 1969, the army followed this strategy of seeking the enemy and inflicting heavy casualties on the National Liberation Front (South Vietnamese communists) and North Vietnamese troops took center stage. Yet only 10 percent of all those "search-and-destroy" missions actually found the enemy. While US military forces did, in fact, inflict horrific losses on enemy forces, the strategy ultimately failed to secure South Vietnam.[44]

The failures of American military strategy did not lessen the horrors of combat for the troops during their tour of duty. Two salient features mark

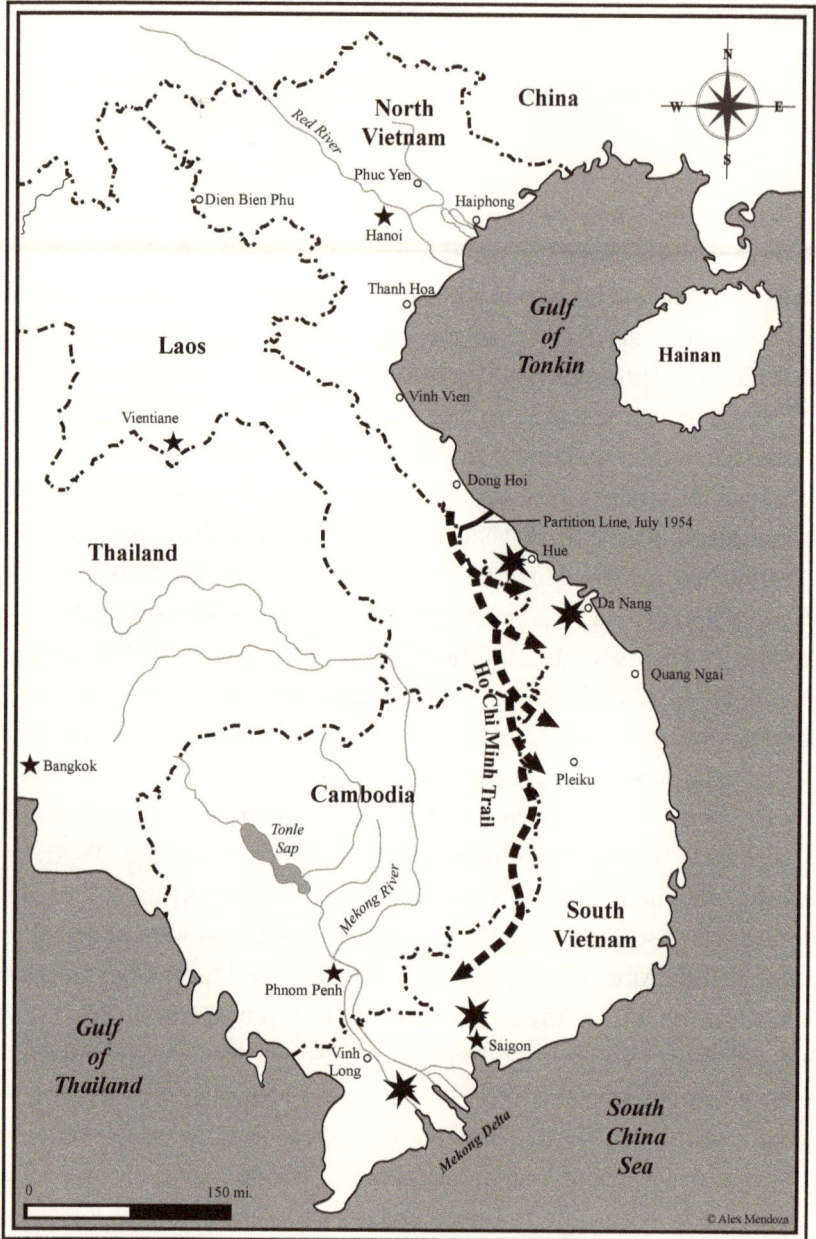

The Vietnam War

the American war experience in Vietnam. The first was the horror of combat, the brutality of war. The second was how long those memories lasted. Fred Castañeda, who was drafted into the army in 1970, maintained that combat seemed to numb him after his first engagement with the enemy. "You now know what combat is like, and you've seen the brutality and experienced the sheer terror," Castañeda recalled. "This is what is called the thousand-yard stare" he said when looking at a wartime photo of him in an apparent daze.[45] Tejano soldiers often remarked that the confusion of strategy and tactics and the difficulty of locating and identifying the enemy proved extremely stressful. "The thing I remember about Vietnam was a lot of uncertainty and confusion," José Antonio Dodier recalled. "At times, we questioned what we were doing." Yet, Dodier and other soldiers relied on one another to persevere. "We are going to get each other through this," he remembered repeating to himself and his comrades as a sort of mantra. "'We are here to take care of each other; we will look out after each other.'"[46] That sense of camaraderie was not unique to Vietnam. It upheld enduring values of loyalty and kinship shared by the rank and file. This experience was common to the American military, as veterans and historians have often cited the importance of group cohesion and camaraderie to explain the willingness to fight and the numerous acts of bravery in the face of the terrifying madness of combat.[47] "We promised to get each other through," Dodier recalled about his wartime experience in a postwar interview. "I promised."[48]

An additional source of stress was dealing with the excess number of landmines and improvised explosive devices found in booby traps while soldiers searched for the enemy. Soldiers encountered these booby traps everywhere on patrol—in rice fields, in villages, in the jungles, hidden beneath corpses, laid against food rations, in huts, and in tunnels. The effects of a simple tripwire and hook could prove devastating to a platoon of men searching for the enemy. "Nothing could prepare you for the sight of the mangled bodies," one combat nurse recollected.[49] Bernardino "Ben" Sáenz of Houston still remembered his experience with land mines decades after the war. One time, Sáenz and a close friend were on a "search-and-destroy" mission, when his fellow soldier stepped on a land mine. The explosion killed his comrade instantly and threw Sáenz fifty feet in the air. Since he was covered in blood and unresponsive, his platoon mates thought that he was also dead. It took a few minutes for his fellow soldiers to understand that Sáenz was only stunned and covered in the friend's blood, rather than his own. "The birds started coming and eating the flesh" of his friend, Sáenz recalled. "So, we started shooting the birds . . . to this day I still remember that."[50]

Booby traps proved nerve-racking for all who encountered them. One day in 1969 when out on patrol, a Mexican American soldier, David Valladolid, serving as a combat radio operator for the 199th Light Infantry Brigade, saw a dead North Vietnamese soldier with grenades attached to his body. He reported it to his superiors, but he and his comrades received orders to remove and detonate the grenades so they could not harm additional US troops. As the soldiers approached the body, Valladolid noticed a formation of stacked rocks near the body. Recognizing it as a warning for explosives used by enemy troops, he yelled at his friends to stop. But it was too late. A booby trap exploded and sent the other soldiers flying through the air. Valladolid was badly hurt as his eardrums were blown out and his eyesight damaged from the blast. After three surgeries, with no guarantees he would ever see again, he regained his eyesight and hearing.[51]

American troops also agonized over the unconventional guerrilla war that replaced large-scale operations. Unlike the world wars, which saw soldiers fighting enemy units and holding established front lines, the war in Vietnam was characterized by hit-and-run raids, ambushes, and chaos. Battles ended as quickly as they broke out, and soldiers were left without an enemy they could easily track down and kill, as insurgents simply melted away into the countryside. Alpine native Eduardo Fierro noted this difference in a postwar account: "Mostly in WWII, Korea, when you went and fought out and you were in a battle, you always had a front. It was territory that you had gained. You left your troops there and that was in control of the U.S.," said Fierro. "In Vietnam, it was a completely different situation because they would take you out to fight a village. You would fight the Viet Cong [South Vietnamese communists] in the village, and then they would pull you out and you wouldn't have control of the village. So the

Viet Cong overnight would go ahead and reinfiltrate into that (village). . . .
In a sense, why fight them there in the first place?"[52] The uncertainty of
not being able to readily locate the enemy frustrated many of the troops.
"Jungle warfare was more than difficult," Valladolid recalled in a postwar
account. "We were taking enemy fire, being ambushed and exposed to
a number of enemy land mines. I witnessed atrocities and vowed that I
never again would be in a situation where somebody could control me,
tell me what to do, when to do it and how to do it."[53]

The uncertainty wore on the men. "Day to day, you didn't know if
you were going to live or die," said Ben Sáenz, an infantryman in the
US Army. "You hardly ever saw any of the enemy. You knew they were
there because they were shooting at you. After the firefight, we would
go out there and see blood trails. That's what a grunt's life was," Sáenz
maintained.[54] The unpredictability of the ambush frazzled many men. On
March 25, 1967, the marines in Antonio Flores Alvarado's company were
on a cleanup operation, marching in a straight line about halfway across
an open field, when they received enemy fire. With nowhere to hide, the
marines hit the ground. Their sergeant told them to get up and move
forward. Soon thereafter, the enemy fired a mortar round that exploded
about ten meters away. Alvarado suffered a leg wound that kept him in
the hospital for nearly two weeks. Several marines were killed in that
engagement, and more than half a dozen wounded. "A machine gunner's
eyes hung out of his head," recalled Alvarado.[55] Eddie Reyes of Dallas had
a similar experience. In June 1970, Reyes had been in combat for seven
months. But one day, his platoon was mistakenly fired upon by American
artillery, who would regularly saturate particular geographic areas with
artillery rounds before troops were deployed on the ground. "Somebody
got the time wrong, and as soon as we got off of the helicopters, the shells
started coming in," Reyes said. "That whole moment stays burned in your
memory forever. The smell. The sound."[56]

The horrors of combat remained so pronounced that many soldiers
felt guilty for merely surviving the various engagements they participated
in. José Dodier survived stepping on a mine while on patrol with his
platoon. Though he felt his men were in a precarious position, exposed

to the enemy, Dodier's superiors told him to forge ahead, nonetheless. The platoon walked into a minefield that shattered his unit. After being airlifted to safety, he remembered that he was never the same. "I became very quick-tempered after I came back and could never understand why. Especially when people don't listen to what I say," Dodier maintains.[57] Tejano infantryman Sergeant Daniel Hinojosa confirmed the effects of war in describing his PTSD. "I have crazy dreams," Hinojosa mentioned in a postwar interview. "Sometimes for days, I only sleep an hour or two. I get very antsy, very panicky sometimes."[58] Tejano veterans tried their best to cope with the return to civilian life after the war. Some succeeded more than others. Jesús Zamora of El Paso struggled after the war. At one point in his life, he would buy cheap cars and go crash them in the demolition derbies. He felt it helped him cope with the anxiety and the nightmares he suffered from after Vietnam.[59]

Others were impacted by the death of a close friend in their unit. Corporal Alvarado, for instance, recalled that after one battle, snipers wreaked havoc on his platoon, killing twenty-two of thirty men. Alvarado tried to save his injured friend, Roland Lee Lyvere, by pulling him to a safe place, but to no avail. Lyvere succumbed to his injuries and died. Alvarado noted how "deeply that death affected him."[60] Eduardo Fierro recalled that he felt survivors' guilt after the war. Fierro, who had his right arm amputated after a horrific attack in May 1968, struggled to cope after surviving an attack that killed many other soldiers. "I had too many flashbacks from the war in Vietnam," said Fierro.[61]

Laredoan Eduardo Teniente noted that the memories of his friend and fellow soldier in the 503rd Airborne, Ignacio "Nacho" Torres, remained strong more than thirty years after the war. The two young men hailed from the same neighborhood on the Texas-Mexico border. "It was a very heart-lifting experience to see each other in a faraway land. We were from the same neighborhood and went to the same high school," Teniente recalled. The two men bonded singing Tejano songs in the jungles of Vietnam, half a world away. "Now we are really going to end this war," Torres told Teniente at one point. Despite being together in many firefights, a battle near Dak To, in November 1967, ended Torres's life. Teniente also felt survivors' guilt, holding on to a letter that Torres wrote to his sister for decades and not being able to meet with Torres's parents because of the harsh pain it would bring. "I want to go and pay my respects to the parents of my friend," Teniente said. "Hopefully, with God's help, my nightmares will continue fading away and I can finally say farewell to a fellow Laredoan, Martinite, friend and Sky 'Soldier.'"[62]

As soldiers fought an enemy they could not find or understand, many displayed individual sacrifice and heroism in Vietnam, though not everyone received a medal or commendation. Perhaps no one exemplified the notion of laudable pride and bravery like Raúl "Roy" Pérez Benavidez of Cuero, Texas. Born of Mexican and Yaqui Indian descent, Benavidez moved to El Campo after his parents died at an early age. Like many Tejanos of that era, Benavidez dropped out of school as a teenager and worked a variety of labor-intensive jobs until he joined the army in 1955. Frustrated by racial discrimination, Benavidez vowed to master English and improve his lot in life. He changed his name from Raúl to Roy and strived for an education. Master Sergeant Benavidez left for Vietnam in 1965 to serve as an advisor for the ARVN. He was wounded shortly thereafter when he stepped on a landmine. Nevertheless, he returned to active duty three years later to earn a Distinguished Service Cross for his bravery during a firefight near Loch Ninh on May 2, 1968. Benavidez exposed himself to enemy fire while rescuing comrades and retrieving vital documents left in a helicopter that had carried American troops to action. Benavidez received thirty-seven wounds and fought off enemy soldiers in hand-to-hand combat. Army doctors initially thought he was dead and placed him in a body bag. Benavidez had to spit blood in their faces to show them he was still alive. Surviving his wounds, Benavidez received the Congressional Medal of Honor years later. In his later years, Benavidez toured the country giving speeches on honor, bravery, and patriotism. He ultimately became arguably the most celebrated Tejano war veteran, as his image was used for a *G.I. Joe* action figure and his name used for schools and US naval vessels. Benavidez even had a commemorative US Postal Service stamp in his honor. He published two autobiographies describing his rise from poverty to war hero.[63]

Benavidez may have been the most popular Tejano to serve in Vietnam, but he was not the only Mexican Texan who distinguished himself for bravery. US Marine Corps Sergeant Alfredo "Freddy" González of Edinburg and Corporal Miguel Keith of San Antonio earned the Medal of Honor for their actions in Vietnam. In both cases, the two men received mortal wounds while in battle; their Medals of Honor awarded posthumously. Both men received additional honors, including the naming of schools, buildings, and González's case, a US naval destroyer, the USS *Gonzalez*. Tejanos earned three of the seventeen Medal of Honor awards given during the conflict. Isaac "Ike" Camacho, a native of El Paso, was captured by the South Vietnamese communists in November 1963 after a skirmish and remained a prisoner for twenty months until he escaped in July 1965, receiving the Silver Star and the Bronze Star for his actions.[64] Sonora native Juan Carlos González received the Bronze Star with Valor for his service during the Tet Offensive. González, who saved the life of fellow soldiers during the assault, offered a poignant response about why he put his life in harm's way for another soldier: "It is every soldier's job to take care of their own."[65]

Some soldiers received awards posthumously. Corsicana native Candelario García braved enemy fire when he charged two machine gun bunkers to protect his fellow soldiers and then rejoined his company to continue the assault against the enemy. Observers felt it was an act worthy of the Medal of Honor. Yet, García never received that honor. He died in his hometown in 2013, suffering from PTSD and alcoholism. In 2014, President Barack Obama corrected that omission when he ordered that García and twenty-three others receive the Medal of Honor, noting that it was discrimination against Latinos, Jews, and African Americans that kept them from receiving their proper accolades. The message was well received by García's family. García's younger brother, Manuel Flores, said Candelario won just about every other award, including a Purple Heart and the Distinguished Service Cross. It was fitting, he said, because García's own father died in World War II in France. "My brother was an American hero," Flores said with pride.[66]

Acts of bravery notwithstanding, Tejano soldiers did not face battle alone and interacted with people from different geographic areas and backgrounds. Sometimes, this led to friction based on old stereotypes and discrimination. Charley Trujillo, a Mexican American soldier whose family came from Sweetwater, noted that the racial hostilities could be tense. "[It was] a whole melting pot of the working class of the United States. And then you [had] these honky guys from the South that [were] sympathetic to the Ku Klux Klan . . . Everybody carried knives!"[67] San Antonio native Daniel M. Hinojosa was all too familiar with discrimination and was not surprised to encounter it in the military soon after he was drafted into the army. "It was nothing new," Hinojosa recollected. "Very few guys really had choices, and those who did have choices were not Latino or Black and that was very visible."[68] Mexican American servicemen found themselves as the middle group in the recently integrated military. The initial encounters with racism and discrimination occurred at basic training. Frank Reyes described one such encounter at Fort Benning, Georgia. "We went to the movies [on base] and that night we were confronted by about four or five white guys . . . They kept calling me 'beaner' and all kinds of things . . . But we walked away, and they didn't."[69] In some cases, Tejano soldiers remained helpless when they were discriminated against by their own officers. Plácido Salazar had received a recommendation for a bronze star for saving the life of a fellow soldier. Unfortunately, a colonel destroyed the recommendation paperwork, according to Salazar. "This colonel didn't know me and I did not know him, but only because I was a Mexican, he ripped the nomination to pieces," Salazar recounted.[70]

Others noted simple pranks and stereotypes. John Sánchez, for instance, despised being called "Speedy Gonzales," the cartoon character who was supposedly the fastest "Mouse of all Mexico." But he made it a point to let his displeasure known, and the behavior ultimately stopped. Others like Adam Nieto simply chose to ignore discrimination and nip it in the bud. "Discrimination. I guess, it does exist everywhere, every day, in any place, but if you just ignore it, I guess, or—because the more attention you paid [to] it, the deeper you go into the hole," he reminisced.[71] When troops were transferred to Vietnam, the behavior generally improved, as soldiers had to rely on unit cohesiveness and camaraderie in a hostile land.[72]

Not every Tejano felt the sting of intolerance. Some avoided discrimination altogether based on what they looked like. Rolando Ríos, for instance, claimed that he was aware of discrimination, but it seemed to skip him because he looked white. "I saw it a lot, but I was kind of treated a little different because I didn't look Hispanic," said Ríos. "It was kind of like [being] inside looking out, but not experiencing a lot of what my friends did."[73] Richard Brito had similar memories. "For me, [racial discrimination] was not a particularly significant issue," Brito said. "I'm sure in some people's minds it was, but I was never aware of it."[74] Oscar García remembers his service in much the same way "Everyone was affected the same," García recalled about experience in Southeast Asia. "There was [*sic*] no Latinos, there was no blacks, there was no whites in the military. We all bleed red, and we all go through the same hardships together."[75]

Soldiers also noted how discrimination seemed to dissipate when they served in Vietnam but returned when they came back stateside. Waco native John Aleman recalled that discrimination was a part of his daily life prior to his service. He went to college, earned a degree, and joined the Air Force rather than wait to be drafted into the army. As the lone Mexican American airman who went to officer training school, he remembers how the military afforded him the "same opportunities as everyone else." When he left the service and returned to Texas, he found that discrimination remained prevalent as he struggled to rent a home and return to civilian life. As a former Air Force officer, Aleman found this contrast "humiliating and contrary to his idea of American culture."[76] Uvalde native Sergio Porras, who was a Chicano activist in his hometown, experienced the sharp edge of bias and discrimination prior to joining the military. While serving, he noted no such prejudice. But when he returned home, he found biases persisted. "There still is discrimination in Uvalde, but it's less visible," he recollected.[77] While some men in uniform dealt with acts of discrimination from their fellows and superiors, a more insidious form of bias was built into the draft. Conscription, which was based on the Selective Service Act of 1948, was not without its problems.

Local draft boards determined which young men would be conscripted into service. The draft boards of the 1960s were mostly white and tended to defer white, middle-class men, opting instead to draft poor, working-class minorities. According to historian Geoff Wawro, of the 27.5 million Americans eligible only 1.7 million would be drafted and sent to Vietnam. Draft boards exempted college students, those with family hardships, and those who opted for the clergy or missionary work. Those who went to fight were disproportionately poor. Although African Americans made up only 11 percent of the population, they made up more than 20 percent of the combat troops in Vietnam. Hispanics, though no longer tabulated by ethnicity and lumped in with the white troops, may have made up as much of 20 percent of all combat troops (80,000–100,000 men).[78]

The various exemptions and deferments allowed middle- and upper-class families to avoid service. The exemption for college students placed the burden on working-class families who could not afford college. Certain jobs also kept some men from being drafted. Teachers, public officials, and those who held critical government jobs were among those who received deferments. While married men with children were also supposed to be excluded, some Mexican American draftees found no such latitude. In 1969, Mexican American draftee Tony Moreno was recently married and with a newborn son, but he failed to obtain an exemption. "I had to go, and I went . . . I [also] think it had a lot to do with being a minority, being Hispanic," he observed, "because there was a lot of people that I knew that were white that didn't have to go . . . probably 'cause they knew people and we didn't."[79] West Texan Robert Lee Polanco also failed to receive consideration for exemption when he was drafted in 1970, despite being recently married with a newborn daughter.[80] The Vietnam War thus received the reputation of being a "working-class war." Those with affluence and social connections could influence local draft boards or obtain doctor's recommendations to avoid military service. People without wealth and connections had to fight in Vietnam, regardless of race or ethnicity. In past wars, Tejanos avoided military service by fleeing to Mexico and escaping conscription. Certainly, in the late 1960s, some felt ambivalent about fighting a war that they did not understand. Richard Manríquez of

Houston resented the idea of the government sending him to fight a war to spread democracy, a concept he cared little about. When he received his draft notice, he reported for duty as directed. Later, when he stood waiting for his plane to training camp, his mother approached him with an offer. She insisted on walking with him alone on the tarmac. Once they were together, she pulled out an envelope with $40,000 in cash and a plane ticket to Mexico. She implored her son not to go to Vietnam. "Son, this is not your war," she told him. Manríquez was taken aback, but he remained committed to seeing his service. He boarded his plane to Southeast Asia. "I am not a draft dodger," he explained.[81] Others tried to avoid the draft by going to a *curandero* (faith healer or shaman) to see if they could help them fail the physical exam. Reportedly, that worked for one draftee.[82]

By the late 1960s, the growing Chicano movement in California and the Southwest challenged the idea of a loyal and faithful population of Mexican Americans that would remain docile. In fact, the new wave of Chicano leaders focused their attention on various injustices. Among one of their criticisms was the disproportionate number of Mexican Americans who died in the conflict. In one case study, figures revealed that 66 percent of San Antonio's casualties in 1966 had Spanish surnames even though the city's total population of Tejanos stood at 41 percent. Tejanos also noted that no Mexican Americans sat on draft boards despite the fact that they composed more than 50 percent of the population in some areas of the Río Grande valley.[83]

Conclusions

In all, more than 2.7 million Americans served in Vietnam. Out of those, 47,364 were killed in action. Texas claimed 3,450 of the dead. Of the 8,167 soldiers from Texas, Arizona, New Mexico, and California who suffered casualties between 1961 and 1969, 19 percent were deemed of Hispanic descent, a figure higher than the 11.8 percent of the population Hispanics made up in those four states. In Texas, out of the 3,450 killed, 777 had Spanish surnames, a figure that represents 22 percent of the total figure, which was slightly higher than the Tejano representation in the Lone Star State's population in 1970.[84]

The high casualty counts had little impact on the leading Mexican American civil rights organizations in Texas, as LULAC and the American GI Forum rallied behind the American war effort in Vietnam. For instance, War II veteran and LULAC activist, John J. Herrera, a native of Houston, approved of the war to stop communism. Héctor P. García, the founder of the American GI Forum, concurred, contending that "the majority if not the total Mexican-American people approve of the present course of action in Vietnam." In 1968, the organization even sponsored a tour to shore up support for the war among Mexican American families. García even collected letters from soldiers in Vietnam describing their support for the war. In one letter, Texan S. B. Sánchez spoke of the need to be a "good citizen" and argued that the war was America's responsibility as a "great country." Sánchez maintained that it was necessary to go to war "to defend our freedom and heritage." The feelings Sánchez expressed echoed those of Benavidez, who later said that he fought as a proud American.[85] The themes of nation and patriotism continued to resonate loudly with the Tejano community. "Latinos fought, and they never complained when it came time for them to fight," said Fred Castañeda. "They didn't do it because they wanted to be brave. It just had to be done."[86]

Yet, the conversation about military service shifted in the 1960s and 1970s. Dallasite Eddie Reyes admitted that he went into the war with a "blind sense of patriotism," but his feelings began to change when he left the army.[87] The Chicano movement, which leaned into the previously disparaging term, *Chicano*, which was a slur against anyone of Mexican descent, developed a more militant approach to fighting against persistent racism. A new civil rights movement had emerged, and it questioned the Mexican American devotion to the principles of integration and assimilation. Chicanos/as denounced US institutions, and the more radical elements of the movement broached the idea of separatism, an antithetical premise to those who aspired to the American dream. The emerging movement rejected the assimilation efforts of older civil rights organizations like LULAC and the American GI Forum. *El movimiento* embraced the Mexican and indigenous roots of Mexican Americans.

This meant that they identified more with the invaded people of Vietnam than they did with the invaders and more actively resisted the discrimination that persisted into the Vietnam War era.[88] Chicano activists protested the political and social constructs that continued to hamper the Mexican American community. In Texas, they walked out of schools, marched in protest to gain political rights, and held labor strikes to object lower wages.[89]

However, protests by the Mexican American community in Texas against the military establishment or against military service remained subdued. The Tejano community seemed to understand that military service provided social and political gains during the civil rights era. As historian Lorena Oropeza maintains, the GI Forum kept a tally of the Mexican American casualties as a means of highlighting the "ethnic group's sacrifices on behalf of the war effort."[90] Initially, Chicano activists critiqued the war on humanitarian grounds and generally eschewed antiwar dissent. Yet, as the antiwar movement gained traction across the country by the late 1960s, Chicanos in Texas no longer hesitated to criticize the war directly. In October 1969, Mario Compean, the chairman for the Mexican American Youth Organization, spoke out against the war, and to "give up all this patriotic [obscenity]."[91] The fact that a leader of the Mexican American community had shunned the notion of patriotism, a cornerstone of military service for Tejanos for the last fifty years, resonated deeply. For many Tejanos, the war in Vietnam inspired them to become more politically active due to their experiences in the war. After the war, men like Eduardo Cavazos Garza joined La Raza Unida Party in South Texas, an alternative to the two major parties.[92] Others simply paid more attention to politics and social justice in the wake of their military service. "We weren't really political because, during that time, especially in those small towns, they didn't teach us anything about Vietnam," recalled one Mexican American veteran. "It was just the war was there, it was on TV, and they make more *escándalo* [fuss] about little incidents now than they did about Vietnam in many ways."[93]

Ultimately, the Tejano war experience in Vietnam demonstrated the growing visibility of the Mexican American community. According to the US Federal Census, by 1970, the Tejano population was estimated at approximately two million, about 20 percent of Texas's total population, spread throughout the state. This growth meant diversity within the Tejano community as well as in the military experience. For some, the war meant the Stars and Stripes and a family tradition of serving in the armed forces. For others, it was a means to escape their prewar lives, whether it be poverty, strife, or even a relationship. To be certain, many of those who were drafted felt they had no alternative but to report for duty rather than live with the stigma of being a draft dodger. Importantly, Tejanos were no longer labeled disloyal, cowardly, or questioned about their motives as they had been in previous wars. Rather, they had become part of the American experience, for better or for worse. The war's failures had nothing to do with the collapse of the individual soldier or their want of bravery. Tejanos fought for themselves and for the men next to them. When they returned home, they tried to reintegrate back into society as best they could and tried to manage the memories of war as they saw fit. Dallas Tejano Eddie Reyes believed it was the love of his family that pulled him through. "If it wasn't for the love of our families, I don't think half of us would have survived," Reyes said. "You know how Latinos are. We hug. We kiss . . . I think what really saved me was the love of my family."[94]

CONCLUSION

In Laredo, on July 4, 2004, city officials, veterans of past wars, and other local dignitaries gathered to unveil a statue and consecrate a memorial plaza to recognize the forty-one Hispanic veterans who had received the Congressional Medal of Honor, the nation's highest award for military service. After gathering at the site of the plaza, near the International Bridge II and downtown Laredo, attendees took turns taking photos of the monument on its granite pedestal as they consumed Mexican *pan dulce* (sweet bread) adorned with red, white, and blue decorations. Local leaders made speeches about the long-standing legacy of Tejano patriotism and valor, as reflected by the military service of Hispanic veterans from the Civil War to Vietnam. Local leaders insisted on the Fourth of July holiday for the ceremony, moving up its dedication from the originally planned Veterans Day in November.

The theme of American patriotism rang loud at the celebration. Ironically, though, the attendees stood in the shadow of a three-hundred-foot-tall Mexican flag that flew a few hundred yards to the south on the south bank of the Río Grande. In response, the city of Laredo erected a gigantic version of the US flag. This massive Stars and Stripes has flown over Laredo since the 1990s and is among the tallest in the country. Approximately two hundred Laredo dignitaries and their guests celebrated the unveiling of the bronze statue of World War I hero David Barkley Cantú, whose Tejano heritage remained unknown for over half a century after his death. Despite the initial excitement, the monument and its location soon fell into disrepair. Twenty years later, local leaders moved the site of the monument and memorial to the nearby Laredo Community College, once the site of Fort McIntosh, due to the decrepit conditions of the original site.[1]

Barkley Cantú Memorial, 2010. In 2003, the city of Laredo commissioned local artist Armando Hinojosa to build a memorial to honor all Hispanic Medal of Honor recipients. Perched atop of the monument is a statue of local Tejano World War I veteran David Bennes Barkley (Cantú), who posthumously received the Medal of Honor for his actions in the Great War. The names of all Hispanic Medal of Honor recipients are engraved in a plaque on the base of the memorial. Author photo.

Laredo was not alone in its civic celebration of Mexican American servicemen. Four years after the unveiling of the memorial to Hispanic Congressional Medal of Honor recipients, El Paso unveiled its own public monument dedicated to its famed Company E, the US Army's first and only unit composed entirely of Mexican Americans. Located in south-central El Paso, about a quarter mile north of the Río Grande, the memorial stood in the middle of a large recreational park, surrounded by warehouses and small residential homes. The memorial was an eight-by-fourteen-foot wall with bronze plaques on either side. On one side, a bronze engraving showed the men of Company E crossing the Rapido River in Italy. A bronze helmet placed at the wall's base stood as a

The Barkley Cantú Memorial Statue in its new location on the Laredo College campus in 2024. Due to neglect, the memorial to honor Hispanic Congressional Medal of Honor recipients was moved to the Laredo College campus almost twenty years after it was first unveiled. The granite plaque commemorating the names of all Hispanic Medal of Honor recipients received a permanent crack during the move. Author photo.

stark reminder of the soldiers' sacrifice. The opposite side displayed four bronze plaques, which contained a list of all the members of the company from El Paso. The memorial struck a chord with many neighborhood residents since most of the men hailed from that part of the city. The park, later renamed World War II Veterans Park, served as a reminder of the service of the Tejano troops.

After a few years, some El Paso residents grumbled that the memorial had little to no visibility. The Tejano heroes needed more. "We have to remember them," El Paso Mayor Dee Margo told the *El Paso Times*. Accordingly, a decade after the dedication of the first monument, city officials ordered a new one, which was to be located in the more tourist friendly downtown area, near the new Mexican American Cultural Center. Unveiled in 2022, the new monument was an eight-by-fourteen-foot bronze statue atop a large marble base. The statue was entitled *The Treacherous Crossing*, and depicts three GIs crossing the Rapido, pulling a wounded soldier across. A new and updated plaque includes more names than the original memorial. "After World War II, these guys proved they were just as American as anybody else and many died serving this country," said Martín Luna, one of the organizers of the push for a second monument and descendant of Company E veteran First Sergeant Lorenzo M. Luna.[2]

Both the Laredo and El Paso commemorations emphasized patriotism and bravery. Yet, amid the flag waving and the patriotic rhetoric, attendees never paused to consider the shifting views of nationalism as in relation to the history of Tejano military service. Tejano military service up to the World War I era often had less to do with patriotism than the soldiers' local allegiances and desires to defend their homes, escape from peonage, find adventure, and gain socioeconomic improvement. By the mid-twentieth century, Mexican Texans found additional motives for their decisions to fight. Among these were patriotism and the desire to refute their relegation to second-class status. Adding to the complexity of their motivations, many Tejanos were also encouraged to join the military to demonstrate their "warrior tradition," the idea that through battle, the rights to citizenship could be confirmed. In essence, by the Second World War, Tejanos who joined the military shed their "Mexicanist" identity and adopted the characteristics of American nationalism. These sentiments would only be expanded during the Cold War–era conflicts in Korea and Vietnam.

The complexity of Tejano military service is an evolving story that contributes to the rich fabric of American military history. Tejanos participated in four major wars and several other smaller conflicts in the nineteenth century. Throughout these wars the Mexican Texan population maintained a sense of ambivalence. During the Texas Revolution, for instance, some Tejanos identified with the rebels due to shared economic and political concerns.[3] Others remained loyal to Mexico because it was part of their cultural history. Other Tejanos tried to remain neutral during the conflict's early stages, perhaps hoping to later align themselves with the winning side. There were varying degrees of loyalty, which moved beyond supporting or rejecting the Texas secession movement. As historian Raúl Ramos notes, interpretations of Tejano identity need to consider the "multiple roles played by Tejanos and their underlying position as mediators in a culturally complex place."[4]

These same sentiments were evident as Texans participated in the Mexican-American War (1846–48), the American Civil War (1861–65), the Spanish-American War, and other conflicts in the nineteenth century. The Tejano population's participation in these conflicts would be influenced by the fact that Mexican Texans maintained a bicultural identity that remained loyal to both American and Mexican nationalities. A third group of Tejanos during the nineteenth century even considered themselves *libres fronterizos* (free border people), an identity that transcended national loyalties and emphasized the inviolability of individual autonomy and liberty. This identity was one in which true loyalty was to the region along the Río Grande and not the nation-states with their flags and national symbols.[5]

This notion of a bicultural identity was clearly lost on the Anglo-American majority, particularly after the Mexican-American War. Yet, in the struggle for peace and security, Tejanos chose to define their identities and loyalties. There are multiple narratives to consider when dealing with people who straddle a borderland. The fact that Tejanos had lived in a contested area forced them to regularly move from one classification system to another. For instance, in Laredo, on the north

Company E Memorial in El Paso's World War II Memorial Park, 2019. Author photo.

bank of the Río Grande, the border between Mexico and the United States after the Treaty of Guadalupe Hidalgo, Tejano city leaders petitioned former Texas Republic President Mirabeau M. Lamar, the American military commander in the city at the time, to allow the city to remain part of Mexico. Lamar was dumbfounded. He could not understand why anyone would be willing to reject living under the American system. Laredoans had "enjoyed the greatest liberty, prosperity, and peace under the laws and institutions of the United States," Lamar scolded the leading Laredo Tejanos who wrote the petition. Lamar's view of national loyalty was framed around his belief that Laredo had been part of Texas since 1836 and had prospered since the Americans' arrival at the onset of the Mexican-American War. It was a narrow view that defined identity and nationalism in stark, black-and-white terms.[6]

Tejano enlistment in that conflict and the Civil War remained minimal. In the Mexican-American War, as more than 8,000 Texans volunteered,

Company E Memorial in downtown El Paso, 2024. In the previous years, The city of El Paso has moved the memorial from a park in a residential neighborhood to a more centralized location downtown, near a minor league baseball stadium.
Photo courtesy of Gilbert Contreras.

only a few Tejanos volunteered to fight, mostly serving in the capacity of guides and spies. The majority of the Tejano population chose to await the outcome of the latest hostilities, as less than two dozen Spanish-surnamed volunteers served in the ranks of Texas forces, all of them in the enlisted ranks.[7]

A similar trend was found during the Civil War more than a decade later. By that point, the Tejano population numbered as high as 25,000, and it was mostly concentrated along the border and in central Texas. But when Texas decided to cast its lot with the Confederacy and secede from the United States, the call for troops placed Tejanos in a quandary. On the one hand, they could aid Confederate Texas, a state that had regarded them as little better than the people the Anglo population fought to keep enslaved in the wake of President Abraham Lincoln's election. Or, on the other hand, they could join the Federal forces and the nation responsible for Manifest Destiny and the transformation of the Mexican north into the American Southwest. With that choice, they could, in essence, fight against Texas, which had overseen the eclipse of Hispanic political and economic influence by joining the US Army. Either way, the decision would not be easy. After all, they had fought on the winning side and lost before. Ultimately, Mexican Americans in Texas joined the ranks of both forces as more than 2,500 enlisted in the Confederate army and an estimated 958 Tejanos fought for the Union.[8]

In the Civil War, the motivations of Tejanos generally did not involve the issues that had fractured the nation. A number of factors influenced the decisions of Tejano volunteers as war came to their native land for the third time in a generation. The defense of their homes and families made for the primary motivating factor as Tejanos joined volunteer forces throughout the state. Others joined the ranks of the Union or Confederate armies because they saw military service as an economic opportunity, just as did the Anglo soldiers who became known as Billy Yank or Johnny Reb. Others followed local political or economic leaders in hopes that their service would be rewarded following the war. A final group of Tejanos, those who lived along the border, viewed the conflict through the prism of a *libre fronterizo* identity and fought for their own best interests. Most of the Tejano population tried to avoid the conflict because they had no ideological or political motivation to fight on either side. This proved a challenge for Confederate Texas leaders as they attempted to rally support for their cause.[9]

Complicating emotions related to military service was the fact that many Tejanos still retained loyalty to Mexico. Even though Tejanos were regarded as American citizens in the wake of Treaty of Guadalupe Hidalgo and they participated in the social and economic life of the United States, they still retained a cultural connection to their ancestral homeland. In his study of Mexican workers in Texas at the turn of the twentieth century, historian Emilio Zamora outlined this dual identity as it pertains to Tejanos. Zamora maintains that Mexican workers undertook circular migrations across the Texas-Mexico border that shaped their "Mexicanist" identity. Many Tejanos, particularly those in South Texas, subscribed to this sense of identity out of a profound love for and loyalty to Mexico.[10]

The Anglo population of Texas questioned the loyalty of Mexican Texans at the onset of the Spanish-American War in 1898. Ambivalence defined the response of most Tejanos to this conflict. The influx of Mexican immigrants into Texas at the turn of the twentieth century had made the Tejano population numerically stronger than in previous years, and they moved into new areas and began to participate more freely in the state's economic and political activities. But these immigrants reinforced the Tejanos' bicultural identity, as most returned to Mexico and never thought to make their position permanent.[11] This perceived lack of allegiance to the United States was not lost on the Anglo population of Texas.

Ambivalence was not the only response among Mexican Texans. Some Tejanos volunteered to fight in one of the four infantry regiments and one cavalry unit: the First, Second, Third, and Fourth Regiments, Texas Volunteer Infantry (United States Volunteers); and the first regiment, Texas Volunteer Cavalry (United States Volunteers). However, out of the approximately four thousand soldiers the Lone Star State provided to support the war, less than 1 percent were of Mexican descent.[12]

In the first decade of the twentieth century, the Tejano population remained fragmented. Elite Tejanos had seen their influence wane at the end of the nineteenth century as the modernizing influence of railroads and economic progress tied Texas to the rest of the nation. Moreover, the arrival of immigrants displaced by Mexico's Revolution pulled Tejanos away from American nationalism. Yet, many Mexican Texans still accommodated to the Anglo-American culture, symbols, and values through the process of assimilation. Their attempts to demonstrate loyalty to Texas and the United States were evident despite a violent anti-Mexican backlash to subversive activities and banditry at the border between the United States and Texas.[13]

US entry into World War I in April 1917, once more swept Mexican Texans into the maelstrom of conflict. During the Great War, the Tejano community, in the words of historian José A. Ramírez, "demonstrated patriotism, but also disloyalty." On one side, some Tejanos fled the state to avoid military service. On the other, more Mexican Texans chose to enlist for service, eager to demonstrate their loyalty to the United States. Mexican Texans even wrote the authorities in Washington to inquire about the possibility of organizing Spanish-speaking companies in the American military.[14]

Tejanos of all classes answered the nation's call to arms during the Great War. Individual reasons varied, but they generally revolved around four motivations: patriotism and support for the United States.; a desire to escape poverty, ethnic pride and demonstrating the worthiness of the *Mexicano* people; and the aspiration for adventure in a foreign war.[15] In Laredo, Benjamin Ramos of *El Demócrata Fronterizo* urged his readers to support the war effort "for honor, for patriotism, for gratitude, for our own best interests," because as residents of the United States "we have benefited from her liberties."[16]

After Mexican American soldiers sacrificed their lives for the United States, some members of Tejanos community dedicated themselves to fighting for civil rights. The Mexican American generation of the 1920s and 1930s "became increasingly insistent on their right to enjoy the privileges guaranteed them under the United States Constitution."[17] Middle-class Mexican Texans created a new organization, the League of United Latin American Citizens. LULAC saw military service as a way of bridging the gap between the American creed and everyday practice. As part of its push for civil rights, LULAC stressed assimilation. More Texans of Mexican descent accommodated themselves to American traditions and values. As the 1930s drew to a close, Mexican Americans in Texas had a stronger sense of belonging to the United States than ever before.[18] When the United States entered World War II after the Japanese attack on Pearl Harbor on December 7, 1941, the Tejano population was once again plunged into conflict. But unlike in past wars, the Tejano community responded to the Second World War with the same patriotic fervor of their Anglo-American neighbors. As many as 750,000 Texans served in the armed forces during the war, a proportionally larger percentage than any other state. Of those, it is estimated that more than 100,000 Tejanos served in the United States armed forces. Historians often refer to the Second World War as the watershed moment for Mexican Americans and their quest for social and political equality.[19] Accordingly, the Tejano population sought to become "genuine Americans," to prove oneself in battle while the family sacrificed for the war effort at home.[20] As in the previous world war, Tejanos viewed service in the military as a means to achievement and recognition unobtainable by Mexican Texans in everyday life. These feelings were exemplified by Luis Leyva, born in Mexico but a resident of Texas, who was an undocumented citizen and was not drafted. Nevertheless, Leyva volunteered. "I know no other country," he explained. "This is my country; this is where I live."[21] Many Tejanos felt a strong patriotic sentiment. San Antonio native Manuel C. Vara, who served in the Pacific, felt this patriotism:

> I was eager to get into the war. I may not have understood it, but I saw it as someone attacking our country, and our response was that the proper thing to do was to fight back. We understood that [joining the military] was the patriotic thing to do, and for me at least, it was not a question of trying to get revenge against Japan, but simply that they needed to be stopped or else who knows where it would end if [Japan] was not stopped on their side of the Pacific.[22]

The feelings of Vara epitomized how many Tejanos now felt.[23] Although some enlisted for the sake of romantic adventurism, to get out of jail, or for financial opportunities, most Mexican Texans were much like their Anglo-American comrades, joining the military for honor and country.[24]

Following the Second World War, Tejanos served in Cold War conflicts in Korea and Vietnam. In some respects, the patriotic fervor that marked enlistment in World War II was absent from the Korean War despite the fact that nearly 148,000 Hispanics served in the military during the conflict. During that period, Tejanos found themselves in an improved social, political, and economic climate. The foremost civil rights organizations, LULAC and the American GI Forum, fought hard against the remaining vestiges of discrimination and segregation during the 1950s and 1960s, making strides, but not eradicating prejudice entirely. In the midst of these improvements, the Tejano community continued to view military service as a way out of poverty and a demonstration of national pride and bravery.[25]

Tejanos even proved willing to demonstrate their loyalty and nationalism, despite reports that a disproportionate number of Hispanic soldiers suffered casualties in Vietnam.[26] War II veteran and LULAC activist John J. Herrera, a native of Houston, approved of the war to stop communism. Héctor P. García, the founder of the American GI Forum, concurred, contending that "the majority if not the total Mexican American people approve of the present course of action in Vietnam."[27] Texan S. B. Sánchez described military service as a way to be a "good citizen" and the war as America's responsibility as a "great country." Sánchez maintained that it was necessary to go to war "to defend our freedom and heritage."[28]

This nationalism was epitomized by two Tejano Air Force pilots, Captain Albert and Major Andrés Tijerina from San Angelo. Albert, two years older than Andrés, told his younger brother, "We're going to fight for those people who did let us into schools. We're going to fight for the teachers who did help us and did reward us when we did well. . . . And we're going to fight for those people who defended our rights and allowed us to grab at the big American pie. These are the people, and these are the institutions we're going to fight to defend." They were not alone. The state's most decorated Tejano Vietnam veteran, Sergeant Roy P. Benavidez, a recipient of the Congressional Medal of Honor, always maintained he fought for the nation he loved.[29]

By the turn of the twenty-first century, the Tejano military experience came to mirror that of their Anglo neighbors. Nationalism and patriotism mean different things to different people. LULAC leaders suggested that patriotism was always present in the Mexican American community. This was not entirely accurate, as many Tejano soldiers of World War I and World War II gave a variety of rationales for their military service. For Mexican Texans, they viewed the love for their nation through the prism of the American dream, and military service offered a path to secure it. Most Mexican Texans were not champions of social justice in most of the wars they participated in. In the Civil War, they helped capture runaway slaves for the Confederacy. In the First World War, they expressed disdain for the African American troops who served alongside them. In World War II, they demonstrated ethnic prejudices like many of their Anglo counterparts. In the Cold War era, they spurned the recently integrated armed forces as they found themselves in the middle of hostility between white and Black troops. The civic commemorations and public spaces that paint a uniform sense of patriotism and nationalism as the sole reason Mexican Texans served in the armed forces fail to consider the complexity and diversity of the Tejano community.

In the post-Vietnam era, Tejanos emphasized the things that had long defined patriotic military service: bravery and patriotism. US Army Major General Freddie Valenzuela underscored these notions in his book, *No Greater Love: The Lives and Times of Hispanic Soldiers* (2008). Valenzuela, a graduate of Thomas Jefferson High School in San Antonio, argues that all Hispanics, not just Mexican Texans, are special to the American armed forces because they have always been confronted with questions about their "loyalty" even though they demonstrate a profound love for this country. "This love affair with our nation defies description," he states.[30] Service in the armed forces also served as a focal point of "*Veteranos*: A Legacy of Valor," a play that combined theater, music, dance and Department of Defense footage to tell the story of four soldiers in four wars. "*Veteranos*"

creator and director Enrique Castillo argued that his film had deep implications for the Mexican American community. "The reason all people
need to see this is that we [Latinos] didn't start with the Alamo, and we're
still here, and we have always been here. If you are a good American, it's
important to know the history of this country, which includes the culture
of our young men," Castillo maintained.[31]

Castillo's sentiments underscored an important aspect of Mexican
Texans' military service by the late twentieth century—the meaning of
nationalism to the Tejano community. To some, by the Vietnam War
era, it meant they felt free to criticize the government's efforts in a murky
war with no end in sight. To others it meant an opportunity to teach the
community about their past. While historians have studied the intrinsic
factors that made Tejanos adopt American values and a nationalistic ideology, there were extrinsic factors present as well. Specifically, the Tejano
community reacted to Anglo Texans' claims that they were disloyal by
the turn of the twentieth century. As such, community groups and civic
rights organizations played an additional role in defining how Tejanos
viewed military service. Each war modified how Tejanos defined their
martial spirit and shifted their motivations to join the armed forces.[32]

Military service in the wars of the twentieth century integrated Tejanos
into the mainstream of American society. Through military service, Tejanos gained access to educational and economic opportunities previously
unavailable to them prior to the early twentieth century. The portrait that
emerges from recent scholarship offers a more comprehensive view of
how Mexican American soldiers in Texas rationalized military service,
moving beyond a simplified depiction of Anglo-Mexican or Anglo-Tejano
relations based on race and class conflict to one that embraces a disparate
set of paradigms that include cultural identity and nationalism.[33] Mexican Texans sought to alter perceptions that viewed them as foreigners
in the land of their birth and tried to prove loyalty to the nation. They
also appreciated how military service could provide in their struggle for
political and social equality.

Tejano military service was not a hegemonic experience forged through
the prisms of assimilation and patriotism. Rather, Mexican Texans altered

their motivations over the twentieth century, shifting them based on a complex set of intrinsic and extrinsic values. The story that emerges from the Tejano military experience is one of bravery, perseverance, and honor. The questions of Tejano loyalty that marked early American military history are not heard in the twenty-first century. The accomplishments and determination of Mexican Texans defined the pivotal role they played in the history of the state and nation.

NOTES

Introduction

1. Raúl M. Chavarría, interview by author, August 1, 2009 (translation by author).
2. Arnoldo De León, *Mexican Americans in Texas: A Brief History* (Wheeling, IL: Harlan Davison, Inc., 2009), 108.
3. Aaron E. Sánchez, *Homeland: Ethnic Mexican Belonging Since 1900* (Norman: University of Oklahoma Press, 2021), 107.
4. Freddie Valenzuela with Jason Lemons, *No Greater Love: The Lives and Times of Hispanic Soldiers* (Austin: Ovation Books, 2008), xiii, xvii, 4.
5. George Mariscal, "Mexican Americans and the Viet Nam War," in Marilyn B. Young and Robert Buzzanco, eds., *A Companion to the Vietnam War* (Malden, MA: Blackwell Publishers, 2002), 27.
6. Ethan Rice, "Compañías Volantes," *Handbook of Texas Online*, accessed February 9, 2023, https://www.tshaonline.org/handbook/entries/companias-volantes.
7. Charles D. Grear, *Why Texans Fought in the Civil War* (College Station: Texas A&M University Press, 2010), 158–159.

Chapter 1

1. The term *Tejano* (and, in turn, *Tejana*) is used to identify ethnic Mexicans who lived in Texas, regardless of nationality. In many cases, these Texans of Mexican origin chose to reside in Texas would later claim, to varying degrees, a distinct identity as Tejanos. For the sake of simplicity, I use the terms "Tejanos," "Mexican Americans," "Mexican Texans," and "Hispanic Texans" interchangeably. In the case of people born in Mexico, I use the terms "Mexican," "*Mexicanos*," or "Mexican immigrant" interchangeably. Tejanos/as sometimes referred to themselves as *Mexicanos* or Mexicans, regardless of where they were born.
2. William T. Austin, "Account of the Campaign of 1835 by William T. Austin, Aid[e] to Gen. Stephen F. Austin & Gen. Ed Burleson," *Texana* 4 (Winter 1966): 297; Stephen L. Hardin, *Texian Iliad: A Military History of the Texas Revolution* (Austin: University of Texas Press, 1994), 28.
3. "Texian" refers to the Anglo-American settlers who lived in Mexican Texas and later in the Republic of Texas.

4. Hardin, *Texian Iliad*, 5.

5. Raúl A. Ramos, *Beyond the Alamo: Forging Mexican Ethnicity in San Antonio, 1821–1861* (Chapel Hill: University of North Carolina Press, 2008); Andrés Reséndez, *Changing National Identities at the Frontier: Texas and New Mexico, 1800–1850* (New York: Cambridge University Press, 2005); Benjamin Huber Johnson, *Revolution in Texas: How a Forgotten Rebellion and Its Bloody Suppression Turned Mexicans into Americans* (New Haven: Yale University Press, 2003); Elliott Young, *Catarino Garza's Revolution on the Texas-Mexico Border* (Durham, NC: Duke University Press, 2004).

6. Andrés Tijerina, *Tejanos and Texas Under the Mexican Flag, 1821–1836* (College Station: Texas A&M University Press, 1996), 5.

7. Donald E. Chipman, *Spanish Texas, 1519–1821* (Austin: University of Texas Press, 2010), 86–104, 105, 110–112, 121–127, 169.

8. Randolph B. Campbell, *Gone to Texas: A History of the Lone Star State* (New York: Oxford University Press 2003), 62–63 (quotation on page 62); Todd F. Smith, *From Dominance to Disappearance: The Indians of East Texas and the Near Southwest, 1786–1859* (Lincoln: University of Nebraska Press, 2005), 16–17; Thomas A. Britten, *The Lipan Apaches: A People of Wind and Lightning* (Albuquerque: University of New Mexico Press, 2009), chapter 2.

9. Francis X. Galán, *Los Adaes: The First Capital of Spanish Texas* (College Station: Texas A&M University Press, 2020), 190–196.

10. Campbell, *Gone to Texas*, 83.

11. Maurine T. Wilson and Jack Jackson, *Philip Nolan and Texas: Expeditions to the Unknown Land, 1791–1801* (Waco: Texian Press, 1987).

12. Gerald E. Poyo, ed., *Tejano Journey, 170–1850* (Austin: University of Texas Press, 1996), 12; Campbell, *Gone to Texas*, 84.

13. Nemecio Salcedo to Viceroy, December 29, 1802, Bexar Archives, Bexar County Courthouse, Reel 30, frames 947–949.

14. Stephen L. Hardin, "Efficient in the Cause," in Poyo, *Tejano Journey*, 50; Rice, "Compañías Volantes."

15. Tijerina, *Tejanos*, 9–10; Jesús F. de la Teja, "Rebellion on the Frontier," in Poyo, *Tejano Journey*, 16.

16. Randell G. Tarín, "Second Flying Company of San Carlos de Parras," *Handbook of Texas Online*, accessed April 1, 2023, https://www.tshaonline.org/handbook/entries/second-flying-company-of-san-carlos-de-parras.

17. Harris Gaylord Warren, "Gutierrez-Magee Expedition," *Handbook of Texas Online*, accessed April 7, 2023, https://www.tshaonline.org/handbook/entries/gutierrez-magee-expedition.

18. Ramos, *Beyond the Alamo*, 7–8; Randell G. Tarín, "Second Flying Company of San Carlos de Parras," *Handbook of Texas Online*, accessed May 2, 2023, https://www.tshaonline.org/handbook/entries/second-flying-company-of-san-carlos-de-parras.

19. Ramos, *Beyond the Alamo*, 58.

20. Robert D. Wood, *Life in Laredo: A Documentary History from the Laredo Archives* (Denton: University of North Texas Press, 2004), 86–88.

21. Campbell, *Gone to Texas*, 94–97.

22. Gerald Horne, *The Counter-Revolution of 1836: Texas Slavery & Jim Crow and the Roots of U.S. Fascism* (New York: International Publishers, 2023), 38–40.

23. Torget, *Seeds*, 160.

24. Campbell, *Gone to Texas*, 104–118.

25. Tijerina, *Tejanos*, 130–132; Torget, *Seeds*, 160–161.

26. Torget, *Seeds*, 160.

27. Burton Kirkwood, *The History of Mexico* (Santa Barbara, CA: Greenwood Press, 2010), 94–95.

28. Campbell, *Gone to Texas*, 124–125.

29. Campbell, *Gone to Texas*, 129–130; Hardin, *Texian Iliad*, 6–7.

30. Hardin, *Texian Iliad*, 10–12; Ramos, *Beyond the Alamo*, 132–134; Campbell, *Gone to Texas*, 130; Loyd Uglow, *A Military History of Texas* (Denton: University of North Texas Press, 2022), 93–94.

31. Campbell, *Gone to Texas*, 131–133.

32. Campbell, *Gone to Texas*, 135–136.

33. Campbell, *Gone to Texas*, 138.

34. H. W. Brands, *Lone Star Nation: How a Ragged Army of Volunteers Won the Battle for Texas Independence—and Changed America* (New York: Doubleday, 2004), 281; Hardin, *Texian Iliad*, 28; Gregg Cantrell, *Stephen F. Austin: Empresario of Texas* (New Haven: Yale University Press, 1999) 319 (quotation).

35. Juan N. Seguín, *Personal Memoirs of John N. Seguín: From the Year 1834 to the Retreat of General Woll from the City of San Antonio in 1842* (San Antonio: Ledger Book Office, 1858), 6.

36. Craig H. Roell, "Benavides, Plácido," *Handbook of Texas Online*, accessed March 3, 2024, https://www.tshaonline.org/handbook/entries/benavides-placido.

37. Stephen L. Hardin, "Plácido Benavides: Fighting Tejano Federalist," in Jesús F. de la Teja, ed., *Tejano Leadership in Mexican and Revolutionary Texas* (College Station: Texas A&M University Press, 2010), 58–61.

38. Hardin, "Plácido Benavides," 61–62.

39. Hardin, "Plácido Benavides," 62; Samuel C. A. Rogers Reminiscences, Dolph Briscoe Center for American History, University of Texas at Austin (hereafter cited as CAH).

40. De León, *Mexican Americans in Texas*, 29–30; Hardin, "Plácido Benavides," 63.

41. Ramos, *Beyond the Alamo*, 144–145, 157; De León, *Mexican Americans in Texas*, 33.

42. David McDonald, *José Antonio Navarro: In Search of the American Dream in Nineteenth-Century Texas* (Denton: Texas State Historical Association Press, 2010), 126–128.

43. Uglow, *Military*, 101–103; Alwyn Barr, *Texans in Revolt: The Battle for San Antonio, 1835* (Austin: University of Texas Press, 1990), 11.

44. Uglow, *Military*, 104–105; Hardin, *Texan Iliad*, 88–91.

45. McDonald, *José Antonio Navarro*, 128.

46. Henry Stuart Foote, *Texas and the Texans: Or, Advance of the Anglo-Americans to the Southwest*, vol. 2 (Philadelphia: Thomas Copperthwait, 1841), 101 (first quotation), 103 (second quotation).

47. Hardin, *Texan Iliad*, 90; McDonald, *José Antonio Navarro*, 128; Brands, *Lone Star Nation*, 315–317.

48. Ramos, *Beyond the Alamo*, 151–152; De León, *Mexican Americans in Texas*, 23–24; Jesús F. De la Teja, "Seguín: Federalist, Rebel, Exile," in De la Teja, *Tejano Leadership in Mexican and Revolutionary Texas*, 224; Paul Andrew Hutton, "The Alamo as Icon," in Joseph Dawson, ed., *The Texas Military Experience: From the Texas Revolution Through World War II* (College Station: Texas A&M University Press, 1995), 19–20.

49. Uglow, *Military*, 108–109, 110–112; Hardin, *Texan Iliad*, 119.

50. Hardin, *Texan Iliad*, 120–121; Uglow, *Military*, 112.

51. Ramos, *Beyond the Alamo*, 156.

52. Henry Smith to Council, December 12, 1835, in *Papers of the Texas Revolution*, ed. John Holmes Jenkins, 10 vols. (Austin: Presidial Press, 1973), 3: 1,459.

53. Ramos, *Beyond the Alamo*, 155–156; De León, *Mexican Texans*, 35–36; McDonald, *Navarro*, 128.

54. De la Teja, "Seguín," 224; Uglow, *Military*, 112–113.

55. Raúl Casso IV, "Damacio Jiménez: The Lost and Found Alamo Defender," *Southwestern Historical Quarterly* 96, no. 1 (July 1992): 88.

56. Hardin, *Texas Iliad*, 136; Uglow, *Military*, 114–117.

57. Brands, *Lone Star Nation*, 363–364.

58. Campbell, *Gone to Texas*, 149; Brands, *Lone Star Nation*, 388–390; Uglow, *Military*, 118–119.

59. Hardin, "Plácido Benavides," 66.

60. Hardin, "Plácido Benavides," 66.

61. Jimmy L. Bryan, "The Enduring People: Tejano Exclusion and Perseverance in the Republic of Texas, 1836–1845," *Journal of the West* 47 (Summer 2008): 42.

62. Campbell, *Gone to Texas*, 152–154.

63. Uglow, *Military*, 127–128.

64. Uglow, *Military*, 128–129; Brands, *Lone Star Nation*, 443–455, 459–466.

65. Hardin, *Texan Iliad*, 209–213 (quotation); Ruben R. Lozano, *Viva Tejas: The Story of the Tejanos, the Mexican-Born Patriots of the Texas Revolution* (San Antonio: Alamo Press, 1985), 36–37; Lloyd L. MacDonald, *Tejanos in the 1835 Texas Revolution* (Gretna, LA: Pelican Publishing Company, 2009).

66. Ramos, *Beyond the Alamo*, 150.

67. Stanley Siegel, "Navarro, José Antonio," *Handbook of Texas Online*, accessed August 8, 2023, https://www.tshaonline.org/handbook/entries/navarro-jose-antonio.

68. Hardin, *Texian Iliad*, 121; Amelia Williams, "A Critical Study of the Siege of the Alamo and the Personnel of its Defenders," *Southwestern Historical Quarterly* 38, no. 4 (April 1934): 263.

69. Frank Salinas, "Plácido Benavides Narrative, 'the Texas Paul Revere,'" CAH; Ramos, *Beyond the Alamo*, 156–157.

70. David Ryan Barnds, "The Untold Story of the Ximenes Family: A *Tejano* Experience in Béxar Spanning across Generations, 1716–1899" (master's thesis, University of Texas at San Antonio, 2022), 46–47.

71. De León, *Mexican Americans in Texas*, 36, 41.

72. Hardin, *Texan Iliad*, 271.

73. David Montejano, *Anglos and Mexicans in the Making of Texas, 1836–1986* (Austin: University of Texas Press, 1987), 25–26.

74. Rebecca J. Herring, "Córdova Rebellion," *Handbook of Texas Online*, accessed July 7, 2023, https://www.tshaonline.org/handbook/entries/cordova-rebellion; Reséndez, *Changing National Identities*, 146–170; Ramos, *Beyond the Alamo*, 167–191; Montejano, *Anglos and Mexicans*, 26.

75. Montejano, *Anglos and Mexicans*, 28–29; Paul Horgan, *Great River: The Río Grande in North American History* (New York: Rinehart & Company, 1954), 569–585; Noel M. Loomis, *Texan–Santa Fe Pioneers* (Norman: University of Oklahoma Press, 1958); Juan Seguín Memoirs, CAH.

76. Juan Seguín Memoirs, CAH.

77. Tijerina, *Tejanos*, 89–92.

78. David A. Clary, *Eagles and Empire: The United States, Mexico, and the Struggle for a Continent* (New York: Bantam Books, 2009), 47–53.

79. Torget, *Seeds*, 219–222.

Chapter 2

1. Peter Guardino, *The Dead March: A History of the Mexican-American War* (Cambridge, MA: Harvard University Press, 2017), 18–35.

2. A. Brook Caruso, *The Mexican Spy Company: United States Covert Operations in Mexico, 1845–1848* (Jefferson, NC: McFarland and Company, 1991), 83; Jerry D. Thompson, *Vaqueros in Blue and Gray* (Austin: State House Press, 2000), 12; Charles D. Spurlin, *Texas Volunteers in The Mexican War* (Austin: Eakin Press, 1999), 158, 166.

3. Caruso, *Mexican Spy Company*, 83; Spurlin, *Texas Volunteers*, 158, 166; Stanley C. Green, *A Changing of Flags: Mirabeau B. Lamar at Laredo* (Laredo, TX: Border Studies Center, 1990), 3.

4. Mirabeau B. Lamar to Bacilio Benavides, José María Ramón, and María González, and April 8 and 11, 1848, in C. A. Gulick and W. Allen, eds., *The Papers of Mirabeau B. Lamar*, 6 vols. (Austin: A. C. Baldwin, 1973), 4:196–197.

5. Armando C. Alonzo, *Tejano Legacy: Rancheros and Settlers in South Texas, 1734–1900* (Albuquerque: University of New Mexico Press, 1998), 132.

6. Michael L. Collins, *Texas Devils: Rangers and Regulars on the Lower Rio Grande, 1846–1861* (Norman: University of Oklahoma Press, 2008), 7.

7. Douglas W. Richmond, "A View of the Periphery: Regional Factors and Collaboration During the US–Mexico Conflict, 1845–1848," in Richard Francaviglia and Douglas W. Richmond, eds., *Dueling Eagles: Reinterpreting the US–Mexican War, 1846–1848* (Fort Worth: TCU Press, 2000).

8. Guardino, *Dead March*, 352–357.

9. Manuel Callahan, "Mexican Border Troubles: Social War, Settler Colonialism, and the Production of Frontier Discourses, 1848–1880" (PhD diss., University of Texas at Austin, 2003), 2.

10. *The Ranchero* (Corpus Christi), March 24, 1860; Jerry D. Thompson, *Cortina: Defending the Mexican Name in Texas* (College Station: Texas A&M University Press, 2007).

11. Arnoldo De León, *They Called Them Greasers: Anglo Attitudes toward Mexicans in Texas, 1821–1900* (Austin: University of Texas Press, 1983), 38–39, 82–83; Uglow, *Military*, 206–210; De León, *Mexican Americans in Texas*, 42.

12. *Texas House Journal, 8th Legislature Regular Session*, 63, accessed August 5, 2025 .https://lrl.texas.gov/scanned/Housejournals/8/11121859_59.pdf.

13. Torget, *Seeds of Empire*, 264; Montejano, *Anglos and Mexicans*, 31, 40–41; Campbell, *Gone to Texas*, 227–238.

14. Campbell, *Gone to Texas*, 241–243; Grear, *Why Texans Fought in the Civil War*, 14–15.

15. Thompson, *Vaqueros*, 11.

16. Grear, *Why Texans Fought*, 157.

17. Torget, *Seeds of Empire*, 184; McDonald, *José Antonio Navarro*, 250–251.

18. Thompson, *Vaqueros*, 11; Grear, *Why Texans Fought*, 157.

19. De León, *Greasers*, 49–51; Jerry Don Thompson, *Tejano Tiger: José de los Santos Benavides and the Texas-Mexico Border* (Fort Worth: TCU Press, 2017), 74.

20. "Recovery of Runaway Negroes," *The Ranchero*, March 17, 1860.

21. *The Ranchero*, November 17, 1860; "Influence of the Benavides Family," in John Salmon "Rip" Ford Papers, circa 1836–1896, CAH.

22. Uglow, *Military*, 211–212; Grear, *Why Texans Fought*, 159.

23. James M. McPherson, *Ordeal by Fire: The Civil War and Reconstruction* (New York: McGraw Hill, 2013), 163–165.

24. *The Semi-Weekly News* (San Antonio), January 2, 1862.

25. Jerry D. Thompson, ed., *Tejanos in Gray: Civil War Letters of Captains Joseph Rafael de la Garza and Manuel Yturri* (College Station: Texas A&M University Press, 2011), xxii; Campbell, *Gone to Texas*, 246–247.

26. Grear, *Why Texans Fought*, 156–161.

27. Miguel González Quiroga, "*Mexicanos* in Texas During the Civil War," in Emilio Zamora, Cynthia Orozco, and Rodolfo Rocha, eds., *Mexican Americans in Texas History: Selected Essays* (Austin: Texas State Historical Association Press, 2000), 51–62; Grear, *Why Texans*, 156–161.

28. Ralph Edward Morales III, "*Hijos de la Gran Guerra*: The Creation of a Mexican-American Identity in Texas, 1836–1929" (PhD diss., Texas A&M University 2015), 34.

29. Arnoldo De León, *The Tejano Community, 1836–1900* (Dallas: Southern Methodist University Press, 1997), 17.

30. Grear, *Why Texans Fought*, 158–159; Jerry Thompson, *Mexican Texans in the Union Army* (El Paso: Texas Western Press, 1986), xvii–xviii; Riley, "Santos Benavides," 117–118, 226–227; John Denny Riley, "Santos Benavides: His Influence on the Lower Rio Grande, 1823–1891" (PhD diss., Texas Christian University, 1976).

31. Grear, *Why Texans Fought*, 139–142.

32. *Tri-Weekly Alamo Express* (San Antonio), February 11, 1861.

33. Thompson, *Cortina*, 88.

34. Thompson, *Tejanos in Gray*, xi.

35. *Weekly Alamo Express* (San Antonio), May 3, 1861; *The Daily Ledger and Texan* (San Antonio), May 14, 1861.

36. Thompson, *Tejanos in Gray*, xvi–xxiv.

37. Joseph de la Garza to Dear Ellen, August 20, 1862, in Thompson, *Tejanos in Gray*, 9.

38. Joseph de la Garza to Dear Mother, October 27, 1863, in Thompson, *Tejanos in Gray*, 23.

39. Joseph de la Garza to Dear Bart, September 9, 1863, in Thompson, *Tejanos in Gray*, 18.

40. Manuel Yturri to My Dear Wife, May 31, 1862, in Thompson, *Tejanos in Gray*, 33.

41. Manuel Yturri Letter Fragment, in Thompson, *Tejanos in Gray*, 75–76.

42. Manuel Yturri to My Dear Wife, May 31, 1862, in Thompson, *Tejanos in Gray*. 33.

43. Manuel Yturri to My Dear Elenita, May 7, 1865, in Thompson, *Tejanos in Gray*, 71.

44. Thompson, *Tejano Tiger*, 86–90.

45. Thompson, *Tejano Tiger*, 84.

46. Thompson, *Tejano Tiger*, 84.

47. Santos Benavides to John S. Ford, May 23. 1861, in John S. Ford Papers, CAH; US War Department, *The War of the Rebellion: Official Records of Union and Confederate Armies*, 128 vols. (Washington, DC: US Government Printing Office, 1880–1891), Series I, 1:539–540 (hereafter this source will be cited as *OR*, with all references being to Series I unless otherwise indicated, and whenever a volume consists of two or more parts, the part number will follow the volume number); Richard B. McCaslin, *Fighting Stock: John S. "Rip" Ford of Texas* (Fort Worth: TCU Press, 2011), 117–118; Thompson, *Cortina*, 98–101; Thompson, *Tejano Tiger*, 91–94 (black-flag policy on pg. 93).

48. Jerry D. Thompson, "Col. José de Los Santos Benavides and Gen. Juan Nepomuceno Cortina Two Astounding Civil War Tejanos," in Roseann Bacha-Garza, Christopher L. Miller, and Russell K. Skowronek, eds., *The Civil War on the Río Grande, 1846–1876* (College Station: Texas A&M University Press, 2019).

49. Young, *Catarino Garza's Revolution*, 7; Montejano, *Anglos and Texans*, 34–35.

50. Thompson, *Tejano Tiger*, 94 (quotation).

51. Thompson, *Tejano Tiger*, 96–104.

52. Albino López to H. P. Bee, March 15, 1863, *OR*, 15: 1128–1129; "Report on Mexican Border Commission," 67–68; J. B. Magruder to W. R. Boggs, January 6, 1864, *OR*, 34, pt. 2:834; *The Houston Tri-Weekly Telegraph*, July 30, 1862; Riley, "Santos Benavides," 142–144.

53. Grear, *Why Texans Fought*, 158.

54. W. Claude Jones, April 5, 1861, *The Semi-Weekly News* (San Antonio), May 4, 1862.

55. Jerry D. Thompson, *Confederate General of the West: Henry Hopkins Sibley* (College Station: Texas A&M University Press, 1996), 247–248; Jerry D. Thompson, "Valverde, Battle of," *Handbook of Texas Online*, accessed February 4, 2025, https://www.tshaonline .org/handbook/entries/valverde-battle-of; Thompson, *Vaqueros*, 26.

56. Helen Trimpi, *Crimson Confederates: Harvard Men Who Fought for the South* (Knoxville: University of Tennessee Press, 2009), 224–225; Macdonald, *Navarro*, 248–249, 255–256; Thompson, *Tejano Tiger*, 196–197.

57. Walter E. Wilson, *Civil War Scoundrels and the Texas Cotton Trade* (Jefferson, NC: McFarland Press, 2020), 104–106, 110.

58. John S. Ford to Headquarters, *Galveston Tri-Weekly Telegraph*, February 12, 1864.

59. Stephen A. Townsend, *The Yankee Invasion of Texas* (College Station: Texas A&M University Press, 2005), 8–9, 77–78; Thompson, *Tejano Tiger*, 164.

60. Thompson, *Tejano Tiger*, 168.

61. Santos Benavides to John S. Ford, March 21, 1864, in *OR*, 34, pt. 1: 648; Thompson, *Tejano Tiger*, 171.

62. Jerry D. Thompson, "A Stand Along the Border: Santos Benavides and the Battle for Laredo," *Civil War Times*, August 1980, 31–32 (quotation on p. 31); Thompson, *Tejano Tiger*, 171–172.

63. "Benavides Attacked," in John S. Ford Papers, CAH; Santos Benavides to John S. Ford, March 21, 1864, in *OR*, 34, pt. 1: 648 (quotation).

64. "Benavides Attacked," in John S. Ford Papers, CAH; Jerry D. Thompson, *Warm Weather and Bad Whiskey: The 1886 Laredo Election Riot* (El Paso: University of Texas at El Paso Press, 1991), 26–30; Thompson, "A Stand Along the Border," 26–33; Thompson, *Tejano Tiger*, 154; McCaslin, *Fighting Stock*, 185–187.

65. McCaslin, *Fighting Stock*, 187; Thompson, *Tejano Tiger*, 190–195.

66. Napoleon J. T. Dana to December 1, 1863, in *OR*, 26, pt. 1:830.

67. Ana Carolina Castillo Crimm, *De León: A Tejano Family History* (Austin: University of Texas Press, 2003), 94 (quotation); Young, *Catarino Garza's Revolution*, 7; Ramos, *Beyond the Alamo*, 231–237.

68. *Galveston Daily News*, September 26, 1877; Jerry Thompson, "Vidal, Adrián J.," *Handbook of Texas Online*, accessed June 9, 2023, https://www.tshaonline.org/handbook /entries/vidal-adrian-j.

69. Thompson, *Vaqueros*, 81; Grear, *Why Texans Fought*, 158.

70. Dale Baum, *The Shattering of Texas Unionism* (Baton Rouge: LSU Press, 1998), 30–31, 42–43, 68, 69.

71. Thompson, *Vaqueros*, 82–83.

72. Thompson, *Vaqueros*, 82.

73. De León, *The Tejano Community*, 59–61.

74. Thompson, *Vaqueros*, 82–83.

75. John L. Haynes and Edmund J. Davis to Edwin M. Stanton, September 1862, in John L. Haynes Papers, CAH.

76. Letter fragment to General Nathaniel P. Banks, n.d., in John L. Haynes Papers, CAH.

77. Edmund J. Davis to Thomas C. Ord, February 10, 1864, in *OR*, 34, pt. 2:288.

78. Edmund J. Davis to Thomas C. Ord, February 10, 1864, in *OR*, 34, pt. 2:288.

79. Thompson, *Vaqueros*, 92–93.

80. Thompson, *Vaqueros*, 92–93.

81. De León, *Greasers*, 29–32.

82. Collins, *Texas Devils*, 70–86.

83. Frederick Law Olmsted, *A Journey Through Texas: or, A Saddle-Trip on the Southwestern Frontier* (New York: Dix, Edwards, and Company, 1857), 164.

84. Benjamin F. McIntyre, *Federals on the Frontier: The Diary of Benjamin F. McIntyre, 1862–1864*, ed. Nannie M. Tilley (Austin: University of Texas Press, 1963), 254, 347.

85. Andy Najera, "Agency of Mexican/Tejano Union Recruits during the United States Civil War: An Archival Case Study of Private Pedro García" (master's thesis, University of Texas Rio Grande Valley, 2021), 74–75.

86. Santiago Tafolla, *A Life Crossing Borders: Memoir of a Mexican American Confederate*, ed. Carmen Tafolla and Laura Tafolla (Houston: Arte Público Press, 2010), 71.

87. Tafolla, *Life*, 72–74.

88. Letter fragment, 1864, in Thompson, *Tejanos*, 75.

89. Grear, *Why Texans Fought*, 161.

90. Najera, "Agency of Mexican/Tejano Union Recruits," 74–80.

91. McIntyre, *Federals on the Frontier*, 354.

92. John Barry to Dear Sister, October 17 and November 4, 1863, Barry Papers, Southern Historical Collection, University of North Carolina at Chapel Hill.

93. Mark A. Weitz, *More Damning than Slaughter: Desertion in the Confederate Army* (Lincoln: University of Nebraska Press, 2008), 225–232; Grear, *Why Texans Fought*, 120–124.

94. Thompson, *Tejano Tiger*, 183.

95. Edmund J. Davis to Thomas C. Ord, 10 February 1864, in OR, 34, pt. 2, 288; Thompson, *Vaqueros*, 44–47.

96. Thompson, *Vaqueros*, 89.

97. Tafolla, *Life*, 70.

98. Manuel Yturri to My Dear Elenita, February 28, 1865, in Thompson, *Tejanos in Gray: Civil War Letters of Captains Joseph Rafael de la Garza and Manuel Yturri* (College Station: Texas A&M University Press, 2011), 65.

99. Joseph de la Garza to Dear DeWitt, December 9, 1862, in Thompson, *Tejanos*, 13.

100. Thompson, *Vaqueros*, 89.

101. Manuel Yturri to My Dear Elena, July 3, 1864, in Thompson, *Vaqueros*, 50.

102. Tafolla, *Life*, 65.

103. Joseph de la Garza to Dear Mother, October 2, 1862, in Thompson, *Tejanos*, 11.

104. Thompson, *Vaqueros*, 122–123.

105. Manuel Yturri to My Dear Elena, 3 July 1864, in Thompson, *Tejanos*, 50.

106. Manuel Yturri to My Dear Elena, July 3, 1864, in Thompson, *Tejanos*, 53.

107. H. B. Adams to Friend Bart, April 19, 1864, in Thompson, *Tejanos*, 28.

108. Thompson, *Tejano Tiger*, 197–204; McCaslin, *Fighting Stock*, 287.

109. "Report of the Mexican Commission on the Northern Frontier Question," reprinted in Carlos E. Cortés, ed., *The Mexican Experience in Texas* (New York: Arno Press, 1976), 66.

110. Grear, *Why Texans Fought*; Susannah J. Ural, ed., *Civil War Citizens: Race, Ethnicity, and Identity in America's Bloodiest Conflict* (New York: NYU Press, 2010); Benedict Anderson, *Imagined Communities: Reflections on the Origin and Spread of Nationalism* (London: Verso Press, 2006).

Chapter 3

1. Campbell, *Gone to Texas*, 267–269.

2. Thompson, *Tejano Tiger*, 208–212; Morales, "Hijos de la Gran Guerra," 34–38; Andreas Oliver Meng Nielsen, "Leyendecker, John Zirvas," *Handbook of Texas Online*, accessed July 29, 2023, https://www.tshaonline.org/handbook/entries/leyendecker-john-zirvas.

3. Sussanah J. Ural, *Hood's Texas Brigade: The Soldiers and Families of the Confederacy's Most Celebrated Unit* (Baton Rouge: Louisiana State University Press, 2017), 231.

4. Tafolla, *Life*, 81.

5. Manuel Yturri to Dear Elenita, May 15, 1865, in Thompson, *Tejanos*, 73.

6. Carl Moneyhon, *Texas after the Civil War: The Struggle of Reconstruction* (College Station: Texas A&M University Press, 2004), 15–17.

7. Moneyhon, *Texas*, 21–86.

8. Thompson, *Tejano Tiger*, 214; Gilberto Miguel Hinojosa, *A Borderlands Town in Transition: Laredo, 1755–1870* (College Station: Texas A&M University Press, 1983), 88.

9. De León, *Tejano Community*, 29–30; McDonald, *Navarro*, 259–260.

10. McDonald, *Navarro*, 258, 260, 262.

11. McDonald, *Navarro*, 30; William A. Brkich, "Mexican-Texan Club," *Handbook of Texas Online*, accessed January 31, 2023, https://www.tshaonline.org/handbook/entries/mexican-texan-club.

12. Cambell, *Gone to Texas*, 287.

13. Thompson, *Tejano Tiger*, 217, 220–221.

14. Thompson, *Tejano Tiger*, 222–223.

15. "Mexican Border Troubles," in *Governor's Messages, Coke to Ross, 1874–1891: Collections of the Art and History Department of the Texas State Library* (Austin: A. C. Baldwin Printing, 1916), 102.

16. David E. Screws, "Hispanic Texas Rangers Contribute to Peace on the Texas Frontier, 1838 to 1880," in Bruce A. Glasrud, *Tracking the Texas Rangers: The Nineteenth Century* (Denton: University of North Texas Press, 2012), 192, 197.

17. Robert Wooster, *Soldiers, Sutlers, and Settlers: Garrison Life on the Texas Military Frontier* (College Station: Texas A&M University Press, 1987), 48; Uglow, *Military*, 244–250.

18. Robert Wooster, *The Military and United States Indian Policy, 1865–1903* (Lincoln, NE: Bison Books, 1988), 13–40.

19. Uglow, *Military*, 259–262.

20. Bill Yenne, *Indian Wars: The Campaign for the American West* (Yardley, PA: Westholme Press, 2006), 160–163, 168–170; Wooster, *Indian Policy*, 140; Uglow, *Military*, 269–270.

21. Tafolla, *Life*, 41.

22. Edward M. Coffman, *The Old Army: A Portrait of the American Army in Peacetime, 1784–1898* (New York: Oxford University Press, 1986), 331.

23. Hans Peter Nielsen Gammel, ed., *The Laws of Texas, 1882–1897*, vol. 6 (Austin: H. P. N. Gammel, 1898), 190.

24. Gammel, *The Laws of Texas*, 190; Allan Robert Purcell, "The History of the Texas Militia, *1835–1903*" (PhD diss., University of Texas at Austin, 1981), 224–227.

25. James Davidson, *Report of the Adjutant General of the State of Texas, 1871* (Galveston: Newsbook and Job Office, 1871), 5.

26. James Davidson, *Report of the Adjutant General of the State of Texas*, 5.

27. *Journal of the Senate of the State of Texas, Being the First Session of the Sixteenth Legislature, 1879* (Galveston: A. H. Belo and Company, 1879), 391–392.

28. John B. Jones, *Report of the Adjutant General of the State of Texas, 1880* (Galveston: A. H. Belo and Company, 1880), 5.

29. De León, *Tejano Community*, 37–40; Calderón, "Mexican Politics in the American Era," 554–556.

30. De León, *Mexican Americans*, 58–59 (quotation on p. 59).

31. Harry S. Laver, "Refuge of Manhood: Masculinity and the Militia Experience in Kentucky," in Craig Thompson Friend and Lorri Glover, eds., *Southern Manhood: Perspectives on Masculinity in the Old South* (Athens: University of Georgia Press, 2004), 2–5.

32. Ramón Treviño, Texas Adjutant General Service Records, 1836–1935, Texas State Library and Archives, Austin, Texas.

33. Ramón Benavides, Texas Adjutant General Service Records, 1836–1935.

34. De León, *Community*, 188.

35. Patricio Benavides and Cisto Castillo, Texas Adjutant General Service Records, 1836–1935.

36. Jesús Sandoval, Texas Adjutant General Service Records, 1836–1935.

37. William H. Mabry, *Report of the Adjutant General of the State of Texas, 1892* (Austin: Ben C. Jones and Company, 1892), 5; William H. Mabry, *Report of the Adjutant General of the State of Texas, 1894* (Austin: Ben C. Jones and Company, 1894), 4; William H. Mabry, *Report of the Adjutant General of the State of Texas, 1896* (Austin: Ben C. Jones and Company, 1896), 5.

38. Coffman, *Old Army*, 328–330; Evan Anders, *Boss Rule in South Texas: The Progressive Era* (Austin: University of Texas Press, 1982), 9; De León, *Greasers*, 88; Thompson, *Warm Weather*, 141–143.

39. Thomas Ty Smith, *The Garza War in South Texas: A Military History, 1890–1893* (Norman: University of Oklahoma Press, 2023); Stanley Green and Carlos Cuellar, "Mexican Revolutionaries in Laredo 1890–1891" (pamphlet in author's possession, 1991); M. Romero, "The Garza Raid and its Lessons," *North American Review* 155, no. 430 (September 1892): 324–337 (quotation on page 324).

40. Monica Muñoz Martinez, *The Injustice Never Leaves You: Anti-Mexican Violence in Texas* (Cambridge, MA: Harvard University Press, 2018), 14.

41. Martinez, *Injustice*, 14.

42. Young, "Crossing Borders," 165–166, 180–182; Elliott Young, "Deconstructing *La Raza*: Identifying the *Gente Decente* of Laredo, 1904–1911," *Southwestern Historical Quarterly* 98, no. 2 (October 1994): 234–235; *The Laredo Times*, November 10, 1891; Thompson, *Tejano Tiger*, 308–309, 322–324.

43. David Trask, *The War with Spain in 1898* (Lincoln: University of Nebraska Press, 1981), 1–12.

44. Trask, *War with Spain*, 15–23, 25–29; John Joseph Leffler, "From the Shadows into the Sun: Americans in the Spanish-American War" (PhD diss., University of Texas at Austin, 1991), 40–48.

45. *Brownsville Daily Herald*, February 16, 1898; *El Paso International Daily Times*, January 27, 1898; *Houston Daily Post*, February 16, 1898; James M. McCaffrey, "Texans in the Spanish-American War," *Southwestern Historical Quarterly*, 106, no. 2 (October 2002): 254–255; John J. Leffler, "The Paradox of Patriotism: Texas in the Spanish-American War," *Hayes Historical Journal* 8, no. 3 (Spring 1989): 24.

46. *Brownsville Daily Herald*, February 16, 1898.

47. Leffler, "Paradox," 24.

48. Elliott Young, "Red Men, Princess Pocahontas, and George Washington: Harmonizing Race Relations in Laredo at the Turn of the Century," *Western Historical Quarterly* 29 (Spring 1998), 55 (quotation); Stanley C. Green, *A History of the Washington Birthday Celebration* (Laredo: Border Studies Press, 1999); *Laredo Daily Times*, January 18, February 1, February 18, 1898.

49. Leffler, "Paradox," 24.

50. *Galveston Tribune*, February 16, and March 16, 1898; *El Paso Times*, March 3 and 8, 1898.

51. Purcell, "Texas Militia," 282–283; Turpie, "A Voluntary War," 861–862.

52. Trask, *War with Spain*, 155.

53. McCaffrey, "Texans," 257.

54. Turpie, "A Voluntary War," 862–863.

55. McCaffrey, "Texans," 258; Purcell, "The History of the Texas Militia," 281–283.

56. Turpie, "A Voluntary War," 869–870.

57. McCaffrey, "Texans," 280; Turpie, "A Voluntary War," 872–873.

58. Leffler, "Americans," 135–137; Turpie, "A Voluntary War," 873–874.

59. Leffler, "Paradox," 37–40.

60. Muñoz Martinez, *Injustice*, 14–15.

61. Graeme S. Mount, "Nuevo Mexicanos and the War of 1898," *New Mexico Historical Review* 58, no 4 (1983): 390–391.

62. *El Paso International Daily Times*, February 25, 1898.

63. *El Paso International Daily Times*, February 27, 1898.

64. *El Paso International Daily Times*, March 29, 1898.

65. *El Paso International Daily Times*, April 20, 1898.

66. *El Paso International Daily Times*, April 22, 1898.

67. *El Paso International Daily Times*, May 31, 1898.

68. *El Paso International Daily Times*, April 30, May 10 and 27, 1898.

69. N. Ray Gilmore, "Mexico and the Spanish-American War," in *Hispanic American Historical Review* 43, no. 4 (1963): 511.

70. De León, *Mexican Americans*, 58–59; McCaffrey, "Texans," 268.

71. *San Antonio Express News*, April 2, 1898; *El Paso International Daily Times*, April 21, 1898.

72. *The Laredo Daily Times*, March 29, 1898.

73. Young, "Deconstructing *La Raza*," 234–235; *The Laredo Daily Times*, November 10, 1891.

74. *The Laredo Daily Times*, April 26, 1898.

75. *The Laredo Daily Times* April 28, 1898.

76. *The Laredo Daily Times*, May 4, 1898.

77. *The Laredo Daily Times*, June 18, 1898; Lewis E. Daniell, *Personnel of the Texas State Government; With Sketches of Representative Men of Texas* (Austin: Smith, Hicks, and Jones, State Printers, 1889), 551–552.

78. *First Annual Report of the Agricultural Bureau of the Department of Agriculture, Insurance, Statistics, and History* (Austin: Texas State House Press, 1889), xlix; John C. Rayburn, "The Rough Riders in San Antonio, 1898," *Arizona and the West* 3, no. 2 (Summer 1961): 115; McCaffrey, "Texans," 262.

79. Texas Adjutant General Service Records, 1836–1935.

80. Eleno Castillo, George Chávez, Eugene Hernández, and Henry Pérez Service Records, Texas Adjutant General Service Records, 1836–1935.

81. Leffler, "The Paradox of Patriotism," 24–30.

82. *La Fé Católica* (San Antonio), May 7, 1898. (Translation by author.)

83. *El Regidor* (San Antonio), May 26, 1898. (Translation by author.)

84. Augustine De Zavala, Texas Adjutant General Service Records, 1836–1935.

85. Augustine De Zavala to Dear Sister, May 18, 1898, in Adina De Zavala Papers, CAH.

86. Augustine De Zavala to Dear Sister, May 18, 1898.

87. Augustine De Zavala to Dear Sister, May 27, 1898.

88. Augustine De Zavala to Dear Sister, June 21, 1898.

89. *Beeville Bee*, May 6, 1898, May 13, 1898; *Brownsville Daily Statesman*; May 17, 1898; *Houston Daily Post*, May 13, 1898; Texas Adjutant General Service Records, 1836–1935.

90. *Corpus Christi Weekly Caller*, February 18, 1898.

91. Trask, *War with Spain in 1898*, 157.

92. See the respective records in the Texas Adjutant General Service Records, 1836–1935. The figure of Tejanos in the Spanish-American War is derived from examining the pension rolls of over 4,300 veterans. Of these only a dozen indicate their origins as "Mexican." This does not consider soldiers of mixed ancestry.

93. McCaffrey, "Texas and the Spanish American War," 275; Purcell, "The History of the Texas Militia," 283–284; Claudia Hazlewood, "Mabry, Woodford Haywood," *Handbook of Texas Online*, accessed June 19, 2023, https://www.tshaonline.org/handbook/entries/mabry-woodford-haywood.

94. *Laredo Daily Times*, November 24, 1898.

95. McCaffrey, "Texans," 277–278.

96. See Agustine De Zavala to Dear Sister, May 17, 24, 27, June 1, 14, August 1898, in Zavala Papers, CAH.

97. Brian McAllister Linn, *The Philippine War, 1899–1902* (Lawrence: University Press of Kansas, 2000), passim.

98. Linn, *Philippine*, 125; Jack S. Anderson, "Service Honest and Faithful: The Thirty-Third Volunteer Infantry Regiment in the Philippine War, 1899–1901" (PhD diss., University of North Texas, 2017), 35–36.

99. Anderson, "The Thirty-Third," 48–49.

100. Muñoz Martinez, *Injustice*, 15–18.

101. Alex Mendoza, "Tejanos at War: A History of Mexican Texans and American Wars," in Alex Mendoza and Charles Grear, eds., *Texans and War: New Interpretations of the State's Military History* (College Station: Texas A&M University Press, 2012), 38–62.

102. De León, *Mexican Americans*, 65.

103. Muñoz Martinez, *Injustice*, 16 (quotation).

104. Martinez, *Injustice*, 16.

105. Mendoza, "Tejanos," 48.

Chapter 4

1. Campbell, *Gone to Texas*, 325–326.

2. Zamora, *The World of Mexican Workers*, 10–29.

3. De León, *Mexican Americans*, 61–62, 74; Montejano, *Anglos*, 130–133.

4. Calderón, "Mexican Politics," 1–4; De León, *Mexican Americans*, 62; Montejano, *Anglos*, 129.

5. De León, *Mexican Americans*, 65.

6. Kelly Lytle Hernández, *Bad Mexicans: Race, Empire, and Revolution in the Borderlands* (New York: W. W. Norton, 2022), 29–34.

7. De León, *Mexican Americans*, 80–82.

8. De León, *Mexican Americans*, 74.

9. Ramírez, *To the Line of Fire*, 6–7.

10. Benjamin Heber Johnson, *Revolution in Texas: How a Forgotten Rebellion and its Bloody Suppression Turned Mexicans into Americans* (New Haven: Yale University Press, 2003), 47.

11. Ralph A. Wooster, *Texas and Texans in the Great War* (Buffalo Gap, TX: State House Press, 2009), 107.

12. Muñoz Martinez, *Injustice*, 7.

13. De León, *Mexican Americans*, 56; Muñoz Martinez, *Injustice*, 30–75; Rebeca Anne Todd Koenig, "Rodríguez, Antonio," *Handbook of Texas Online*, accessed March 1, 2023, https://www.tshaonline.org/handbook/entries/rodriguez-antonio.

14. Wooster, *Texas*, 107.

15. Johnson, *Revolution*, 3–4, 73, 79–80; Montejano, *Anglos*, 117; Ramírez, *Line of Fire*, 8–9; Wooster, *Texas*, 20.

16. Montejano, *Anglos*, 118.

17. Johnson, *Revolution*, 82–85; Montejano, *Anglos*, 117.

18. Johnson, *Revolution*, 90–94.

19. Trinidad Gonzales, "The Mexican Revolution, *Revolucion de Texas*, and *Matanza de 1915*," in Arnoldo De León, ed., *War Along the Border: The Mexican Revolution and Tejano Communities* (College Station: Texas A&M University Press, 2012), 111–121; Uglow, *Military*, 289–296.

20. *San Antonio Express*, August 9, 1915; Montejano, *Anglos*, 119.

21. *San Antonio Express*, August 11, 1915.

22. *Brownsville Herald*, September 17, 1915.

23. Muñoz Martinez, *Injustice*, 77; Johnson, *Revolution*, 116–117.

24. Muñoz Martinez, *Injustice*, 78–83.

25. Johnson, *Revolution*, 119.

26. Charles C. Cumberland, "Border Raids in the Lower Rio Grande Valley," *Southwestern Historical Quarterly* 57 (January 1954): 292–293.

27. *Brownsville Herald*, September 17, 1915; Ramírez, *Line of Fire*, 11.

28. *Brownsville Herald*, September 8, 1915.

29. Johnson, *Revolution in Texas*, 121–122; Ramírez, *Line of Fire*, 12.

30. Jeff Guinn, *War on the Border: Villa, Pershing, the Texas Rangers, and an American Invasion* (New York: Simon and Schuster, 2021), 131–140, 156.

31. *San Antonio Express*, January 17, 1916, April 28, 1916; Muñoz Martinez, *Injustice*, 20.

32. *El Paso Daily Times*, February 13, 1916; *San Antonio Express*, February 12, 1916.

33. *El Paso Morning Times*, October 5, 1916; Ramírez, *Line of Fire*, 15.

34. *La Prensa* (San Antonio), July 7, 1916; *El Paso Morning Times* (Spanish-language edition), May 24, 1916.

35. *El Paso Morning Times* (Spanish-language edition), November 7, 1916; *San Antonio Express*, November 14, 1916; *La Prensa* (San Antonio), December 12, 1916.

36. Gregory W. Ball, *Texas and World War I* (Austin: State House Press, 2019), 5–6; Ramírez, *Line of Fire*, 15–16; Wooster, *Texas*, 26–30.

37. *Houston Post*, March 2, 1917.

38. Ball, *Texas and World War I*, 6–7; Wooster, *Texas*, 32–33.

39. Ball, *Texas and World War I*, 7.

40. President Wilson's Declaration of War Message to Congress, April 2, 1917, Records of the United States Senate; Record Group 46, National Archives, Washington, DC.

41. *Houston Post*, April 7, 1917.

42. *El Paso Morning Times*, April 8, 1917.

43. *Cleburne Morning Review*, April 10, 1917.

44. Wooster, *Texas*, 35.

45. Ramírez, *Line of Fire*, 17 (quotation).

46. *La Prensa*, May 30, 1917.

47. Ramírez, *Line of Fire*, 18; Teresa Palomo Acosta, "La Crónica," *Handbook of Texas Online*, accessed June 22, 2023, https://www.tshaonline.org/handbook/entries/la -cronica.

48. Edward M. Coffman, *The War to End All Wars: The American Military Experience in World War I* (Lexington: University Press of Kentucky, 1998), 16–17; David Kennedy, *Over Here: The First World War and American Society* (New York: Oxford University Press, 2004), 107.

49. John S.D. Eisenhower, *The Epic Story of the American Army in World War I* (New York: Free Press, 2001), 24–25.

50. Mendoza, "Tejanos at War," 48–49; Alex Mendoza, "'I Know No Other Country': Tejanos and the American Wars of the Twentieth Century," *Military History of the West* 41 (2011): 34–35.

51. De León, *Mexican Americans in Texas*, 91.

52. De León, *Mexican Americans in Texas*; Carole E. Christian, "Joining the American Mainstream: Texas' Mexican Americans During World War I," *Southwestern Historical Quarterly* 92, no. 4 (April 1989): 572–577, 592–594.

53. Ramírez, *Line of Fire*, 27–30.

54. Editorial, W. E. B. Du Bois, *The Crisis*, July 1918, 111.

55. *El Demócrata Fronterizo*, October 5, 1918. (Translation by author.)

56. *La Prensa* (San Antonio), June 6, 1917; Ramírez, *Line of Fire*, 23.

57. Wooster, *Texas*, 38–39; *San Antonio Express*, August 17, 1917.

58. *San Antonio Express*, August 17, 1917.

59. Ramírez, *Line of Fire*, 23.

60. *San Antonio Express*, August 18, 1918.

61. Ramírez, *Line of Fire*, 31–33.

62. Zamora, *The World of the Mexican*, xi, 197–210.

63. *El Demócrata Fronterizo*, December 1, 1917.

64. Ramírez, *Line of Fire*, 32

65. Ramírez, *Line of Fire*, 19.

66. Ramírez, *Line of Fire*, 20.

67. *San Antonio Express*, August 17, 1917; *Laredo Weekly Times*, July 1, 1917.

68. *Dallas Morning News*, May 1918; *Evolución*, June 17, 1917, November 10, 1917; *New York Times*, May 17, 1918.

69. Ramírez, *Line of Fire*, 33.

70. Jeanette Keith, "The Politics of Southern Draft Resistance, 1917–1918: Class, Race, and Conscription in the Rural South," *Journal of American History* 87, no. 4 (March 2001): 1357; *Houston Post*, January 4, 1918; Ramírez, *Line of Fire*, 33.

71. Ramírez, *Line of Fire*, 34.

72. Ramírez, *Line of Fire*, 35.

73. *Corpus Christi Caller*, September 11, 1918; *Brownsville Herald*, September 11, 1918; *The San Antonio Express*, May 5, 1917.

74. Morales, "*Hijos de la Gran Guerra*," 88.

75. Kennedy, *Over Here*, 61.

76. Christian, "Mainstream," 562, 568–570.

77. Ramírez, *Line of Fire*, 35.

78. *Corpus Christi Caller*, September 11, 1918.

79. *Laredo Weekly Times*, April 15, 1917.

80. *La Prensa*, September 18, 1918.

81. *Corpus Christi Caller*, April 5, 1917.

82. *Houston Daily Post*, May 18, 1917.

83. *San Antonio Express*, May 16, 1917.

84. *La Prensa*, September 27, 1918; *Laredo Weekly Times*, July 15, 29, 1917. (Translation by author.)

85. *Evolución*, October 22, 1918 translation by author); *Laredo Weekly Times*, April 21, 1918.

86. Christian, "Mainstream," 584–585; Kennedy, *Over Here*, 114; Ramírez, *Line of Fire*, 60–63.

87. Ramírez, *Line of Fire*, 59.

88. Ramírez, *Line of Fire*, chapter 3.

89. José De La Luz Sáenz, *The World War I Diary of José De La Luz* Sáenz, ed. and trans. Emilio Zamora, (College Station: Texas A&M University Press, 2014), 30.

90. Christian, "Mainstream," 562.

91. Manuel Gamio, "Juan Salorio," in *The Life Story of the Mexican Immigrant: Autobiographic Documents Collected by Manuel Gamio* (Chicago: University of Chicago Press, 1931), 83.

92. *La Prensa*, April 10, 1917.

93. Ramírez, *Line of Fire*, 19, 20, 22–23; De León, *Mexican Americans*, 91, 93.

94. *La Prensa*, October 27, 1918. (Translation by author.)

95. Conrado Mendoza, interview by Mike Acosta, December 4, 1976, Interview No. 252, Institute of Oral History, The University of Texas at El Paso. Mendoza said, "Yo quise ir al servicio . . . [pero] mi dijeron que estaba muy joven." In text translation by author.)

96. *La Prensa*, September 18, 1918.

97. Sáenz, *World War I Diary*, 30.

98. Christian, "Mainstream," 578.

99. *La Prensa*, May 15, 1917. (Translation by author.)

100. *La Prensa*, September 26, 1918.

101. Geoffrey Wawro, *Sons of Freedom: The Forgotten American Soldiers Who Defeated Germany in World War I* (New York: Basic Books, 2018), 30.

102. Wawro, *Sons of Freedom*, 35–38.

103. Geoffrey Wawro, "How 'Hyphenated Americans' Won World War I," *New York Times*, September 18, 2018.

104. Sáenz, *World War I Diary*, 29.

105. Ramírez, *Line of Fire*, 38.

106. Uglow, *Military History of Texas*, 306; Wooster, *Texas*, 40; Eisenhower, *Yanks*, 63.

107. Ball, *Texas and World War I*, 84.

108. Wooster, *Texas*, 41.

109. *El Demócrata Fronterizo*, December 1, 1917 (translation by author); M. J. Exner, M.D., *Prostitution in its Relation to the Army on the Mexican Border* (New York: The American Social Hygiene Association, 1917), 2, 3–15.

110. *Corpus Christi Caller*, September 11, 1917.

111. Byron Farwell, *Over There: The United States in the Great War, 1917–1918* (New York: Norton and Company, 1999), 141–147.

112. Ramírez, *Line of Fire*, 85 (quotation).

113. Kennedy, *Over Here*, 187–189.

114. Coffman, *The War*, 165; Kennedy, *Over Here*, 189.

115. H. A. Morgan Memorandum, "Foreign Legion Companies in Development Battalions," Foreign Speaking Soldier Sub-Section, August 27, 1918, Records of the War Department General and Special Staffs, Entry 65, Box No. 3533, Record Group 165, National Archives Administration; Ramírez, *Line of Fire*, 80; Capt. Edward E. Padgett, "Camp Gordon Plan," *Infantry Journal* 15, no. 5 (1918), 334–335; Dennis Connole, *America's "Foreign Legion": Immigrant Soldiers in the Great War* (Jefferson, NC: McFarland Press, 2018), 93–96.

116. G. B. Perkins to Lt. Colonel Fitch, September 17, 1918, USA Chief of the Military Morale Section, War Department, Office of the Chief of Staff, Box 3533, National Archives.

117. Nancy Gentile Ford, *Americans All!: Foreign-born Soldiers in World War I* (College Station: Texas A&M University Press, 2001), 108–109.

118. *Corpus Christi Caller*, September 11, 1917; E. B. Johns, comp., *Camp Travis and its Part in the World War* (New York: by the compiler, 1919), 13–61.

119. Quoted in Ramírez, *Line of Fire*, 81–82.

120. *La Prensa*, December 4, 1918.

121. Shaffer, *America in the Great War*, 178–179.

122. Ramírez, *Line of Fire*, 82.

123. Garna L. Christian, *Black Soldiers in Jim Crow Texas, 1899–1917* (College Station: Texas A&M University Press, 1995), 199.

124. Ramírez, *Line of Fire*, xiii–xiv.

125. Sáenz, *World War I Diary*, 97; Christian, "Mainstream," 582.

126. Richard Faulkner, *Pershing's Crusaders: The American Soldier in World War I* (Lawrence: University Press of Kansas, 2017), 83.

127. Mark E. Grotelueschen, *The AEF Way of War: The American Army and Combat in World War I* (Cambridge, UK: Cambridge University Press, 2007), 40; Faulkner, *Pershing's Crusaders*, 64–65, 95; Farwell, *Over There*, 103–105; Coffman, *The War*, 30.

128. Ramírez, *Line of Fire*, 91 (quotation)

129. Sáenz, *World War I Diary*, 69.

130. *Laredo Weekly Times*, June 2, 1918.

131. Christian, "Mainstream," 579.

132. Farwell, *Over There*, 65; *San Antonio Express*, February 13, 1918.

133. Farwell, *Over There*, 92.

134. "First U.S. Troops Land in France," *The Sunday Star* (Washington, DC), July 1, 1917.

135. Sáenz, *World War I Diary*, 398.

136. Pablo González to Father and Mother, November 1, 1918, in *Brownsville Herald*, December 9, 1918.

137. Ramírez, *Line of Fire*, 95.

138. Sáenz, *World War I Diary*, 422, 424; Ramírez, *Line of Fire*, 95.

139. Wawro, *Sons of Freedom*, 9; Farwell, *Over There*, 91.

140. Donald Smythe, *Pershing: General of the Armies* (Bloomington: Indiana University Press, 1986), 175–176.

141. Coffman, *The War*, 170; Eisenhower, *Yanks*, 17; Farwell, *Over There*, 89, 100; Kennedy, *Over Here*, 172.

142. Eisenhower, *Yanks*, 80–82.

143. Wooster, *Texas*, 126–127; Ball, *Texas and World War I*, 100–101; Uglow, *Military*, 311.

144. Farwell, *Over There*, 91–94, 100; Eisenhower, *Yanks*, 62, 90–91.

145. Eisenhower, *Yanks*, 84.

146. José de la Luz Sáenz to My Dear Wife, July 30, 1918, in Sáenz, *World War I Diary*, 168.

147. Gamio, "Juan Salorio," 280.

148. *La Prensa*, June 2, 1919. (Translation by author.)

149. Wawro, *Sons of Freedom*, 200–210; Farwell, *Over There*, 181; Wooster, *Texas*, 130–131.

150. *La Prensa*, October 21, 1918. (Translation by author.) See also *Houston Daily Post*, October 1, 1918.

151. Eisenhower, *Yanks*, 173–174.

152. Smythe, *Pershing*, 171; Ford, *Americans All!*, 12; Sarah Jameson, "Ready for Primetime: The American First Army at St. Mihiel, 1918" (PhD diss., University of North Texas, 2023), 67–68; Eisenhower, *Yanks*, 188; Uglow, *Military*, 311; Wawro, *Sons*, 275–300.

153. Sáenz, *World War I Diary*, 203.

154. *Evolución*, October 26, 1918. (Translation by author.)

155. Sáenz, *World War I Diary*, 208.

156. Wawro, *Sons*, 245–246.

157. Account of Private Pablo Cortez, Company M 141st Infantry, 36th Division, October 8, 1918, in Records of the American Expeditionary Forces, World War 1, 1848–1942, Records Group 120, National Archives, Washington, DC (Translation by author). Cortez wrote in Spanish: "Fuimos a andetap [on the top] arriba simia cuando dieron escomecies [sic] y en cuando venía viendo [viniendo] los que caivan [caían] americanos y tan bien bilos [vi los] alemanes que caían mas delante [voltie] y lla [ya] no vi al caporal quello [que yo] llevaba y entonces mas derejira por un sargento dela mis compañia fines es todo lo que [vi]."

158. Account of Sgt. Miguel Barrera, 141st Inf, Co. B, 36th Division, in Records of the American Expeditionary Forces, World War 1, 1848–1942, Records Group 120, National Archives, Washington, DC.

159. Account of Sgt. Miguel Barrera.

160. Eisenhower, *Yanks*, 262–272, 280–283; Uglow, *Military History of Texas*, 310–312.

161. José de La Luz Sáenz to Eulalio Velázquez, July 5, 1918, in Sáenz, *World War I Diary*, 152.

162. Elena Gómez, "Marcelino Serna Became World War I Hero," *Borderlands* 23 (2004–2005): 10; "Medal Still in Limbo for WW I Soldier," *San Antonio Express News*, January 9, 2025; Christian, "Mainstream," 583; Wooster, *Texas*, 117–145; United States Department of Defense, *Hispanics in America's Defense* (Washington, DC: Office of the Deputy Assistant Secretary of Defense for Military Manpower and Personnel Policy, 1988, 25.

163. "Laredo's only Medal of Honor Winner Remembered," *Laredo Morning Times*, November 9, 2002; Craig Phelon, "The Hero Who Hid His Heritage, *Vista* 7, no. 6 (January 4, 1992): 7–25; De León, *Mexican Americans*, 94.

164. Sáenz, *World War I Diary*, 274–275; Ramírez, *Line of Fire*, 26, 102.

165. Ball, *Texas and World War I*, 115.

166. Sáenz, *World War I Diary*, 287.

167. Wawro, *Sons*, 442–443; Ramírez, *Line of Fire*, 103; Ball, *Texas and World War I*, 114–115; Wooster, *Texas and Texans*, 153, 160–161.

168. *Evolución*, November 28, 1918. (Translation by author.)

169. Ramírez, *Line of Fire*, 105.

170. *Evolución*, August 14, 1918.

171. *Evolución*, December 8, 1918. (Translation by author.)

172. *La Prensa*, November 3, 1918. (Translation by author.)

173. *Evolución*, June 24, 1919. (Translation by author.)

174. *Dallas Morning News* June 2, 14, 15. 1919.

175. Mendoza, "I Know No Other Country," 38–39.

176. Emilio Zamora, "Fighting on Two Fronts: José de la Luz Sáenz and the Language of the Mexican American Civil Rights Movement," in Ramón A. Gutiérrez and Silvio Torres-Saillant, eds., *Recovering the U.S. Hispanic Literary Heritage* (Houston: Arte Public Press, 2002), 214–230; Alex Mendoza, "The Warrior Tradition," *LareDOS: A Journal of the Borderlands* 14, no. 4 (April 2008): 65; Ford, *Americans All!*, 144–145; De León, *Mexican Americans*, 108–109; Wooster, *Texas*, 167.

177. Ramírez, *Line of Fire*, 22–23; De León, *Mexican Americans*, 91–102, 110–112; Christian, "Mainstream," 572–577, 592–594; Zamora, "Two Fronts," 214–230.

178. Harry L. Krenek, "A History of the Texas National Guard Between World War I and World War II" (PhD diss, Texas Tech University, 1979), 20–21, 24–27, 30–31, 39–41; Elmer Ray Milner, "An Agonizing Evolution: A History of the Texas National Guard, 1900–1945" (PhD diss., North Texas State University, 1979), 24–31, 35–55, 78–82. It is difficult to specifically delineate exact totals of Tejanos in the US military due to

the government's policy of labeling all soldiers of Mexican descent as "white" during the First World War and beyond. Thus, in the interwar years, specific numbers for Texas military personnel of Mexican descent are difficult to ascertain due to the policy of labeling Tejanos as "white" and the number of Mexican American veterans who came from mixed ancestry (as in the case of David Bennes Barkley/ David Barkley Cantú).

179. Jorge Rodríguez, "A History of El Paso's Company E in World War II" (master's thesis, University of Texas at El Paso, 2010), 27–30.

Chapter 5

1. *Corpus Christi Caller*, June 19, 1919.
2. *Corpus Christi Caller*, June 19, 1919.
3. Pete Leyva, interview by Oscar J. Martínez, July 20, 1976, Interview No. 312, Institute of Oral History, University of Texas at El Paso.
4. Ramírez, *To the Line of Fire*, 119.
5. Leyva interview.
6. Ramírez, *To the Line of Fire*, 22–23; De León, *Mexican Americans*, 91–102, 110–112; Christian, "Mainstream," 572–577, 592–594; Zamora, "Fighting on Two Fronts," 214–230.
7. Franklin D. Roosevelt, "Speech by Franklin D. Roosevelt, New York." Transcript, 1941. https://www.loc.gov/item/afccal000483/.
8. Uglow, *Military*, 320, 322. According to Arnoldo De León, scholars believe "between 500,000 and 1 million Hispanics saw military duty." See Arnoldo De León, "Tejanos: On Two Battlegrounds," in Christopher B. Bean, ed., *Texas and Texans in World War II, 1941–1945* (College Station: Texas A&M University Press, 2022), 128.
9. *Laredo Morning Times*, November 17, 2020; John Valls, interview by Liliana Rodriguez, March 6, 2010, Voces Oral History Center, University of Texas at Austin (hereafter VOHC).
10. Arnoldo De León, "Mexican Americans in Texas," in Ben Proctor and Archie McDonald, eds., *The Texas Heritage*, 4th Edition (Wheeling, IL: Harlan Davidson, 2003), 215.
11. Mendoza, "I Know No Other Country," 38–39.
12. Luis Leyva, interview by Mary Alice Carnes, November 23, 2001, VOHC.
13. David Zimmerman, "Mexican-American Texans," in James Lee War, ed., *1941: Texas Goes to War* (Denton: University of North Texas Press, 1991), 128–143; *Albuquerque Journal*, July 26, 1981; *Houston Chronicle*, April 5, 1999; Rodriguez, "A History of El Paso's Company E," 37, 45–50, 51–61.
14. Arnulfo D. Azios, interview by Paul Zepeda and Ernest Eguia, December 13, 2002, VOHC. See also "Arnulfo D. Azios Obituary," *Houston Chronicle*, March 27, 2013.
15. Randel Fernández, interview by Steven Rosales, June 30, 2004, VOHC.
16. De León, "Two Battlegrounds," 128–129; Mendoza, "I Know No Other Country," 39–40.

17. Mariscal, *Aztlán and Viet Nam*, 27; Luis Álvarez, "Transnational Latino Soldiering: Military Service and Ethnic Politics during World War II: in Maggie Rivas Rodríguez and B.V. Olguín eds., *Latinos/as and World War II: Mobility, Agency, and Ideology* (Austin: University of Texas Press, 2014), 76–77.

18. Alvino Mendoza interview, National Museum of the Pacific War, Fredericksburg, Texas.

19. Reynaldo Benavides Rendon, interview by Juan Martínez, February 14, 2004, VOHC.

20. Bob Sánchez, interview by Marcel Rodríguez, July 7, 2007, VOHC.

21. Ramón Martín Rivas, interview by Maggie Rivas Rodríguez, June 12, 1999, VOHC.

22. Noé Sandoval, interview by Julio Ovando, November 6, 2004, VOHC.

23. Natividad Campos, interview by Beatriz Guerrero, September 1, 2007, VOHC.

24. *Falfurrias Facts*, June 19, 1942.

25. Lee Kennett, *G.I.: The American Soldier in World War II* (Norman: University of Oklahoma Press, 1987), 11–12 (quotation on page 12); Rendon interview, VOHC.

26. Kennett, *GI*, 39–41; Uglow, *Military*, 320.

27. Dave Gutiérrez, *Patriots from the Barrio: The Story of Company E, 141st Infantry: The Only All Mexican American Unit in World War II* (Yardley, PA: Westholme Press, 2018), 46.

28. Uglow, *Military*, 316–319.

29. Kennett, *GI*, 43.

30. 1940 Texas Almanac, City Population History from 1850–2000, accessed August 8, 2025, https://www.texasalmanac.com/drupal-backup/images/CityPopHist%20web.pdf.

31. Kennett, *GI*, 42–47.

32. William R. Ornelas, interview by Dr. Maggie Rivas-Rodríguez, VOHC.

33. De León, "On Two Battlegrounds," 129.

34. Thomas Bruscino, *A Nation Forged in War: How World War II Taught Americans to Get Along* (Knoxville: University of Tennessee Press, 2010), 61–62 (quotation on p. 62).

35. Porfirio Martínez, interview by Yazmin Lazcano, October 15, 2000, VOHC.

36. Joe Villa, interview by Amanda Abrigo, July 24, 2010, VOHC.

37. Raymond Muñiz, interview by Maggie Rivas-Rodríguez, June 25, 2006, VOHC.

38. Campos interview.

39. Davis quoted in Bruscino, *Forged in War*, 79.

40. Bruscino, *Forged in War*, 78–79.

41. Albert Caballero, interview by Steve Treviño, May 3, 2008, VOHC.

42. Steven E. Rosales, *Soldados Razos at War: Chicano Politics, Identity, and Masculinity in the U.S. Military from World War II to Vietnam* (Tucson: University of Arizona Press, 2017), 73–74; Raymond Muníz, Virgilio Roel, Juan Martínez, and Guadalupe "Lupe" Hernandez, interviews, VOHC.

43. Kennett, *GI*, 48–49.

44. Isidro Ramos, interview by Jesse Herrera, July 13, 2007, VOHC.

45. Calixto Ramírez, interview by Karin Brulliard, September 13, 2003, VOHC.

46. Gutiérrez, *Patriots from the Barrio*, 51.

47. Kennett, *GI*, 49–59, 63–64.
48. Lauro Castillo, interview by Manuel Castillo, November 23, 2012, VOHC.
49. José R. Navarro, interview by Veronica Franco and Raquel C. Garza, October 13, 2001, VOHC.
50. Kennett, *GI*, 110–112.
51. Villa interview.
52. Jesse Acuña, interview by Paul Brown, September 15, 2008, VOHC.
53. *The Laredo Times*, February 22, 1942. (Translation by author.)
54. Eliud Acevedo, interview by Eliud Martínez, May 11, 2009, VOHC.
55. Kennett, *GI*, 116.
56. José Eriberto Adame, interview by Christina Perkins, December 8, 2001, VOHC.
57. De León, "On Two Battlegrounds," 130.
58. Geoffrey Perret, *There's a War to be Won: The United States Army in World War II* (New York: Ivy Books, 1991), 129–164.
59. Williamson Murray and Allan Millett, *A War to be Won: Fighting the Second World War* (Cambridge, MA: Belknap Press, 2000), 301–303; 375–381.
60. Fred Gómez, interview by William Luna, September 17, 2002, VOHC.
61. Santiago Craver, interview by Robert Rivas, November 6, 2003, VOHC.
62. Richard Ortiz, interview by Antonio Gil, November 6, 2004, VOHC.
63. Perret, *There's a War to be Won*, 167–169.
64. Gutiérrez, *Patriots from the Barrio*, 66.
65. Rick Atkinson, *An Army at Dawn: The War in North Africa, 1942-1943* (New York: Holt and Company, 2002), 88–91.
66. Eduardo Peniche, interview by Fernando Dovalina, May 17, 2000, VOHC.
67. William R. Ornelas, interview by Maggie Rivas Rodríguez, August 25, 1999, OHC.
68. Murray and Millett, *War to be Won*, 377–387.
69. Roberto Vásquez, interview by William Luna, June 20, 2002, VOHC.
70. "El Paso War Hero Now Leads Quiet Life," *Albuquerque Journal*, July 26, 1981; Gutiérrez, *Patriots from the Barrio*, 30–31; Rodríguez, "A History of Company E," 73–74.
71. Guadalupe Conde, interview by Carlos Conde, September 7, 2002, VOHC.
72. Kennett, *GI*, 72–73.
73. José R. Navarro, interview by Veronica Franco and Raquel C. Garza, October 13, 2001, VOHC.
74. Allen R. Millett and Peter Maslowski, *For the Common Defense: A Military History of the United States of America* (New York: Free Press of America, 1994), 450–451, 458–460; Murray and Millett, *A War to be Won*, 304–355; Emilio Portales, interview by Patricia Portales, May 13, 2008, VOHC.
75. Portales interview.
76. Ricardo Martínez Bustos, interview by Raul R. Zepeda, February 14, 2006, VOHC; Benjamin Alvarado, "Untitled Memoir," in Benjamin Alvarado Collection (AFC/2001/001/32448), Veterans History Project, American Folklife Center, Library of Congress, Washington, DC.

77. Francisco Vega, interview by Juan Martínez, July 2, 2007, VOHC.

78. Johnnie Marino, interview by Paul R. Zepeda, May 22, 2001, VOHC.

79. Mike Silva, interview by Violeta Domínguez, November 2, 2002, VOHC.

80. Ernesto Pedregón Martínez, interview by Jeffrey Lee Johnson, June 28, 2001, VOHC.

81. Millett and Maslowski, *For a Common Defense*, 479–480; Bennie Trujillo, interview by Joseph Padilla, February 19, 2011, VOHC.

82. Kennett, *GI*, 73–74.

83. Margarito Correa, interview by Ismael Martínez, August 20, 2002, VOHC.

84. Abelardo García, interview by Raquel C. Garza, March 21, 2009, VOHC.

85. Alfonso López Dávila interview, April 15, 2017, VOHC.

86. Peniche interview.

87. Randal Zepeda Fernández, interview by Steven Rosales, June 30, 2004, VOHC.

88. William R. Ornelas, interview by Maggie Rivas Rodriguez, August 25, 1999, VOHC.

89. Stephen E. Ambrose, *Citizen Soldiers: The U.S. Army from Normandy Beaches to the Bulge to the Surrender of Germany, June 7, 1944–May 7, 1945* (New York: Touchstone, 1998), 461–463.

90. Marino interview; Juan Martínez interview by Celina Moreno, February 2, 2002, VOHC.

91. Joe G. Lerma, interview by Rene Zambrano, April 11, 2001, VOHC.

92. Harry A. Gailey, *The War in the Pacific: From Pearl Harbor to Tokyo Bay* (Novato, CA: Presidio Press, 1995), 142–145.

93. José Adame, interview by Christina Perkins, December 8, 2001, VOHC.

94. Aaron Mendoza interview, National Museum of the Pacific War, Fredericksburg, Texas.

95. Juan Medina Sánchez, interview by Grace Charles, VOHC.

96. Emiliano Espinosa Gimeno, interview by Joseph Padilla, June 1, 2011, VOHC.

97. John Dower, *War Without Mercy: Race and Power in the Pacific War* (New York: Pantheon Books, 1986), 60–68, 74–75.

98. W. H. Anderson, "The Question of Japanese-Americans," in *Los Angeles Times*, February 2, 1942.

99. Moises Flores, interview by Joe Myers Vásquez, February 2, 2002, VOHC.

100. Dower, *War Without Mercy*, 116, 179–180.

101. Kennett, *GI*, 163–164.

102. Gailey, *War in the Pacific*, 55.

103. Gonzalo Garza, interview by Juan Campos, March 17, 2001, VOHC.

104. Benigno Gaytán, interview by Amanda Peña, August 4, 2007, VOHC.

105. Genovevo Bargas Interview by Raquel C. Garza, August 4, 2007, VOHC.

106. Peter De León, interview by Antonio Gilb, November 13, 2001, VOHC.

107. Alvino Mendoza, interview by Haldun Morgan, October 20, 1999, VOHC.

108. *Laredo Morning Times*, November 18, 2007; Homero Martínez Statement to Claims Committee, 1946, Documents of the Lost Battalion, copy in author's possession.

109. Felipe Ortego, interview by Mario Barrera, March 21, 2008, VOHC.

110. Raul Muñoz Escobar, interview by Raquel C. Garza, November 21, 2007, VOHC.

111. Andrew Aguirre, interview by Rene Zambrano, January 22, 2001, VOHC.

112. Ricardo García, interview by Cheryl Smith Kemp, May 9, 2008, VOHC.

113. Isidro Ramos interview.

114. John Valls interview, VOHC; John Andrew Snyder, "John Valls: Hitler's 'Best Commander' Climbed Down from His Tank and Personally Surrendered to this Laredoan," *LareDOS: A Journal of the Borderlands* 16, no. 4 (April 2010): 16–17, 19.

115. *El Paso Herald-Post*, November 6, 1944; Rodríguez, "A History of Company E," 98; Gilbert Contreras to Alex Mendoza, July 2, 2022, March 12, 2024, emails in author's possession.

116. Paul Ham, *Hiroshima Nagasaki: The Real Story of the Atomic Bombings and their Aftermath* (New York: Harper Collins, 2011), 459–487.

117. Raymond Vega, interview by Violeta Domínguez, December 12, 2003, VOHC.

118. Elias Guajardo, interview by Kristin Henry, March 9, 2001, VOHC.

119. Lorena Oropeza, *¡Raza Sí! ¡Guerra No!: Chicano Protest and Patriotism During the Viet Nam War Era* (Berkeley: University of California Press, 2005), 14–15.

120. Roberto R. Treviño, "Prensa y Patria: The Spanish-Language Press and the Biculturation of the Tejano Middle Class, 1920–1940," *Western Historical Quarterly* 22, no. 4 (November 1991): 454, 464, 466–467 (quotation on p. 467).

121. De León, *Mexican Americans*, 117.

122. Naomi Quiñonez, "Rosita the Riveter: Welding Tradition with Wartime Transformation," in Maggie Rivas-Rodríguez, ed., *Mexican Americans and World War II* (Austin: University of Texas Press, 2005), 245–267.

123. Rafaela Muñiz Esquivel, interview by Joanne Rao & Mario Sánchez, April 12, 2001, VOHC.

124. De León, "On Two Battlegrounds," 133–134.

125. De León, "On Two Battlegrounds," 134.

126. *Falfurrias Facts*, May 29, 1942.

127. *El Paso Times*, December 15, 1941.

128. *Laredo Times*, February 25, 1942.

129. *Corpus Christi Caller Times*, January 28, 1942.

130. Marcelino Ramírez Bautista, tribute by Mercy Bautista-Olvera, daughter of Marcelino Ramírez Bautista, VOHC.

131. Thomas A. Guglielmo, "Fighting for Caucasian Rights: Mexicans, Mexican Americans, and the Transnational Struggle for Civil Rights in World War II Texas," *Journal of American History* 92, no. 4 (March 2006): 1213.

132. Zachary Foust, "Caucasian Race Resolution," *Handbook of Texas Online*, accessed February 2, 2024, https://www.tshaonline.org/handbook/entries/caucasian-race-resolution.

133. De León, "On Two Battlegrounds," 141.

134. *Falfurrias Facts*, July 2, 1942; *Eagle Eye* (Eagle Pass, TX), September 24, 1943.

135. *Laredo Times*, March 8 and 16, 1942.

136. *Laredo Times*, January 12, 1943.

137. Alex Mendoza, "'An Example for the Rest of Texas in the Way of Celebrations': Laredo's Border Olympics and the Move towards Modernization," *Journal of South Texas* 24, no. 2 (Fall 2011): 24–53; *Laredo Times*, January 12, 1943.

138. *Laredo Times*, March 12, 14, 27, 1943; *Laredo Times*, March 7, 16, 19. 1944.

139. *Laredo Times*, February 22, 1942.

140. *La Pitahaya* (Martin High school yearbook), 1942, 1943, and 1944; Alex Mendoza, "Martin High School During the 'Good War,'" in *LareDOS* 15, no. 12 (December 2010): 52.

141. Gutiérrez, *Patriots from the Barrio*, 208; Cleto L. Rodríguez, interview by Oscar J. Martínez and Sarah E. John, 1976, no. 290, Institute of Oral History, University of Texas at El Paso.

142. De León, *Mexican Americans*, 117; *Laredo Times*, undated clipping in author's possession; "Manuel D. Martinez, Enlisted Record and Report of Separation"; "General Orders No. 394," April 30 1945, copies in author's possession (courtesy of Martínez's daughter, Magda M. Martínez).

143. Valentín Aguilar, interview by Peter Mendoza, October 7, 2000, VOHC.

144. Manuel C. Vara, interview by Martha Treviño, March 15, 2001, VOHC.

145. Gonzalo Garza, Oscar Torres, Bob Sánchez, and Luis Leyva interviews, VOHC.

146. "Sergeant José Mendoza López's Medal of Honor," in National World War II Museum, New Orleans, Louisiana; Matt S. Meir and Feliciano Ribera, *Mexican Americans/ American Mexicans: From Conquistadores to Chicanos* (New York: Hill and Wang, 1993), 161.

147. Ernest Eguia, interview by Claudia García, February 3, 2001, VOHC.

148. Patrick J. Carroll, *Felix Longoria's Wake: Bereavement, Racism, and the Rise of Mexican American Activism* (Austin: University of Texas Press, 2003), 55–56; De León, *Mexican Americans*, 127–128, 134.

149. Caballero interview.

Chapter 6

1. "Macario García," *Handbook of Texas Online*, accessed July 29, 2020, http://www .tshaonline.org/handbook/online/articles/GG/fga76.html.

2. Martín Sánchez, interview by Alcario Acevedo, January 10, 2009, VOHC.

3. Joseph Alcoser, interview by Rene Zambrano, no date, VOHC.

4. Estanislado Reyna, interview by Nicole Muñoz, January 29, 2002, VOHC.

5. David Montejano, "The Beating of Private Aguirre: A Story about West Texas During World War II," in Rivas-Rodríguez, *Mexican Americans in World War II*, 51–59; Arnoldo De León, *Mexican Americans in West Texas: The Borderlands of the Edwards Plateau and the Trans-Pecos* (Lubbock: Texas Tech University Press, 2023), 177.

6. Patrick J. Carroll, *Felix Longoria's Wake: Bereavement, Racism, and the Rise of Mexican American Activism* (Austin: University of Texas Press, 2003), 55–56; De León, *Mexican Americans*, 120–121.

7. De León, "Tejanos," 141–142.

8. Montejano, "The Beating," 44.

9. De León, *Mexican Americans*, 121; Rivas-Rodríguez, *Mexican Americans and World War II*, xvii.

10. Paul Kennedy, *The Parliament of Man: The Past, Present, and Future of the United Nations* (New York: Cambridge University Press, 2006), 23–44.

11. Millett and Maslowski, *Common Defense*, 494–499.

12. Brian McCallister Linn, *Elvis's Army: Cold War GIs and the Atomic Battlefield* (Cambridge, MA: Harvard University Press, 2016), 10–12.

13. Millett and Maslowski, *Common Defense*, 502–506; Linn, *Elvis's Army*, 41–43.

14. George Castañeda, interview by Maggie Rivas Rodríguez, October 19, 2002, VOHC.

15. Diana De La Peña (Páez's daughter) to author, October 19, 2023, letter in author's possession.

16. Millett and Maslowski, *Common Defense*, 506.

17. John Lewis Gaddis, *Strategies of Containment: A Critical Appraisal of American National Security Policy During the Cold War* (New York: The Free Press, 2005), 87–93, 97–104, 106–108.

18. Callum A. MacDonald, *Korea: The War Before Vietnam* (New York: The Free Press, 1986), 8–16, 18–34; Stanley Sandler, *The Korean War: No Victors, No Vanquished* (Lexington: University Press of Kentucky, 1999), 54.

19. Terrence Gough, *U.S. Army Mobilization and Logistics in the Korean War* (Washington, DC: Center of Military History, United States Army, 1987); John Andrew Snyder, "Overdue Remembrance: Korean War Ceasefire and Veterans Finally Recognized by Congress," in *LareDOS: A Journal of the Borderland* 15, no. 9 (October 2009): 31.

20. Sandler, *Korean War*, 54–55; John Toland, *In Mortal Combat: Korea, 1950–1953* (New York: William, Morrow, 1991), 168–186.

21. Terrence Gough, *U.S. Army Mobilization and Logistics in the Korean War* (Washington, DC: Center of Military History, United States Army, 1987), 25–35.

22. *La Pitahaya*, 1951 yearbook, students of Raymond and Tirza Martin High School (copy in author's possession).

23. *La Pitahaya*, 1952 yearbook, students of Raymond and Tirza Martin High School (copy in author's possession).

24. Gabriel García, interview by Cheryl Smith Kemp, January 15, 2010, VOHC.

25. Ricardo Vela to author, May 5, 2011 (letter in author's possession); Alex Mendoza, "Korean War Tejanos: Two Men Who Answered the Call," in *LareDOS: A Journal of the Borderlands* 17, no. 6 (June 2011): 45.

26. Rosales, *Soldados*, 70–71.

27. Cleto L. Rodríquez, interview by Oscar J. Martínez and Sarah E. John, 1976, Interview no. 290, Institute of Oral History, University of Texas at El Paso.

28. Julie Leininger Pycior, *LBJ and Mexican Americans: The Paradox of Power* (Austin: University of Texas Press, 1997), 79.

29. Steven Rosales, "*Soldados Razos*: Chicano Politics, Identity, and Masculinity in the U.S. Military, 1940–1975," (PhD diss., University of California, Irvine, 2007), 118–119 (quotation); Rosales, *Soldados*, 73.

30. Felipe Soliz, interview by Susan Miller, October 22, 1999, VOHC.

31. Luis Landin, interview by Raquel Garza, October 3, 2009, VOHC.

32. Carlos R. Quijano, interview by Stephanie De Luna, April 26, 2011, VOHC.

33. Pete Castillo, interview by Raquel C. Garza, January 19, 2010, VOHC.

34. Ford, *Americans All!*, 63–64; Raúl M. Chavarría, interviewed by author, August 1, 2009 (Translation by author).

35. Rosales, *Soldados*, 73–74.

36. Sandler, *The Korean War*, 59–62.

37. Eliseo Cremar, interview by R. J. Molina, June 16, 2016, VOHC.

38. Hinojosa quoted in Rosales, *Soldados*, 80–81.

39. Carlos R. Quijano, interview by Stephanie De Luna, April 26, 2011, VOHC.

40. *Laredo Morning Times*, July 28, 2006.

41. Ernesto Sánchez, interview by Laura Barberena, March 6, 2010, VOHC.

42. Daryl S. Paulson and Stanley Krippner, *Haunted by Combat: Understanding PTSD in War Veterans including Women, Reservists, and Those Coming Back from Iraq* (Westport, CT: Praeger Press, 2007), 2–6, 8–10.

43. Sara Cantú, email to Alex Mendoza, July 16, 2024.

44. Carlos R. Quijano, interview by Stephanie De Luna, April 26, 2011, VOHC.

45. *Laredo Morning Times*, July 28, 2006.

46. Neftalí Zendejas, interview by Raquel C. Garza, January 15, 2010, VOHC.

47. Arnold B. Peinado, interview by Homero Galicia, 2009, no. 1521, Institute of Oral History, University of Texas at El Paso.

48. Eliseo Cremar, interview by R. J. Molina, June 16, 2016, VOHC.

49. Richard Armando Moya, interview by Alsha Khan, November 2, 2013, VOHC.

50. Ernesto Sánchez, interview by Laura Barberena, March 6, 2010, VOHC.

51. Daniel Rothberg, "Obama Will Award Medal of Honor to 24 Overlooked Army Veterans," *Los Angeles Times*, February 21, 2014.

52. *Hispanics in America's Defense*, 34, 59, 60.

53. Joseph Alcoser, interview by Rene Zambrano, no date, VOHC.

54. Martin Sánchez, interview by Alcario Alvarado, January 10, 2009, VOHC.

55. Chavarría interview.

Chapter 7

1. Millett and Maslowski, *Common Defense*, 505–506.

2. Linn, *Elvis's Army*, 56–57.

3. Brian McCallister Linn, *Real Soldiering: The U.S. Army in the Aftermath of War, 1815–1980* (Lawrence: University Press of Kansas, 2023), 148–149.

4. Linn, *Real Soldiering*, 149–150; Linn, *Elvis's Army*, 57.

5. Matthew S. Muehlbauer and David J. Ulbrich, *Ways of War: American Military History from the Colonial Era to the Twenty-First Century* (New York: Routledge, 2014), 435.

6. Linn, *Real Soldiering*, 149.

7. Linn, *Elvis's Army*, 194–196, 338–340.

8. Armando A. Sánchez, interview by Rosa Morales, November 30, 1976, Interview no. 270, Institute of Oral History, University of Texas at El Paso.

9. Oropeza, ¡*Raza Si!*, 35; De León, *Mexican Americans*, 128–132; De León, *West Texas*, 187–192; Sánchez, *Homeland*, 104–109.

10. De León, *West Texas*, 191.

11. *New York Times*, May 17, 1952.

12. *Laredo Daily Times*, May 19, 1950; *Del Rio News Herald*, May 16, 1957.

13. *San Antonio Express News*, May 22, 1955.

14. Acevedo quoted in Rosales, *Soldados*, 94.

15. Mercurio Martínez, interview by Frank Trejo, March 6, 2010, VOHC.

16. Rosales, *Soldados*, 95.

17. Rosales, *Soldados*, 95.

18. Rosales, *Soldados*, 95.

19. Geoffrey Wawro, *The Vietnam War: A Military History* (New York: Basic Books, 2024), 13–16.

20. Muehlbauer and Ulbrich, *Ways of War*, 447–450, 454–458.

21. Wawro, *Vietnam*, 81–82.

22. Raymond García, interview by Andres Salinas, November 6, 2010, VOHC.

23. Plácido Salazar, interview by Lena Price, November 6, 2010, VOHC.

24. Fernando Rodríguez, interview by Maggie Rivas-Rodríguez, November 29, 2009, VOHC.

25. Oropeza, ¡*Raza Si!*, 27–28 (quotations), 42–43.

26. Charley quoted in Lea Ybarra, *Veteranos: Vietnam Veteranos: Chicanos Recall the War* (Austin: University of Texas Press, 2004), 40.

27. John Andrew Snyder, "A Soldier's Story: A Tour in Tophet," in *LareDOS: A Journal of the Borderlands* 12 (November 2006): 6.

28. Richard Brito, interview by Manuel G. Aviles-Santiago, January 21, 2010, VOHC.

29. José Antonio Dodier, interview by Maggie Rivas-Rodríguez, August 1, 2015, VOHC.

30. George Sáenz, interview by Homero Galicia, Interview no. 1533, February 2, 2009, Institute of Oral History, University of Texas at El Paso.

31. Nestor Rodríguez, interview by Ben Wermund, April 29, 2011, VOHC.

32. John Reyes, interview by Julie Rene Tran, April 9, 2011, VOHC.

33. Felipe Ramírez, interview by Desiree T. Hernández, February 26, 2011, VOHC.

34. Richard Pérez, interview by Alex Loucel, April 9, 2011, VOHC.

35. José M. Soto, interview by Liliana Rodríguez, March 6, 2010, VOHC.

36. Rosales, *Soldados*, 94–95.

37. Raymond Saucedo, interview by Jackie Rapp, March 12, 2019, VOHC.

38. Ramírez interview.

39. Christian G. Appy, *Working-Class War: American Combat Soldiers and Vietnam* (Chapel Hill: University of North Carolina Press, 1993), 87–89; Rosales, *Soldados*, 100.

40. Adam Nieto, interview by Kristine Navarro-McElhaney, Interview No. 1477, March 3, 2010, Institute of Oral History, University of Texas at El Paso.

41. Adán Daniel Arrellano, interview by Manuel G. Aviles-Santiago, December 13, 2009, VOHC.

42. Nestor Rodríguez interview.

43. Wawro, *Vietnam*, 169–191, 532–533.

44. Wawro, *Vietnam*, 2–3.

45. Fred Castañeda, interview by Manuel G. Aviles-Santiago, January 18, 2010, VOHC.

46. Dodier interview.

47. Christopher H. Hamner, *Enduring Battle: American Soldiers in Three Wars* (Lawrence: University Press of Kansas, 2011), 3–5.

48. Dodier interview.

49. Quoted in Wawro, *Vietnam*, 163.

50. Ben R. Sáenz, interview by Ben Song, April 9, 2011, VOHC.

51. David Valladolid, interview by Henry Mendoza, June 7, 2011, VOHC.

52. Eduardo Fierro, interview by Frank L. Hernández, August 3, 2010, VOHC.

53. *The San Diego Union-Tribune*, October 22, 2022.

54. Sáenz interview.

55. Antonio Flores Alvarado, interview by Kassandra Ballí, November 6, 2010, VOHC.

56. *Dallas Morning News*, August 2, 2018.

57. Dodier interview.

58. Daniel M. Hinojosa, interview by Amy Bingham, November 6, 2010, VOHC.

59. Jesús Zamora, interview by Yolanda Chávez Leyva, July 26, 2016, no. 1686, Institute of Oral History, University of Texas at El Paso.

60. Alvarado interview.

61. Fierro interview. See also Juan Carlos González, interview by Valerie Martínez, July 30, 2010, VOHC.

62. "Vietnam Veteran Remembers Friend Who Died in War," in *Laredo Morning Times*, June 6, 2009.

63. Undated newspaper clipping in Roy Benavidez Papers, CAH; *San Antonio Express News*, November 8, 1998; Roy Benavidez Biographical Sketch in Benavidez Papers, CAH; *El Campo News Leader*, April 16, 1980, February 21, March 28, 1981, July 28, 2001; *Triad: Published in the interest of Fort McCoy Personnel*, March 24, 1989; Roy P. Benavidez with Oscar Griffin, *The Three Wars of Roy Benavidez* (New York: Ballantine, 1986); Roy Benavidez with John R. Craig, *Medal of Honor: One Man's Journey From Poverty and Prejudice* (Washington, DC: Potomac Books, 1995).

64. John Flores, *When The River Dreams: The Life of Marine Sgt. Freddy Gonzalez* (Bloomington, IN: Author House, 2006); Oropeza, *¡Raza Sí!*, 189.

65. Juan Carlos González interview.

66. *Dallas Morning News*, September 15, 2015.

67. Trujillo quoted in Rosales, *Soldados*, 109.

68. Daniel M. Hinojosa, interview by Amy Bingham, November 6, 2010, VOHC.

69. Rosales, *Soldados*, 109, 113.

70. Salazar interview.

71. Nieto interview.

72. Rosales, *Soldados*, 114.

73. Rolando L. Ríos, interview by Jess Brown, March 29, 2015, VOHC.

74. Brito interview.

75. Armando Oscar García, interview by Grant Abston, August 3, 2010, VOHC.

76. John Aleman, interview by Haley Dawson, April 9, 2011, VOHC.

77. Sergio Porras, interview by Chris Touma, April 9, 2016, VOHC. See also interviews with Dan Arrellano and Armando Oscar García.

78. Wawro, *The Vietnam War*, 75; Rosales, *Soldados*, 90; Ybarra, *Veteranos*, 5; Oropeza, *¡Raza Si!*, 68–69.

79. Tony Moreno quoted in Rosales, *Soldados*, 96.

80. Robert Lee Polanco, interview by Taylor Peterson, August 3, 2010, VOHC.

81. Richard Manríquez, interview by Jordan Haeger, April 9, 2011, VOHC.

82. Ybarra, *Veteranos*, 8.

83. Meier and Ribera, *Mexican Americans*, 218–220; Oropeza, *¡Raza Si!*, 7–8, 67–68, 191–193.

84. *Hispanics in America's Defense*, 38–39. See also Oropeza, *¡Raza Si!*, 216n 85; (Southeast Asia) Combat Area Casualties Current File (electronic record), Records of the Office of the Secretary of Defense, Record Group 330, National Archives; De León, *Mexican Americans*, 122, 136.

85. Oropeza, *¡Raza Si!*, 62–63; *San Antonio Express News*, November 8, 1998.

86. Castañeda interview.

87. *Dallas Morning News*, August 2, 2018.

88. Oropeza, *¡Raza Si!*, 96.

89. De León, *Mexican Americans*, 142–144.

90. Oropeza, *¡Raza Si!*, 62–63.

91. Quoted in Oropeza, *¡Raza Si!*, 103.

92. Eduardo Cavazos Garza, interview by Emily Macrander, April 20, 2011, VOHC.

93. Quoted in Ybarra, *Veteranos*, 40.

94. *Dallas Morning News*, August 2, 2018.

Conclusion

1. The description of events surrounding the Hispanic National Medal of Honor Monument is derived from, *The Laredo Morning Times*, July 5, 2004; María Eugenia Guerra, "What Drove LNB's Decision to Turn Premium Real Estate into a Park Space Honoring Hispanic Medal of Honor Recipients," *LareDOS: A Journal of the Borderlands* 10, no. 12 (December 2004): 11.

2. *El Paso Times*, May 14, 2019; Cindy Ramirez, "New Company E Memorial Raises Questions About Who's Included," *El Paso Matters*, June 27, 2022. See also Rodríguez, "Company E," 110–111.

3. Montejano, *Anglos and Mexicans*, 25–26; Cayetano Castillo to Texas Veterans Association, April 22, 1880, in Texas War Veteran Papers, CAH. Castillo was a veteran of the siege of San Antonio in 1835 under the command of Captain Manuel Leal. Yet, his pension had to be vouched for by Thaddeus W. Smith, who served as a witness to signature by mark. Smith also served as witness to Ygnacio Espinosa. Ramos devotes a chapter of *Beyond the Alamo* to examining the Anglo-Texan mistrust of Tejanos evident in the postwar period.

4. Frank Salinas, "Plácido Benavides Narrative, 'The Texas Paul Revere,'" CAH; Ramos, *Beyond the Alamo*, 157; De León, *Mexican Americans in Texas*, 33.

5. The historical scholarship focusing on the concept of shifting loyalties and identities with Tejanos is found in Ramos, *Beyond the Alamo*; Reséndez, *Changing National Identities*; and Johnson, *Revolution in Texas*.

6. Mirabeau B. Lamar to Bacilio Benavides, José María Ramón, and María González, April 8 and 11, 1848, in C. A. Gulick and W. Allen, eds., *The Papers of Mirabeau B. Lamar*, 6 vols., (Austin: Texas: A.C. Baldwin, 1973), IV, 196–197. In his letter of April 8, Lamar told the Laredo Tejanos that the residents of the city could "choose one of three things: they can submit to the laws of the U.S.; they can leave the country; or they can take up arms; and which of these courses is best?" Three days later Lamar admonished the trio, warning them that "invoking the aid of the public authorities" in Mexico was a dangerous proposition. Laredo Tejanos had a history of trying to forge their own path away from government interference in the years leading up to 1848. See for instance [Mayor] Bacilio Benavides, April 10, 1836, in *Mercurio de Matamoros*, copy in Laredo Archives, UNT. In a letter printed in the Mexican newspaper, Benavides wrote: Para llamar la atención del Supremo Gobierno de la Nación en fin de que los prodiguen la protección que tan justa merecen, no solamente por ser Mejicano, sino por la recomendable cualidad de ser habitantes de la frontera, que como tengo dicho a sus sacrificios é inseguridades deben de gozar los pueblos del interior." With these words, Benavides called on the national government in Mexico City to provide protection that Laredoans deserved, not just because they were Mexican, but because as border residents, they had sacrificed in order for the interior of the country to prosper.

7. A. Brook Caruso, *The Mexican Spy Company: United States Covert Operations in Mexico, 1845–1848* (Jefferson, NC: McFarland and Company, 1991), 83; Thompson, *Vaqueros in Blue and Gray*, 12; Spurlin, *Texas*, 158, 166.

8. Thompson, *Vaqueros in Blue and Gray*, 81.

9. Grear, *Why Texans Fought*, 156–161; González Quiroga, "*Mexicanos* in Texas During the Civil War," 51–62.

10. Zamora, *The World of the Mexican*, xi, 197–210. See also De León, *The Tejano Community*, 23–201; Emilio Zamora, "Mutualist and Mexicanist Expressions of a Political Culture in Texas," in Emilio Zamora, Cynthia Orozco, and Rodolfo Rocha, eds., *Mexican*

Americans in Texas History (Austin: Texas State Historical Association, 2000), 83–101; John Adams, *Conflict and Commerce on the Rio Grande: Laredo, 1755–1955* (College Station: Texas A&M University Press, 2008), 106, 116; Young, *Garza's Revolution*, 80; Elliott Young, "Crossing Borders: Race, Nation, Class, and Gender on the South Texas Border, 1877–1911" (master's thesis, University of Texas at Austin, 1993), 121; M. Romero, "The Garza Raid and Its Lessons," *North American Review* 155, no. 430 (September 1892): 324–337 (quotation on page 324); De León, *The Tejano Community*, 202–206.

11. Zamora, *The World of the Mexican Worker*, 15–19; De León, *Mexican Americans in Texas*, 58–59.

12. McCaffrey, "Texans in the Spanish American War," 257; See the respective records in the Texas Adjutant General Service Records, 1836–1935, Texas State Library.

13. Ramírez, *To the Line of Fire*, 1–3, 6–7, 8–11, 15–18; De León, *Mexican Americans in Texas*, 65; Montejano, *Anglos and Mexicans*, 82–92; Young, "Red Men," 50–51; Young, "Deconstructing *La Raza*," 228.

14. Ramírez, *To the Line of Fire*, 19 (quotation), 20, 22–23; De León, *Mexican Americans in Texas*, 91, 93; Christian, "Mexican Americans During World War I," 572–577, 592–594.

15. Ramírez, *To the Line of Fire*, 27–30.

16. *El Demócrata Fronterizo*, October 5, 1918 (translation by author).

17. De León, "Mexican Americans in Texas," 215.

18. De León, *Mexican Americans in Texas*, 108–109; Bruscino, *A Nation Forged in War*, 30–35, 40–46.

19. Robert A. Calvert et al., *The History of Texas*, 4th edition (New York: Harland Davidson, 2007), 347; *Hispanics in American Defense*, 27. There is difficulty in providing a precise number of Tejanos in World War II due to the fact that under the race categorization on enlistment and discharge papers, Mexican Americans and other Hispanics were often described as "White," "Mexican" and simply, "NA." Beyond Puerto Ricans, this figure is imprecise.

20. Richard Griswold del Castillo, "The War and Changing Identities: Personal Transformations," in *World War II and Mexican American Civil Rights* (Austin: University of Texas Press, 2008), 51; Mario T. García, *Mexican Americans: Leadership, Ideology, and Identity, 1930–1960* (New Haven: Yale University Press, 1989), 114.

21. Luis Leyva interview. See also Griswold del Castillo, "The War and Changing Identities," 51, 56; García, *Mexican Americans*, 114; Christian, "Joining the American Mainstream," 593–594.

22. See Manuel C. Vara Interview.

23. See, for instance, the interviews of Gonzalo Garza, Oscar Torres, Bob Sánchez, and Luis Leyva in VOHC.

24. Reynaldo B. Rendon (Corpus Christi) joined the military to get out of jail for a previous transgression; Bob Sánchez (Laredo) thought service would be a "bit romantic"; while Ramón M. Rivas (Eagle Pass) joined the US Army to make a little more money than he was earning with the Works Progress Administration. See Rendon, Sánchez,

and Rivas oral interviews in VOHC. Other Tejanos shirked the duty to serve, to be sure. See *Falfurrias Facts*, June 19, 1942.

25. De León, *Mexican Americans in Texas*, 128–132.

26. Oropeza, *¡Raza Sí! ¡Guerra No!*, 216n85.

27. Oropeza, *¡Raza Sí! Guerra No!*, 62.

28. Oropeza, *¡Raza Sí! Guerra No!*, 63. For views of Vietnam veterans, see Ybarra, *Vietnam Veteranos*.

29. Andrés Tijerina, "Becoming Aggie: The Tijerina Brothers, Albert '65 and Andrés '67," accessed October 10, 2010, http://siempre.tamu.edu/index.php?pg=56&nav=7; Benavidez and Craig, *Medal of Honor*. Biographical information on Benavidez derived from the Roy P. Benavidez Papers in CAH.

30. Freddie Valenzuela with Jason Lemons, *No Greater Love: The Lives and Times of Hispanic Soldiers* (Austin: Ovation Books, 2008), xiii, xvii.

31. *The Laredo Morning Times*, October 16, 2002.

32. *The Laredo Morning Times*, September 22, 2002, May 11, 2003, July 5, 2004; Guerra, "Honoring Hispanic Medal of Honor Recipients," 11; De León, *The Tejano Community*, 2002–205.

33. Ramírez, *To the Line of Fire*, 86–89; Christian, "Joining the American Mainstream," 559–595; Oropeza, *¡Raza Sí! ¡Guerra No!*; Rosales, *Soldados Razos*. Additional works pertinent to Tejanos include Thompson, *Vaqueros in Blue and Gray*; Thompson, *Mexican Texans in the Union*; Rivas-Rodríguez, *Mexican Americans and World War II*; Charley Trujillo, *Chicanos in Viet Nam* (San Jose, CA: Chusma House Publications, 1990); and Lea Ybarra, *Vietnam Veteranos*; Alex M. Saragoza, "Recent Chicano Historiography: An Interpretive Essay," *Aztlan* 19, no. 1 (Spring 1988–90): 1–77; David G. Gutierrez, "Significant to Whom?: Mexican Americans and the History of the American West," *Western Historical Quarterly* 24 (November 1993): 519–539. For older works dealing with Hispanic military service, see Harley L. Browning et al., "Income and Veteran Status: Variations Among Mexican Americans, Blacks, and Anglos," *American Sociological Review* 38 (1973): 74–85; Raúl Morín, *Among the Valiant: Mexican-Americans in WWII and Korea* (Los Angeles: Borden, 1963); Lea Ybarra and Nina Genera, *La Batalla Esta Aqui (The Battle is Here): Chicanos and the War* (El Cerrito, CA: Chicano Draft Help, 1972).

BIBLIOGRAPHY

Archives

Adina De Zavala Papers. Dolph Briscoe Center for American History. University of Texas at Austin.

Héctor P. García Papers. Special Collections Archive. Jeff and Mary Bell Library. Texas A&M University-Corpus Christi.

Institute of Oral History. University of Texas at El Paso.

Institute of Texan Cultures. University of Texas at San Antonio.

Juan Seguín Memoirs. Dolph Briscoe Center for American History. University of Texas at Austin.

National Museum of the Pacific War. Fredericksburg, Texas.

Records of the American Expeditionary Forces, World War 1, 1848–1942. Records Group 120, National Archives. Washington, DC.

Records of the United States Senate. Record Group 46, National Archives. Washington, DC.

Records of the War Department General and Special Staffs. Record Group 165, National Archives Administration. Washington, DC.

Samuel C. A. Rogers Reminiscences. Dolph Briscoe Center for American History. University of Texas at Austin.

South Texas Archives and Special Collections. Texas A&M University-Kingsville.

Texas Adjutant General Service Records, 1836–1935. Texas State Library and Archives. Austin, Texas.

Texas Military Forces Museum. Camp Mabry. Austin, Texas.

UNT Oral History Program. University of North Texas, Denton, Texas.

Voces Oral History Center. University of Texas at Austin.

Newspapers

The Alamo Express (San Antonio)

Austin Statesman

Beeville (Texas) Bee

Brownsville Daily Statesman

Brownsville Herald

Cleburne (Texas) Morning Review

Corpus Christi Caller
Dallas Morning News
El Demócrata Fronterizo (Laredo)
El Paso Herald
El Paso Morning Times
El Paso Times
El Regidor (San Antonio)
Evolución (Laredo)
Galveston Tribune
Houston Post
Houston Tri Weekly Telegraph
La Fé Católica (San Antonio)
La Prensa (San Antonio)
Laredo Daily Times
Laredo Morning Times
Laredo Sun
San Antonio Herald
Semi-Weekly News (San Antonio)

Books, Articles, and Dissertations

Aguirre, Frederick P., Linda Martínez Aguirre, and Rogelio C. Rodríguez. *Undaunted Courage: Mexican American Patriots of World War II*. Orange, CA: Latino Advocates for Education, 2005.

Allsup, Carl. *The American GI Forum: Origins and Evolution*. Austin: University of Texas Press, 1982.

Ambrose, Stephen E. *Citizen Soldiers: the U.S. Army from Normandy Beaches to the Bulge to the Surrender of Germany, June 7, 1944–May 7, 1945*. New York: Touchstone, 1998.

Anderson, Jack S. "Service Honest and Faithful: The Thirty-Third Volunteer Infantry Regiment in the Philippine War, 1899–1901." PhD diss., University of North Texas, 2017.

Bailey, Beth. *America's Army: Making the All-Volunteer Force*: Cambridge, MA: Harvard University Press, 2009.

Baime, A. J. *The Arsenal of Democracy: FDR, Detroit, and an Epic Quest to Arm an America at War*. Boston: Houghton Mifflin, 2014.

Ball, Gregory W. *Texas and World War I*. Austin: State House Press, 2019.

Barnds, David Ryan. "The Untold Story of the Ximenes Family: A Tejano Experience in Béxar Spanning Across Generations, 1716–1899." Master's thesis, University of Texas at San Antonio, 2022.

Barr, Alwyn. *Texans in Revolt: The Battle for San Antonio, 1835*. Austin: University of Texas Press, 1990.

Bean, Christopher B., ed. *Texas and Texans in World War II, 1941–1945*. College Station: Texas A&M University Press, 2022.

Benavidez, Roy, and Oscar Griffin. *The Three Wars of Roy Benavidez*. San Antonio: Corona, 1986.

Brager, Bruce L. *The Texas 36th Division: A History*. Austin: Eakin Press, 2002.

Brands, H. W. *Lone Star Nation: How a Ragged Army of Volunteers Won the Battle for Texas Independence—and Changed America*. New York: Doubleday, 2004.

Britten, Thomas A. *The Lipan Apaches: A People of Wind and Lightning*. Albuquerque: University of New Mexico Press, 2009.

Brooks, Jennifer E. *Defining the Peace: World War II Veterans, Race, and the Remaking of the Southern Political Tradition*. Chapel Hill: University of North Carolina Press, 2004.

Bruscino, Thomas. *A Nation Forged in War: How World War II Taught Americans to Get Along*. Knoxville: University of Tennessee Press, 2010.

Bryan, Jimmy L. "The Enduring People: Tejano Exclusion and Perseverance in the Republic of Texas, 1836–1845." *Journal of the West* 47 (Summer 2008): 42–48.

Calderón, Roberto R. "Mexican Politics in the American Era, 1846–1900: Laredo, Texas." PhD diss., University of California, Los Angeles, 1993.

Campbell, Randolph B. *Gone to Texas: A History of the Lone Star State*. New York: Oxford Press 2003.

Carrigan, William D. *The Making of Lynching Culture: Violence and Vigilantism in Central Texas, 1836–1916*. Urbana and Chicago: University of Illinois Press, 2004.

Carroll, Patrick J. *Felix Longoria's Wake: Bereavement, Racism, and the Rise of Mexican American Activism*. Austin: University of Texas Press, 2003.

Chipman, Donald E. *Spanish Texas, 1519–1821*. Austin: University of Texas Press, 2010.

Coffman, Edward M. *The Old Army: A Portrait of the American Army in Peacetime, 1784–1898*. New York: Oxford University Press, 1986.

———. *The War to End All Wars: The American Military Experience in World War I*. Lexington: University Press of Kentucky, 1998.

Collins, Michael L. *Texas Devils: Rangers and Regulars on the Lower Rio Grande, 1846–1861*. Norman: University of Oklahoma Press, 2008.

Connole, Dennis. *America's "Foreign Legion": Immigrant Soldiers in the Great War*. Jefferson, NC: McFarland Press, 2018.

Cooke, James J. *Pershing and His Generals: Command and Staff in the AEF*. Westport, CT: Praeger, 1997.

———. *The All-Americans at War: The 82nd Division in the Great War, 1917–1918*. Westport, CT: Praeger, 1999.

Christian, Carole E. "Joining the American Mainstream: Texas' Mexican Americans During World War I." *Southwestern Historical Quarterly* 92, no. 4 (April 1989): 559–95.

Daniell, Lewis E. *Personnel of the Texas State Government; With Sketches of Representative Men of Texas*. Austin: Smith, Hicks, and Jones, 1889.

D'Este, Carlo. *Eisenhower: A Soldier's Life*. New York: Henry Holt and Company, 2002.

De la Teja, Jesús F., ed. *Tejano Leadership in Mexican and Revolutionary Texas*. College Station: Texas A&M University Press, 2010.

De León, Arnoldo. *Ethnicity in the Sunbelt: Mexican Americans in Houston.* College Station: Texas A&M University Press, 2001.

———. *Mexican Americans in West Texas: The Borderlands of the Edwards Plateau and the Trans-Pecos.* Lubbock: Texas Tech University Press, 2024.

———. *They Called Them Greasers: Anglo Attitudes toward Mexicans in Texas, 1821–1900.* Austin: University of Texas Press, 1983.

———, ed. *War Along the Border: The Mexican Revolution and Tejano Communities.* College Station: Texas A&M University Press, 2012.

Dower, John W. *War Without Mercy: Race and Power in the Pacific War.* New York: Pantheon, 1986.

Eisenhower, John S. D. *Yanks: The Epic Story of the American Army in World War I.* New York: Free Press, 2001.

Farwell, Byron. *Over There: The United States in the Great War, 1917–1918.* New York: Norton and Company, 1999.

Faulkner, Richard S. *Pershing's Crusaders: The American Soldier Experience in World War I.* Lawrence: University Press of Kansas, 2017.

Flores, John. *When The River Dreams: The Life Of Marine Sgt. Freddy Gonzalez.* Bloomington, IN: Author House, 2006.

Flynn, George Q. *The Draft: 1940–1973.* Lawrence: University Press of Kansas, 1993.

Foos, Paul. *A Short, Offhand, Killing Affair: Soldiers and Social Conflict During the Mexican-American War.* Chapel Hill: University of North Carolina Press, 2002.

Foley, Neil, ed., *Reflexiones: New Directions in Mexican American Studies.* Austin: University of Texas Press, 1998.

Ford, Nancy Gentile. *Americans All!: Foreign-Born Soldiers in World War I.* College Station: Texas A&M University Press, 2001.

Frazier, Donald S. ed. *The United States and Mexico at War: Nineteenth-Century Expansionism and Conflict.* New York: Macmillan Reference USA, 1998.

Friend, Craig Thompson, and Lorri Glover, eds., *Southern Manhood: Perspectives on Masculinity in the Old South.* Athens: University of Georgia Press, 2004.

García, Mario T. *Desert Immigrants: The Mexicans of El Paso.* New Haven, Yale University Press, 1981.

———. *Mexican Americans: Leadership, Ideology, and Identity, 1930–1960.* New Haven: Yale University Press, 1989.

Gonzales, Manuel G. *Mexicanos: A History of Mexicans in the United States.* Bloomington: Indiana University Press, 1999.

Governor's Messages, Coke to Ross, 1874–1891: Collections of the Art and History Department of the Texas State Library. Austin: A. C. Baldwin Printing, 1916.

Grear, Charles D. *Why Texans Fought in the Civil War.* College Station: Texas A&M University Press, 2010.

Griffith Jr., Robert K. *Men Wanted for the Army: America's Experience with and All-Volunteer Army Between the World Wars.* Westport, CT: Greenwood Press, 1982.

Grotelueschen, Mark E. *The AEF Way of War: The American Army and Combat in World War I*. Cambridge, UK: Cambridge University Press, 2007.

Guinn, Jeff. *War on the Border: Villa, Pershing, the Texas Rangers, and an American Invasion*. New York: Simon and Schuster, 2021.

Gutiérrez, Dave. *Patriots from the Barrio: The Story of Company E, 141st Infantry: The Only All Mexican American Unit in World War II*. Yardley, PA: Westholme Press, 2018.

Gutiérrez, David. *Walls and Mirrors: Mexican Americans, Mexican Immigrants, and the Politics of Ethnicity*. Berkeley: University of California Press, 1995.

Hastings, Max. *The Korean War*. New York: Touchstone Press, 1987.

Harris, Charles H. and Louis R. Sadler. *The Texas Rangers and the Mexican Revolution: The Bloodiest Decade, 1910–1920*. Albuquerque: University of New Mexico Press, 2004.

Henderson, Harry McCorry. *History of the 141st Infantry, 36th Infantry Division Texas National Guard*. San Antonio: Naylor Company, 1950.

Hernández, José Angel. "Contemporary Deportation Raids and Historical Memory: Mexican Expulsions in the Nineteenth Century." *Aztlan: A Journal of Chicano Studies* 35, no. 2 (Fall 2010): 123–124.

Hernández, Kelly Lytle. *Bad Mexicans: Race, Empire, and Revolution in the Borderlands*. New York: W.W. Norton, 2022.

———. *Migra! A History of the U.S. Border Patrol*. Berkeley: University of California Press, 2010.

Hoganson, Kristin. *Fighting for American Manhood: How Gender Politics Provoked the Spanish-American and Philippine-American Wars*. New Haven: Yale University Press, 1998.

Huebner, Andrew J. *The Warrior Image: Soldiers in American Culture from the Second World War to the Vietnam War Era*. Chapel Hill: University of North Carolina Press, 2008.

Johnson, Benjamin Heber. *Revolution in Texas: How a Forgotten Rebellion and its Bloody Suppression Turned Mexicans into Americans*. New Haven: Yale University Press, 2003.

Kaplowitz, Craig. A. *LULAC, Mexican Americans, and National Policy*. College Station: Texas A&M University Press, 2005.

Keene, Jennifer D. *Doughboys, the Great War and the Remaking of America*. Baltimore: John Hopkins University Press, 2001.

Kennedy, David M. *Over Here: The First World War and American Society*. New York: Oxford University Press, 2004.

Kennett, Lee. *G.I.: The American Soldier in World War II*. Norman: University of Oklahoma Press, 1987.

Krenek, Harry L. "A History of the National Guard in Texas Between World War I and World War II." PhD diss., Texas Tech University, 1979.

Lee, James Ward, Carolyn N. Barnes, Kent A. Bowman, and Laura Crow. *1941: Texas Goes to War*. Denton: University of North Texas Press, 1991.

Leffler, John Joseph. "From the Shadows into the Sun: Americans in the Spanish-American War." PhD diss., University of Texas at Austin, 1991.

Lengel, Edward G. *Thunder and Flames: Americans in the Crucible of Combat, 1917–1918.* Lawrence: University Press of Kansas, 2015.

Linn, Brian McAllister. *Elvis's Army: Cold War GIs and the Atomic Bomb Battlefield.* Cambridge, MA: Harvard University Press, 2016.

———. *The Echo of Battle: The Army's Way of War.* Cambridge, MA: Harvard University Press, 2007.

———. *The Philippine War, 1899–1902.* Lawrence: University Press of Kansas, 2000.

MacDonald, L. Lloyd. *Tejanos in the 1835 Texas Revolution.* Gretna, LA: Pelican Publishing Company, 2009.

McCaffrey, James M. "Texans in the Spanish-American War." *Southwestern Historical Quarterly* 106, no. 2 (October 2002): 255–279.

McDonald, David. *José Antonio Navarro, In Search of the American Dream in Nineteenth Century Texas.* Denton: Texas State Historical Association Press, 2010.

Mansoor, Peter R. *The GI Offensive in Europe: The Triumph of American Infantry Divisions, 1941–45.* Lawrence: University Press of Kansas, 1999.

Meir, Matt S. and Feliciano Ribera, *Mexican Americans-American Mexicans: From Conquistadores to Chicanos.* New York: Hill and Wang, 1993.

Mendoza, Alexander. "'For Our Own Best Interests': Nineteenth-Century Laredo Tejanos, Military Service, and the Development of American Nationalism." *Southwestern Historical Quarterly* 115, no. 2 (October 2011): 125–152.

———. "'I Know No Other Country': Tejanos and the American Wars of the Twentieth Century." *Military History of the West* 4 (2011): 31–59.

Mendoza, Alexander, and Charles Grear, eds. *Texans at War: A New Military History of the Lone Star State.* College Station: Texas A&M University, 2012.

Millett, Allan R., and Peter Maslowski. *For the Common Defense: A Military History of the United States of America.* New York: Free Press of America, 1994.

Milner, Elmer Ray. "An Agonizing Evolution: A History of the Texas National Guard, 1900–1945." PhD diss., North Texas State University, 1979.

Montejano, David. *Anglos and Mexicans in the Making of Texas, 1836–1986.* Austin: University of Texas Press, 1987.

Morales, Ralph Edward III. "The Tejano-Anglo Alliance: Tejanos, Ethnicity, and Politics in Texas, 1832–1865." Master's thesis, Texas A&M University, 2008.

Morín, Raúl. *Among the Valiant: Mexican-Americans in WWII and Korea.* Los Angeles: Borden, 1963.

Muñoz Martinez, Monica. *The Injustice Never Leaves You: Anti-Mexican Violence in Texas.* Cambridge: Harvard University Press, 2018.

Muehlbauer, Matthew S., and David J. Ulbrich. *Ways of War: American Military History from the Colonial Era to the Twenty-First Century.* New York: Routledge, 2014.

Najera, Andy. "Agency of Mexican/Tejano Union Recruits During the United States Civil War: An Archival Case Study of Private Pedro García." Master's thesis, University of Texas Río Grande Valley, 2021.

Nelson, Christian G. "Texas Militia in the Spanish-American War." *Texas Military History* 2 (August 1962): 193–234.

Offner, John L. *An Unwanted War: The Diplomacy of the United States and Spain Over Cuba, 1895–1898*. Chapel Hill: University of North Carolina Press, 1991.

O'Leary, Cecilia Elizabeth. *To Die For: The Paradox of American Patriotism*. Princeton: Princeton University Press, 1999.

Olson, Bruce A. "The Houston Light Guards: Elite Cohesion and Social Control in the New South, 1873–1940." PhD diss., University of Houston, 1989.

Oropeza, Lorena. *¡Raza Si! ¡Guerra No!: Chicano Protest and Patriotism during the Viet Nam War Era*. Berkeley: University of California Press, 2005.

Orozco, Cynthia E. *No Mexican, Women, or Dogs Allowed: The Rise of the Mexican American Civil Rights Movement*. Austin: University of Texas Press, 2010.

Perales, Alonso S. "Some Places Where Mexicans are Discriminated Against in Texas Either by Denying them Service or by Segregating them from Anglo-Americans," *Recovering the U.S. Hispanic Literary Heritage Digital Collections*, https://usldhrecovery.uh.edu/files/original/1/108/pera0080_001.jpg.

Pérez, Louis A., Jr. *The War of 1898: The United States and Cuba in History and Historiography*. Chapel Hill: University of North Carolina Press, 1998.

Poyo, Gerald E., ed. *Tejano Journey, 170–1850*. Austin: University of Texas Press, 1996.

Purcell, Allan Robert. "The History of the Texas Militia, 1835–1903." PhD diss., University of Texas at Austin, 1981.

Ramírez, José A. *To the Line of Fire!: Mexican Texans and World War I*. College Station: Texas A&M University Press, 2009.

Ramos, Henry A. J. *The American GI Forum: In Pursuit of a Dream, 1948–1983*. Houston: Arte Público Press, 1998.

Ramos, Raúl A. *Beyond the Alamo: Forging Mexican Ethnicity in San Antonio, 1821–1861*. Chapel Hill: University of North Carolina Press, 2008.

Reséndez, Andrés. *Changing National Identities at the Frontier: Texas and New Mexico, 1800–1850*. New York: Cambridge University Press, 2005.

Rivas-Rodríguez, Maggie, ed. *Mexican Americans and World War II*. Austin: University of Texas Press, 2005.

Rodríguez, Jorge. "A History of El Paso's Company E in World War II." Master's thesis, University of Texas at El Paso, 2010.

Romero, M. "The Garza Raid and its Lessons," *The North American Review* vol. 155, no. 430 (September 1892): 324–337.

Rosales, Steven. *Soldados Razos: Chicano Politics, Identity, and Masculinity in the U.S. Military, from World War II to Vietnam*. Tucson: University of Arizona Press, 2017.

———. "*Soldados Razos*: Chicano Politics, Identity, and Masculinity in the U.S. Military, 1940–1975." PhD diss., University of California, Irvine, 2007.

Salyer, Lucy E. "Baptism by Fire: Race, Military Service, and U.S. Citizenship Policy, 1918–1935." *Journal of American History* vol. 91, no. 3 (2001): 847–876.

Sáenz, José De La Luz. *The World War I Diary of José De La Luz Sáenz*. Edited and translated by Emilio Zamora. College Station: Texas A&M University Press, 2014.

Sánchez, George J. *Becoming Mexican American: Ethnicity, Culture, and Identity in Chicano Los Angeles, 1900–1945*. New York: Oxford University Press, 1993.

Schaffer, Ronald. *America in the Great War: The Rise of the War Welfare State*. Oxford, UK: Oxford University Press, 1991.

Seguín, Juan N. *Personal Memoirs of John N. Seguín: From the Year 1834 to the Retreat of General Woll from the City of San Antonio in 1842*. San Antonio: Ledger Book Office, 1858.

Smith, Thomas Ty. *The Garza War in South Texas: A Military History, 1890–1893*. Norman: University of Oklahoma Press, 2023.

Smith, Todd. *From Dominance to Disappearance: The Indians of East Texas and the Near Southwest, 1786–1859*. Lincoln: University of Nebraska Press, 2005.

Snell, Mark A., ed. *Unknown Soldiers: The American Expeditionary Forces in Memory and Remembrance*. Kent: Kent State University Press, 2008.

Stout, Joseph A., Jr. *Border Conflict: Villistas, Carrancistas and the Punitive Expedition, 1915–1920*. Fort Worth: TCU Press, 1999.

Thompson, Jerry Don. *Cortina: Defending the Mexican Name in Texas*. College Station: Texas A&M University Press, 2007.

———. *Mexican Texans in the Union Army*. El Paso: Texas Western Press, 1986.

———. *Tejano Tiger: José de los Santos Benavides and the Texas-Mexico Borderlands, 1823–1891*. Fort Worth: TCU Press, 2017.

———. *Vaqueros in Blue and Gray*. Austin: State House Press, 2000.

Tijerina, Andrés. *Tejanos and Texas Under the Mexican Flag, 1821–1836*. College Station: Texas A&M University Press, 1994.

Torget, Andrew J. *Seeds of Empire: Cotton, Slavery, and the Transformation of the Texas Borderlands, 1800–1850*. Chapel Hill: University of North Carolina Press, 2015.

Torget, Andrew J., and Gerardo Garza-Lavalle, eds. *These Ragged Edges: Histories of Violence along the U. S.-Mexico Border*. Chapel Hill: University of North Carolina Press, 2022.

Trask, David F. *The AEF and Coalition Warmaking, 1917–1918*. Lawrence: University Press of Kansas, 1993.

———. *The War with Spain in 1898*. Lincoln: University of Nebraska Press, 1981.

Treviño, Roberto R. "*Prensa y Patria*: The Spanish-Language Press and the Biculturation of the Tejano Middle Class, 1920–1940." *Western Historical Quarterly* 22, no. 4 (November 1991): 451–472.

Trujillo, Charley. *Chicanos in Viet Nam*. San Jose, CA: Chusma House Publications, 1990.

Turpie, David C. "A Voluntary War: The Spanish-American War, White Southern Manhood, and the Struggle to Recruit Volunteers in the South." *Journal of Southern History* 80, no. 4 (November 2014): 859–892.

Tyler, Ronnie C. *Santiago Vidaurri and the Southern Confederacy*. Austin: Texas State Historical Association, 1973.

Uglow, Loyd. *A Military History of Texas*. Denton: University of North Texas Press, 2022.

United States Department of Defense. *Hispanics in America's Defense*. Washington, DC: Office of the Deputy Assistant Secretary of Defense for Military Manpower and Personnel Policy, 1988.

United States War Department. *Records of the Office of Secretary of War, Records Group 107*. Washington: Government Printing Office, 1863–1877.

Valenzuela, Freddie, with Jason Lemons. *No Greater Love: The Lives and Times of Hispanic Soldiers*. Austin: Ovation Books, 2008.

Wagner, Robert L. *The Texas Army: A History of the 36th Division in the Italian Campaign*. Austin: Robert Wagner, 1972.

Wawro, Geoffrey. *Sons of Freedom: The Forgotten American Soldiers Who Defeated Germany in World War I*. New York: Basic Books, 2018.

———. *The Vietnam War: A Military History*. New York: Basic Books, 2024.

Weigley, Russell F. *The American Way of War: A History of United States Military Strategy and Policy*. Bloomington: Indiana University Press, 1973.

White, Lonnie J. *The 90th Division in World War I: The Texas-Oklahoma Draft Division in the Great War*. Manhattan: Sunflower University Press, 1996.

Woodward, David R. *The American Army and the First World War*. Cambridge, MA: Cambridge University Press, 2014.

Wooster, Ralph A. *Texas and Texans in the Great War*. Buffalo Gap, TX: State House Press, 2009.

Ybarra, Lea. *Vietnam Veteranos: Chicanos Recall the War*. Austin: University of Texas Press, 2004.

Ybarra, Lea, and Nina Genera. *La Batalla Esta Aqui (The Battle is Here): Chicanos and the War* El Cerrito, CA: Chicano Draft Help, 1972.

Yenne, Bill. *Indian Wars: The Campaign for the American West*. Yardley, PA: Westholme Press, 2006.

Young, Elliott. *Catarino Garza's Revolution on the Texas-Mexico Border*. Durham, NC: Duke University Press, 2004.

———. "Deconstructing *La Raza*: Identifying the *Gente Decente* of Laredo, 1904–1911," *Southwestern Historical Quarterly* 98, no. 2 (October 1994): 226–259.

Zamora, Emilio. "Fighting on Two Fronts: José de la Luz Sáenz and the Language of the Mexican American Civil Rights Movement." In *Recovering the U.S. Hispanic Literary Heritage*, edited by Ramón A. Gutiérrez and Silvio Torres-Saillant. Houston: Arte Público Press, 2002.

———. *The World of the Mexican Worker in Texas*. College Station: Texas A&M University Press, 2000.

Zamora, Emilio Cynthia Orozco, and Rodolfo Rocha, eds. *Mexican Americans in Texas History*. Austin: Texas State Historical Association, 2000, 83–101.

Zieger, Robert H. *America's Great War: World War I and the American Experience*. Lanham, MD: Rowman and Littlefield Publishers, 2000.

Zillich, Emily Tessier. "History of the National Guard in El Paso." Master's thesis, Texas Western College, 1958.

INDEX

www.ingramcontent.com/pod-product-compliance
Lightning Source LLC
Chambersburg PA
CBHW020445100426
42812CB00036B/3452/J